D1593817

PIECES OF TIME
Peter Bogdanovich
On the Movies

Also by Peter Bogdanovich

ALLAN DWAN: THE LAST PIONEER (1971)
FRITZ LANG IN AMERICA (1969)
JOHN FORD (1968)
THE CINEMA OF ALFRED HITCHCOCK (1963)
THE CINEMA OF HOWARD HAWKS (1962)
THE CINEMA OF ORSON WELLES (1961)

PIECES
OF
TIME

Peter Bogdanovich
On the Movies

An Arbor House/Esquire Book

For C.S.

"An' that's the thing—" said Jimmy Stewart, *"that's the great thing about the movies . . . After you* learn *—and if you're good and Gawd helps ya and you're lucky to have a personality that comes across—then what you're doing is—you're giving people little . . . little, tiny pieces of* time *. . . that they never forget."*

Contents

Acknowledgments

MY THANKS TO EVERYONE mentioned in this book, either for speaking with me or simply for existing. Especially to Harold Hayes, former editor of *Esquire*, for making it possible (as a reading of the various headnotes to the pieces will make clear); all the articles printed here first appeared, with minor changes, in his magazine. (The dates that follow each of them indicate the issue in which they were first published.)

For their invaluable contributions, in various important ways, I'd like also to thank Orson Welles, the late Eugene Archer, Andrew Sarris, Mae Woods, Richard Waltzer. And, particularly, for her encouragement and contribution to those pieces written between 1962 and 1966, Polly Platt.

P.B.

Introduction

FOR MY MONEY, *The Man Who Shot Liberty Valance* is one of the worst movies ever made. Peter Bogdanovich thinks it is one of the best. We have argued this difference over the past twelve years we have known each other, and since most people now regard Bogdanovich as one of the most talented filmmakers of the day, I am prepared to grant the possibility that he may be in possession of certain criteria which elude me. Until he made *The Last Picture Show*, it was still possible for me (an editor) to regard him as just another writer—a prejudice for *Liberty Valance* was one of those inexplicable quirks you grew to expect, like Gay Talese's habit of scanning his rough draft through binoculars. But Bogdanovich has moved on to another dimension. He is still a writer, as this book eloquently confirms, but he is on to his sixth film now, each one of them having been strikingly different from the others, and each more successful than the last. These movies bring joy to the lives of millions and vast sums to the pockets of his sponsors. For the moment then, I will let the question rest: if Bogdanovich wants to go on making a ninny of himself over *Liberty Valance*, he has, I suppose, earned the right.

Clearly, if he has other inadequacies, they are, against the background of his accomplishments, even less visible: at twenty-seven, the second unit director of *The Wild Angels;* at twenty-nine, the producer-director of *Targets;* at thirty-one, *The Last Picture Show* and a feature-length documentary, *Directed by John Ford;* at thirty-one and a half, the brilliant fifteen-minute compression of the Chaplin *oeuvre* for Chaplin's special Oscar presentation; at thirty-two, *What's Up, Doc?;* at thirty-three, *Paper Moon*. And earlier, before he began to mark time by his film release dates, six books on cinema as well as a major volume in preparation on the career of Orson Welles.

Not so long ago, I was in his suite at the Plaza (in New York he always stays at the Plaza and always in a suite), and he looked just wonderful—not a week older than when I had first met him. In those days he was always crunching on gelusils to soothe his ulcer but now, the ulcer having given way to the radiance of success, he was puffing a big fat cigar —"A Shakespeare," he said grandly, fixing his taste for to-bacco somewhere in the same ballpark with his taste for *Liberty Valance*. The phone rang and Peter picked it up.

"What kind of car are you sending?" Pause. "No, no dear. *Not* an Impala. A limousine with a driver. I can't go there in a rental car. It's uncomfortable. You can't stretch your legs and your pants get all wrinkled. No, no, no. Get a Lin-coln or a Cadillac and have the driver wait outside."

The first car he ever owned was one my wife had located for him through a fellow tenant on Riverside Drive. It was a 1951 Ford convertible, with good rubber, and it cost $150. He put his wife in it and her mongrel dog, named "Puppy," and headed west for heaven. "The car turned out to have a cracked block which meant that it overheated at almost any speed," Peter said at the Plaza. "So we took to coasting in neutral down any excuse for a hill to cool off the motor. Going through Kansas, this became a problem. There are no hills. There is barely even an occasional rise. When I came to make *Paper Moon* and decided hot flatlands would be good for the story, I didn't have a hard time remembering those days we'd spent getting across Kansas."

Ten years later, sitting there forty blocks south of the point of his original departure, younger than Monroe Stahr and in a near state of asphyxiation from his own cigar, he certainly didn't look any more like The Hope of a Dying Industry than he had when he left. Despite the radical change in his circumstances, the Hollywood Bogdanovich still acts and talks just like the Upper West Side Bogdanovich, his character out there on his sleeve. There may be other facets to it but those that interest me are: a) an obsessive temperament; b) love of craft; c) reverence for the past; d) sentiment; e) ingenuity; f) charm and/or chicanery. Some of these attributes have been noted by others, some have not. Since this is a book *by* a movie director and not about one, however, I feel obliged to go into these matters here as they are perfectly germane to the prose you will soon be reading. Furthermore, I labor under the prejudice that any author worth his beans is always more interesting than his subject matter. While this is a tough point to make when you put Bogdanovich up against, say, Marlene Dietrich, I submit it nevertheless. There is a good deal, too, to be said about his reportorial technique—clear, direct and without a whit of self-consciousness—but as always, technique speaks for itself. It is a natural talent with him—he didn't make it; he just has it. The subject of these remarks is Bogdanovich's progress as a culture force.

I still can't believe it.

First, a) the obsessive temperament. Some points are not worth laboring. His obsessiveness no doubt accounts for the precision of detail in his films. I wouldn't know about that. My own experience with it may be summarized briefly in relation to the problem of titling this book. The last I heard, it would be called "Picture Shows." Perhaps it still is. I do not know because I have washed my hands of it. Peter has called me twenty-seven times about it, nineteen times from Beverly Hills and eight times from London. I disclaim any involvement in its outcome beyond persuading him that a prospective subtitle, "Hollywood Now and Then," would not be appreciably strengthened by a change to "Hollywood Then and Now."

As for the rest of it, the years from adolescence through *Targets* demonstrate the evolution of character from b) through f). His formal education ended just short of his high school diploma but, to his great fortune, at Collegiate School for Boys, one of the best private schools in New

York City. "I hadn't passed algebra but they didn't want to embarrass me, so I went up on the stage like everyone else, moved my tassel from one side of the mortar board to the other and was handed an envelope just like everyone else. I wondered what could be inside. When I got back to my seat, I opened it. It was a piece of cardboard."

The more serious phase of his education began on 89th and Broadway two blocks from his father's apartment at The New Yorker Theater, owned and operated by Daniel Talbot, a former critic who had built his modest business by showing the movies he thought people ought to see. Peter had written a film column for his high school paper and now sought to extend his knowledge of the form.

"I knew a guy who told me the way to get into movies was to write movie reviews. Then they would send you free tickets. I started writing so I could get to see free movies —that was the only reason. Honest. A small magazine called *Ivy*—it was supposed to be read by ivy league college students—ran some of my stuff and the screening notices began to come in. But I wanted to see The New Yorker's older movies too, so I went around to see Talbot.

" 'Hi,' I said. 'I'm Peter Bogdanovich. I live just around the corner and I want to see if there is any way I can get in to see your movies free.'

" 'Yeah," Talbot said, 'I've heard of you. I've read some of your stuff.'

" 'You have?'

" 'Yeah, I read something you wrote about *Intolerance*. I hated it.' "

Nevertheless, Talbot agreed to put Peter to work writing program notes in mimeograph for hard-core buffs who wanted to know more about the films than the credits. Happily Bogdanovich set to work, eventually persuading Talbot not only to program those movies he wanted particularly to see but to charge five cents for the program notes so that he might enjoy an income as well.

Since the record shows that Bogdanovich has seen some

45,000 of the 60,000 films made in Hollywood, it is to be assumed The New Yorker billing in those days offered a funky fare. One day, to his astonishment, he received a call from the late Richard Griffith, curator of films for The Museum of Modern Art. Griffith had read his five-cent mimeograph on Orson Welles' *Othello*, was impressed by Peter's knowledge of the subject and asked him to write a 25,000-word monograph to accompany a forthcoming Museum retrospective on Welles. The fee would be $125.

Some years before all this, at fifteen, having lied about his age and cut his gym class to make time available (f), Peter had begun to study with Stella Adler, commencing an acting career which ultimately would interweave his career as a taste maker for The New Yorker Theater: summer stock in Traverse City, Michigan; Stratford, Connecticut; and Phoenicia, New York. In 1959, at nineteen, he somehow managed to raise the money to stage an off-Broadway production of Clifford Odets' *The Big Knife*. Meanwhile, his polysyllabic by-line began to emerge in print, wherever he could manage to place it—*Ivy*, of course, *Frontier*, *Film Culture*, and one review in *The Village Voice*.

In 1962, he decided he wanted to see all of Howard Hawks' films. Paramount was about to release *Hatari!* "I called Saul Cooper, the publicity man at Paramount, and I said, 'If I can get the Museum to assign me to write a monograph on Hawks and then do a retrospective to tie in with the release of *Hatari!*, would you foot the bill?' 'Sure,' Cooper said. So then I called Dick Griffith and said, 'If I can get Paramount to foot the bill, would you be interested in doing a retrospective on Hawks to coincide with the release of *Hatari!* and assign me to do the monograph?' 'Sure,' Griffith said. I saw almost all of Hawks' movies and got paid for it." (The following year, he did the same number on Universal with Hitchcock's *The Birds*.)

Thus inspired, Paramount invited a few editors, myself among them, to dinner preceding the preview at a restaurant in New Rochelle, twenty miles from New York City. To this day, I do not understand why the dinner was held in New Rochelle unless it somehow suited the purposes of Bogdanovich, who of course was there.

The next phase of his career, the phase between the ages of twenty-two and twenty-nine with which I am most familiar, may be examined in the pages of this book. Shortly after that dinner, he mentioned an article he had written about Hollywood which had been turned down by *Harper's*. I asked to see it, bought it and led the August 1962 issue of *Esquire* with it. We called it "Talkies"; it was as good as anything we ever ran on the subject.

Jerry Lewis, Ford, Bogart, Jimmy Stewart—the rest of the major profiles followed in rather predictable sequence. His interests in the world outside Hollywood or the theater were provincial but within the film form, wildly eclectic. I can't remember a Hollywood assignment he rejected (though three of my enthusiasms—Sonny and Cher, Tony Randall and Jack Lemmon—insufficiently challenged his imagination and I later had to turn the completed assignment down). For a writer so possessed, the source material seemed inexhaustible. Had he chosen to go on as a journalist, *Esquire* would be running Bogdanovich's all-star profiles to this day.

Yet despite the consistency of his obsession, the books lining the walls of his Riverside Drive apartment were choice whatever the category, and all of them freebies, like his screening privileges. Since thousands of books are published each year, it takes great discernment to know which free books to throw out. Peter has good instincts in this respect, and with only an occasional exception, he has always seemed to me to know precisely what he should take along and what he should leave behind.

My wife and I had dinner at his apartment one evening, and found him and his then wife Polly hollering and carrying on over a large, bedraggled green plant they had been given on their wedding; it was dying. They had cleaned the dirt away from the roots, washed it in the bathtub and now they were pouring back in fresh dirt they had dug out of the park across the street. The plant responded more to their sentiments than to the treatment, and it flourished.

More than any other, this slight memory seems to me at the heart of his magic. For the contemporary "communicator," sentiment was something we all had to outgrow. J. D. Salinger was too soft, Adlai Stevenson too much the bleeding heart, Arthur Miller too corny and so on. The sixties put an end to sentiment, except that Bogdanovich, growing paler by the day in the darkness of his local second-run movie house, somehow failed to get the word. Sentiment dominates the films of the thirties (more than any other, his artistic point in time) and it has much to do with his own nature. The dog "Puppy" had one eye and a heritage obscenely bizarre even in a city overrun with some weird specimens of dog. When the Bogdanovichs went out for the evening, "Puppy" went with them. At Christmas and on birthdays, with no income in sight, they each splurged with O. Henry abandon on gifts for the other. They were both tough-minded and demanding of themselves and their work. But there was an ancient sweetness about them altogether out of keeping with their generation. Possessing this value he has learned to work with it, and it is his mastery of sentiment—hovering dangerously on the edge of sentimentality but never quite going over—that so brilliantly in these hard-assed seventies informs his work. It is there when Timothy Bottoms cries over the broken body of the idiot boy in *Picture Show* and at the end of *Paper Moon* when Ryan O'Neal finally relents and lets his nine-year-old bastard daughter tag along with him into the future. His audiences weep for all the reasons Peter wants them to weep, and as well, no doubt, for the simple pleasure of being able to weep at the movies again.

There is in his possession, too, the oft-cited reverence for the past. The pages to follow are filled with it; not just respect for the glory of those who have preceded him but a craftsman's awareness of just how good they *were*. He is Hollywood's first faithful child, and even with less talent he would be the apple of his home town's eye. As has ever been the case, most of the money powers out there now are pragmatists: you are no better than your latest box office, etc. Thus great innovators are wasted before they are through because the measurable index of popular taste seems against them. But not on Bogdanovich, they aren't. He writes for them and about them, and his work demands their echo be heard. At the Warner's commissary a year or so ago, we entered the room and looked for a table. A distinguished director of the forties and fifties rushed over to him, pathetically solicitous: "Peter, how *are* you? When can you come by the house and watch some movies with me?" Robert Benton and David Newman, the screenwriters, tell with awe of the time he finally broke through and was invited by Columbia to discuss a three-picture contract. He is reported to have said to a flustered executive: "Why are you guys getting so excited about a kid like me when men like John Ford can't get work out here?"

When finally he decided to move to the coast, there was little more my magazine could do for him than he could now do for himself. So long as he wanted to write for *Esquire*, there would always be space available, and of course he would be closer to his subject matter in L.A. than in New York. So he shipped his books on ahead, piled into his convertible and took off.

He stayed in touch but I was never quite sure what he was up to out there. When Dwight Macdonald quit as our movie reviewer, he suggested himself as replacement (*Liberty Valance*!?!) but I gently deflected him toward more profiles. The ill-fated Sonny and Cher assignment fell through, and he tells what happened next:

"On Wednesday, my agent called to say *The Saturday Evening Post* was taking the Sonny and Cher piece you had rejected. You had paid a $200 reject fee. They paid $2000 for the piece *you* would have paid $1,000 for.

"On Thursday, you called me and said the Jimmy Stewart

piece I'd just turned in was the best thing I'd ever written. "On Friday, Roger Corman called and offered me $125 a week to work as his general assistant on *The Wild Angels*." All the strings at last were in his hands, and Peter began to pull them with great dexterity. Upon completion of *The Wild Angels*, Corman was sufficiently impressed with his work to let him produce his own film so long as he consented to certain conditions:

a) The film must come in under $125,000.

b) A part must be found for Boris Karloff, who owed Corman two days shooting time.

c) Use would be made of eighteen minutes of an old Karloff horror movie Corman already had somewhere in the can.

Otherwise, Bogdanovich would be "free" to make whatever picture suited him. Shortly thereafter he came to New York and we had breakfast at the Plaza. I knew none of the above, only that he had an opportunity to make a low-budget movie and that he was looking for a story. It was in the summer of 1966, several weeks after the traumatic Whitman killings from the tower of the University of Texas. Why not something on that, I suggested with the enthusiasm of a man who would not have to cope with the problem. Peter went on pushing at his eggs.

Targets, produced, directed and written by Peter Bogdanovich, co-starring Boris Karloff and Peter Bogdanovich, made its appearance some eighteen months later. It was the story of an aging horror actor who apprehends a psychopathic sniper. Happily it was a minor release, which assured its viewing by the more serious film critics, and before you knew it, Peter was basking under the white hot sun of the New York media.

You know as much about what happened *after* that as I do.

What none of us still knows, however, is where Peter will take us next. Of all his spiritual forebears, Orson Welles is the one whose talent seems the most appropriate measure for his ambitions. While the darkness in Welles seems deeper than the darkest moments in Bogdanovich's few films, including *The Last Picture Show*, the joyousness in Bogdanovich's films, including *The Last Picture Show*, is something all his own, and precious. It accounts no doubt for his immense popularity in the baleful mood of the early seventies.

Recently a major film executive was lecturing me on our scarifying national temper: "People don't want to be reminded of their problems. They want to be diverted and entertained. They want a *Paper Moon* by Bogdanovich, not a reprise on the tragedy of Bobby Kennedy." Up to a point, he is right. Thus far, Bogdanovich's films have for the most part been exercises in sensibility—a preoccupation with the distinctions inside his people rather than outside. But he is wrong that Bogdanovich reflects the appalling shutdown going on around us. Peter is making the movies he wants to make. It is a coincidence that they match our desire of the moment to flee inward. *Targets*, his little-known exegesis of a psychopathic killer, is in itself a comment on the *Zeitgeist*. It is also an indication of his range and power. There is more to come, and I doubt that any of us, including Peter, will be able to predict either the subject matter or his handling of it. Which is finally a lot to say for any artist.

Meanwhile this book, and what a blessing for all of us— readers, editors and nonfilmgoers, if there are any left—that he writes so well!

—Harold Hayes

1

FIRST
IMPRESSIONS

Somewhat pompously, I originally called my first piece for Esquire, "Notes on A Maiden Voyage," since is described my first visit to Hollywood. Appropriately, it was over a year in the making. I had written for a few tiny film magazines and for one or two other minuscule publications and, through some set of circumstances I can no longer remember, had met Mr. Robert Silvers, who was then an editor at Harper's Magazine (he has since, of course, become the guiding father of the New York Review of Books). I told Mr. Silvers late in 1960 that I was planning to go to Hollywood on business—I was all of twenty—and would he give me an assignment to do a piece. Well, he said he'd give me a letter saying he was "anxious to read any piece I might write." Not quite the same thing, but enough to help me to be convincing when I told the various P.R. people that I was doing an article on Hollywood for Harper's. The truth was that I wanted to go West to meet Clifford Odets, whose play, The Big Knife, I had revived off-Broadway the previous season. Though he'd allowed me to produce and direct his play, we'd never met; I asked him once why on earth he gave me the rights simply on the basis of one long, enthusiastic letter I'd written him, and he said with characteristic ambiguity, "I took a drop in the ocean." What I wanted now was to convince him to let me revive another play of his, Night Music, and at the same time—I make an unconscionable habit of always trying to kill at least two birds with one stone—to try to meet some Hollywood folk with the vague idea of either a) being "discovered" or b) getting acquainted with some childhood heroes. One way or another, I somehow scraped up enough money for the trip and took off in early January 1961. It was also my first plane flight.

I stayed two weeks (that's when the money ran out), meeting a score or two of famous people, taking three sizable *pads full of notes, failing to convince Odets about the other play, and having a terrific time. I had one quite bad attack of smog, coughing and sneezing, but otherwise it was a fascinating adventure for someone who'd grown up wanting to be a part of the movies—which in those days only meant Hollywood. The notebooks intimidated me, however, and I didn't write a word of the article for about nine months—not until long after a lovely season of summer theatre during which I directed four plays and fell in love and was very happy.*

Back in the city again, with nothing to do and few prospects, I finally sat down and wrote what turned out to be a mammoth seventy-page journal of the trip that must have covered every single scribble in those three notepads. Bob Silvers actually did read it and then spent a couple of hours with me one afternoon making brilliant suggestions for how I should cut it down, which I did gladly. Silvers' boss, however, turned the revised piece down. After it was shown to Dwight Macdonald, who liked it (about the last production of mine he has liked) and sent it on for me to The Atlantic Monthly, *which also rejected it, the article retreated to a closet in my apartment where it stayed for several weeks.*

One evening, at a dinner that preceded a press preview of Howard Hawks' Hatari! *(I was doing a monograph on him for the Museum of Modern Art), I was seated next to a handsome Southern gentleman who said he was with* Esquire, *and we got into a discussion about movies, during the course of which I believe I insulted him and his taste about fifteen times. But it was all very friendly and funny, really, and I liked him enormously, even though I thought he didn't have the foggiest notion of what a good movie was. As we were leaving the restaurant, I asked him what it was he did at* Esquire. *"Managing editor," he said. It was Harold Hayes.*

A week later I phoned him. "Hi," I said, "I'm the fellow that insulted you all through dinner last week." He remembered me. I told him the history of the article I'd done and asked if he would like to see it. He would, he did, and another ten days later he called me: "Hi, buddy," he said. "Hey, we're gonna buy that piece and we want you to go on to Hollywood and do another one for us right away. It was the beginning of many good things for me.

Talkies

Now i'm in hollywood—staring in disbelief at Grauman's Chinese, trying to understand those funny-looking trees—and it's all true, everything I'd heard, all the clichés. They make airplanes out here, and missiles. But, above all, they make movies.

One of my first interviews was with Alfred Hitchcock, the director, who ushered me gingerly into his expansive office at Paramount Pictures; he was wearing a dark suit, white shirt, dark tie, holding a large cigar, and looking very heavy indeed. "I work in an office," he told me in his carefully enunciated, British way, often breaking up his words by syllables. "The writer and I plan out the entire script down to the smallest detail, and when we're finished all that's left to do is shoot the film. Actually, it's only when one enters the studio that one enters the area of compromise. Really, the novelist has the best casting since he doesn't have to cope with the actors and all the rest."

"From the point of view of suspense and character" he thought *Shadow of a Doubt* was his best film, and *Psycho* "technically the most satisfying." Concerning *Under Capricorn*, a favorite of the French New Wave but a failure in America, Hitchock said he didn't like to do costume pictures. "(a) I'm not very good at it," he explained, "and (b) I cannot imagine anyone in a costume picture ever going to the bathroom."

A young woman came into the office with a cup of coffee and handed it to me as the director went on to explain that his attitude toward *Psycho* was essentially humorous. "I couldn't make a film like that seriously. One can't," he said rationally. "If I had wanted to make the film seriously, I would have had to go *inside* it, and show the inner workings of the character. But, you see, I showed it from the outside." To prove his point of view on *Psycho*, he asked his assistant,

Peggy Robertson, to call for a print of the preview-trailer he
had shot for the film so he could screen it for me.

While this was being arranged, I asked about *North by
Northwest* and his preference for Cary Grant, who has
starred in several Hitchcock pictures. "I was very amused,"
he said smiling, "when I read some critic referring to *North
by Northwest* as 'unconsciously funny.' Well, my dear, the
film is sheer fantasy. Our original title, you know, was *The
Man in Lincoln's Nose*. Couldn't use it, though. They also
wouldn't let us shoot people on Mount Rushmore. Can't de-
face a national monument," he added sarcastically. "And it's
a pity too, because I had a wonderful shot in mind of Cary
Grant hiding in Lincoln's nose and having a sneezing fit."
He chuckled happily and went on. "Cary is marvelous, you
see. One doesn't direct Cary Grant, one simply puts him in
front of a camera. And, you see, he enables the audience to
identify with the main character. I mean by that, Cary Grant
represents a man we know. He's not a stranger. If you are
walking down a street and you see a man hit by a car and
you don't know him, you stop and look for a moment and
you say, 'Tut, tut, that's too bad,' and you pass on. Now if
the person hit were your brother, well, there's a different
situation altogether. It's the same thing, you see, as Cary
Grant in a film versus an unknown actor." He paused to re-
light his cigar. "I want to cause the audience to emote," he
continued. "To do that one must throw them into the picture completely, win them over to your way of thinking.
Often, you see, when a character is doing wrong, the audience still will want him to succeed. That only works if they
are totally involved with the picture and the character." He
regarded his cigar a moment. "I like to exploit the fine line
between comedy and tragedy; I like to take the ordinary
and make it extraordinary. I believe in pure cinema," he said,
pronouncing it cin-e-maa, and taking a puff on his cigar.
"Some people say that cinema is action, but that is a miscon-
ception. Movement is only a part of cinema. Spectacle is not
cinema, either. Nor is photographing actors acting. Relying

on the actor is borrowing from the stage. I think that montage is the essential thing in a motion picture. You take a shot of Jimmy Stewart, say, looking; then a shot of what he sees; then his reaction. But you see, it's like the old Pudovkin test. He took the same shot of an actor looking downward with a blank expression, and spliced it between a shot of a baby playing and a shot of an open grave. The audience that saw it marveled at the subtlety of expression and emotion the actor's face had shown. But in reality it was the same identical shot of the actor after both the baby and the grave. Only montage has that power of audience suggestion. I'm very keen on that method of storytelling."

The phone rang and he answered it. His secretary came in quietly and removed my empty cup and saucer. "Mr. Hitchcock can't stand the sight of dirty dishes," she whispered. As soon as he hung up, the director went on. "As far as I'm concerned, you see, the content is secondary to the handling; the effect I can produce on an audience rather than the subject matter." He paused and puffed twice on his cigar. "When I was making *Psycho*, Paramount made for me a whole torso out of rubber for the shower scene. When one plunged a knife in it, blood would spurt out. Oh, it was wonderful," he said merrily. "But I wouldn't use it. That would have been too simple. Instead I spent one week shooting that sequence and the knife never touches the body on the screen. We give the impression that it does, but actually it doesn't. The effect is achieved, you see, through montage. Also there is no part of the woman's body shown that might be considered taboo. The illusion of nudity is achieved through montage as well. There are seventy different setups in forty-five seconds." Hitchcock paused to let this impressive fact sink in and to puff twice again on his cigar.

I asked why he had chosen to have Janet Leigh stabbed to death in the shower, and how he had controlled the amount of exposure. "Well, that's what life is like," he answered reasonably. "Things happen out of the blue. You may say I'm going downtown to the movies, but on the way you might be killed. One must never set up a murder. They must happen unexpectedly, as in life." He paused. "All you see of Janet Leigh," he went on, "is her hands, her shoulders, and head. The rest is a model."

Here the director put his cigar on an ashtray and stood up to illustrate his story. "You see, I filmed the shots with the nude and the camera both moving in slow motion. As she moved up this arm, you see," he said, slowly raising his left arm, "we cover up this breast. And as she moved the other arm up," he demonstrated again, "we cover the other breast. After all, one can't show breasts on the screen, can one?" He sat and picked up his cigar again. "Now, when the footage was projected at regular speed it looked as though the girl's arms were moving fast. Shooting it in slow motion, however, enabled us to control the exposure of the body."

In making his kind of film, the director told me, there were certain rules. "When making a suspense picture," he said, "one must never confuse the audience. Always give them the fullest facts. Occasionally one even provides the audience with information the character doesn't know. That builds suspense as well. But one must always play fair with the audience. Take a look at *Psycho* a second time. It's honest; you can check all the details; all the clues are provided during the picture. All-important, however, is the fact that cinema is a visual medium. In *Psycho*, for example, I wanted to express desperation visually. The girl and her lover are desperate. And the first time we see them, they are half-undressed in the middle of the day. How better to express that kind of desperation?"

Word came that the print he had ordered was ready, and Hitchcock led the way down a long corridor to a small projection room where I was shown the trailer for *Psycho*. In it, the director himself meandered jauntily about the locale in which the film took place, pointing out where the two murders took place, giving sly little hints, and saying things like, "Oh, it's horrible and bloody," mock-seriously to the camera. All the while his television theme-music played, conjuring up a syncopated elephant prancing along a narrow side street in London.

When the short was over, he stood up and said, "You see what I meant?"

Later on, back in his office, he told me about actors. "I once said that actors are cattle," he smiled. "But that's a joke. However, actors *are* children, and they're temperamental, and they need to be handled gently and sometimes . . ." he paused for emphasis ". . . slapped. I always talk things over with them in the dressing room before we go on the set. Otherwise, one too often has all the drama on the set and none in the scene. I go out of my way to make them feel relaxed." He took a few reflective puffs on his cigar. "One day," he continued, "Ingrid Bergman was making a film in England, and she came over to my hotel and began telling me how terribly upset she was, and how worried and miserable. I just looked at her. And she said, 'Oh, Hitch, I know what you're going to say. Don't say it!' Well, what I was going to say was simply what I always say: 'Ingrid, it's *only* a movie.'"

Billy Wilder, director-writer-producer (*One, Two, Three; The Apartment*), pacing the carpeted floor of his office at the Samuel Goldwyn studios: "In film making, I like the normal setup, like Wyler uses, like John Ford, like Chaplin. I'm against this fancy-schmancy stuff. It reminds an audience that artisans have intruded. I don't want them to grab their partner and say, 'My God, look at *that!*' Besides, we tried all those things in the old UFA days," he added, referring to the famous German studio of the twenties.

Later, concerning his old films, which he doesn't like to see: "I want to climb up there and change everything," he said, smiling. "It's like meeting a girl you slept with fifteen years ago. You look at her and you think, 'My God, did I go to bed with that?'"

Warner Brothers. Gordon Douglas, a contract director in a white captain's cap, on the set of *Claudelle Inglish* as an army of technicians puts the final touches on a setup: "It's kinda not as much fun as it was in the old days. Too many people. In the old days, for a simple shot like this, I'd only need about half the people that're around here now. It's the union thing, you know. You gotta have somebody to move the chair, somebody else to move the tie rack. It's ridiculous."

Diane McBain, the young star of the picture, came over to the director and asked how he thought she looked. He said he thought she looked just fine. Then she told him how much fun she'd had over the weekend playing with Clue, a game, and her ouija board. He said he was glad to hear it.

After a short rehearsal of the scene with the actors, and three or four loud requests for less noise from the technicians, Douglas walked jauntily past me as further noisy adjustments were being made, and mumbled from the corner of his mouth: "It's all a lotta shit, isn't it?"

John Sturges, director of *Sergeants 3* and *By Love Possessed*, discussed his favorite subject: "Western characters must not be glamorized," he said with emphasis. "I'm a Westerner myself, and I can tell you I don't go for that Stuart Lake baloney. You can't make a Western if it's pretty. The men look like chorus boys, for Christ's sake. Always use a lot of back lighting, and don't let the star talk too much. John Ford, you know, made John Wayne a star by not letting him talk. But the absolute must for a Western is isolation. The man must be God. And you've gotta take issues that can only be resolved by guns."

On pace: "For some reason," he said frowning, "in America they think you can't begin a picture slow. They want to hook the audience before they get bored. Now, for Christ's sake, how can anyone get bored in the first five minutes of a picture? They haven't been there long enough, for Christ's sake." He smiled. "Charlie Brackett summed it up beautifully, I think, when he said that in Europe you could open a picture with clouds, dissolve slowly to clouds, and dissolve again to more clouds. In America, though, he said, you open with clouds, you then dissolve to an airplane, and in the next shot the airplane's gotta explode."

Dean Martin, actor and singer, in his dressing room on the Metro-Goldwyn-Mayer lot: (a) On Broadway: "Doin' the same thing ev'y night? Jesus, how borin'. I wouldn't mind tryin' it for about three nights, but I'd sure as hell hate to be in a hit." (b) On acting: "I just kinda think the way the part is, you know. I kinda think back to somethin' that's happened to me. Like in *Rio Bravo*, there was a scene I was supposed to be very sad in, supposed to cry even. So I thought about a time I was unhappy, time my son, little Dino, was very sick, and that helped me. I kinda used those feelin's I had then." He sighed deeply. "Before I started the picture, I went to Brando and he helped me out a little bit. Told me to listen. Actin' is reactin', you know. Think that you're thinkin'." (c) On the many jokes made about his drinking: "They don't bother me, but they're a little silly. If anyone drank that much, how long you think people'd keep hirin' him?" He paused, but not for an answer. "Oh, don't get me wrong, I drink. But I hardly ever get drunk. I don't mind the jokes though. Matter of fact, they kinda help the image, you know what I mean?"

William Goetz, a producer for many years (*Sayonara, Me and the Colonel*), discussed picking properties: "It all depends on how it interests me. I am not interested in any one type of picture. I don't mind copying someone else as long as I don't copy myself; and I don't mind someone copying me." He smiled. "But mainly I am interested in books as properties, because you can see the whole thing clearer. An original story, for example, can't be seen in toto. And books, best sellers, are presold, they already have an audience. A play hasn't got that kind of presell. In a year, maybe 800,000 people see a play, but books, you see, have a much wider circulation. And how can people have an interest in something they don't know anything about?"

He paused for a moment and added: "A picture should also be a fine time. If you want to send messages, call Western Union, as somebody said once."

One morning at Paramount, I was taken to *The Ladies' Man* sound stage where Jerry Lewis was directing, producing, and starring. The area was buzzing with technicians, actors, actresses, signs, props, television cameras and electrical equipment, TV monitors, motion picture cameras, cables, booms, chairs, and other paraphernalia. At the far end of the stage, dominating the area, was a gigantic, four-story, fully furnished, completely practical (including an elevator), three-wall set of the boardinghouse in which most of the picture's action took place; with a fourth wall added, it could easily have been lived in.

Atop a huge crane, with an added extension, at the end of which was the camera, sat Jerry Lewis, screaming instructions, insults, jokes, and exchanging quips with the cast and crew. Painted in large white letters on the side of this mountainous piece of equipment was the notice: JERRY's TOY. Next to the camera was an old-fashioned car horn that Lewis intermittently sounded as a sign of approval or anger. When he wished to get down to the ground, he screamed to a man at the rear of the machine, who controlled the crane's raising and lowering. Whenever Lewis was making a movie, I was told, it was "a free-for-all set," and yet *The Bellboy*, made under even more haphazard circumstances, was one of the studio's biggest money-makers.

I watched Lewis throw cigarettes down at technicians and then demand them back. Almost at the opposite end of the stage, facing the boardinghouse and running from one wall to the other, was a huge banner colorfully lettered: VERY HAPPY HOLIDAYS FROM THE LOUSY PRODUCER-DIRECTOR, followed by a caricature of Lewis' profile, which, I noticed, was also to be found on walls, pieces of equipment, instruments, and even on the shirts of some of the personnel. Suddenly Lewis screamed: "That's no damn good! Two demerits for Jim!"

On the side of Lewis' portable dressing room there was a bulletin board marked with a sign, LITTLE BITS OF INFORMATION WE COULDN'T DO WITHOUT, surrounded by a jumble of ads, press layouts, stills, and so forth, from Lewis' last two comedies. Near the set were two rows of bleachers where, someone informed me, children were allowed to watch shooting; two or three small children were there now along with a couple of bewildered parents. Nearby was a large display cabinet filled with old comedy and vaudeville props, each separately labeled. On a side wall were some hundred fifty coffee mugs, each with a person's first name under it; at Lewis' request, each member of the cast and crew had his own cup.

After a little while, Lewis dismounted his crane, changed his shirt, and was ready for a take. He called for quiet, climbed the spiral staircase in the boardinghouse, entered a second-story room, and comically began cleaning with a feather duster. The camera recorded his moves. Suddenly he stopped. "Cut!" he screamed. "What the hell is this crap doing here?" he demanded, indicating a little table on which stood a small spray bottle. "Hey, Jim," he yelled, "what are you, some kind of a *nut?*" A heavyset technician lumbered into the room and Lewis started squirting him with the contents of the atomizer. Running away, the man cried, "Hey, come on, Jerry, cut it out! Hey, cut it out, Jerry!" Instead, Lewis chased him zanily around the set as other technicians and actors chuckled wearily. Then, hiding behind a jog, he waited until the winded man rounded the corner and gave him a good squirt full in the face.

This attended to, the comedian repeated the scene, expressing satisfaction with the take when it was completed, and went into his dressing room, followed by an entourage of five or six. A bit later, he reappeared in an insane Indian disguise, which, I was told, was not for the picture but for the general amusement. After checking a new setup, he took the costume off, and looked at some rushes of the day's shooting on a large screen behind his dressing room.

I asked him why the three or four television sets were on the stage. "We use them to set up the shots," he answered seriously. "We can see better what the shot'll look like with them." Then, grabbing a baseball, he began tossing it around the area with some technicians. I lingered long enough to see him mischievously set up an inflatable toy clown behind a large carton and amuse the company, as, seemingly on its own rubber legs, he made it rise and fall from behind the box like a grotesque dwarf. Exchanging some droll comments with it, he called him Melvin. A moment later he was screaming instructions again, and climbing aboard his expensive "Toy," from where he could survey his make-believe kingdom.

In the Polo Lounge of the Beverly Hills Hotel, Jack Lemmon, the actor, told me why he thought his Columbia films had not been as successful as those (*The Apartment*, *Some Like It Hot*) he had made on loan-out. "Some of the Columbia pictures were damned good, but I think what screwed them up were the titles. No, really, titles are important. Look at the ones I've been stuck with: *It Should Happen to You, You Can't Run Away From It, Phffft.*" He smiled. "When we were shooting *Phffft*, they stopped production right in the middle of the day so they could discuss that title. Everyone waited while they went into a two-and-a-half hour huddle upstairs. When they broke, I asked the director about it, and he said they'd decided to take out one 'f.' "

Later, in front of the hotel, waiting for our cars to be brought from the parking lot, Lemmon looked at me, smiled, and said, "You know, I'll tell you something. Here I am at thirty-five and—though, believe me, everything's wonderful that's happened—I can only play two parts a year. I yearn for those days when I was doing a different TV role every week. You know, I'm an actor, I like to work."

The cars arrived, we said good-by, and both of us drove away. We met again at the first red light. From his convertible sports car, he yelled, "Driving is wild in this town, isn't it?" And we raced down Sunset Boulevard until a red light separated us and he raised his fist in the air with the middle finger extended in a gesture of comic defiance as he sped away from me down the dark, empty boulevard.

At the Universal-International studios, Gail Gifford, of the publicity department, discussed the aims of Ross Hunter, one of the most successful producers to release through Universal, with such box-office hits as *Imitation of Life* and *Midnight Lace*. Hunter, she explained, was unique among current producers in his belief that glamor had been taken out of films for too long. His formula, she said, was elegance: rich, lush sets, expensive clothes, real jewels and real flowers. "Ross always says," she quoted, "that 'It's just as easy to commit a murder on an Oriental rug as on linoleum.' And his grosses bear him out. His pictures make fantastic amounts of money. Like *Portrait in Black*. It was a bad picture, and he knows it, but it did fantastically."

Later, in Miss Gifford's office, I noticed some publicity sheets on her desk, headed: "Picture Layouts for *Lover, Come Back*," followed by several photo story ideas, listed: "1. How to recognize a drunk—Tony Randall. 2. How to make a chocolate Easter egg—Doris Day. 3. Sunday with Rock."

Cary Grant, wearing a white dress shirt open at the collar and a pair of slacks, both of which looked as though he had slept in them, sat behind his large, paper-strewn desk at Universal, a day's stubble on his face, his grey-flecked dark hair disheveled, having just finished a long story conference on his own production, *That Touch of Mink*. He spoke as kindly of Hitchcock as the director had spoken of him: "Oh, Hitch is great! You walk on his set for a scene and the set is everything you thought it would be, just as you envisioned it— never anything out of place or wrong," he said in that unique, Bristol-born fashion so popular with impersonators. He smiled. "And he's so patient. I'll never forget when we were shooting *Notorious* with Ingrid. In the morning we started a scene that was quite difficult because, you see, Ingrid had to say some of her lines a certain way so that I could imitate her readings. Well, anyway, we started," he continued, leaning forward and acting out the situation, "and Ingrid just couldn't get it. We went over and over the scene and she was in some sort of daze. You know, she just wasn't *there*. But Hitch, he didn't say anything. He just sat there next to the camera, pulling on his cigar." Grant laughed slightly at the recollection. "Finally around eleven o'clock, I began to see in Ingrid's eyes that she was starting to come around. And for the first time all morning, the lines were coming out right. And just then Hitch said, 'Cut.'" He stopped and did a fast, downward take to the left, as though looking amazed, at Hitchcock. "And I thought," he said, looking back at me, "what on *earth* is he stopping for *now?* Hitch just sat and looked up at Ingrid and said, quietly, '*Good* morning, Ingrid.'"

Leaving Universal, I passed a young secretary sorting fan mail, a great deal of it, from all over the world, almost none of which would be seen by the star to whom it was addressed. "They all begin the same way," she said, " 'I've never written to a movie star before.' "

In his private cottage at Paramount, Laurence Harvey, the British actor of *Room at the Top*, played a phonograph record of two slightly bawdy songs he had sung in an English movie, *The Long and The Short and The Tall* (called *Jungle Fighters* in America). While they played, he leaned against a wall, smiling occasionally to himself. Then we walked to the studio commissary, now deserted, and Harvey asked a waitress if he might have some cottage cheese, crackers and tea. "I'm very sad," he said, "that New York isn't a big film community. It's such an exciting city and everything happens there. Just as London is the cultural center of England." He broke a cracker into his cottage cheese and began to speak as though he were dictating. "Out here in Hollywood, you understand, domesticity settles in more than anywhere else in the world. But, aside from that, Hollywood is still unquestionably *the* movie capital of the world. The technical facilities out here are fantastic." He gazed at his plate a moment, moving the spoon around the edges. "And, you know, I've found that in America everything is done and directed toward the actor. Here, I mean, the technicians work for the actor. In England, it's the other way around."

Leaning back in his chair, he lit a cigarette, and went on. "I think that Hollywood has been able to get together as many talents as there are in the world—it's destroyed as many. When people talk of the world of the jungle, Africa or New York City. . . ." He sipped his tea. "Why, here, the beast roams on beautifully manicured front lawns and swimming pools that are kept the same temperature the year round, defying all laws of Mother Nature." He drew on his cigarette. "I hope you'll quote exactly," he said. "The stakes are so high in Hollywood, the competition is keener, and it is so much harder to survive. The only way *to* survive is to be honest with yourself and evaluate what you can give as a person and an artist, and not be involved with all the b.s. of this place." He finished his tea, and again leaned grandly back in his chair. "In Hollywood, the studios feed you with an extraordinary amount of gilt-edged words. And if one is a weak personality, one grows to believe this and thinks the whole world outside will act the same way, and, of course, it doesn't. After all, the artist must satisfy his own soul. All you can lose is your reputation. And, anyway, the public has the final say."

Walking back to his cottage, Harvey told me, "There's really only one thing I don't like about pictures." He smiled. "I hate getting up so early. I'm such a whore, I can't stay in bed *long* enough."

At his own Buena Vista studios, I told Walt Disney, creator of Mickey Mouse, Donald Duck, and producer of *Snow*

White and the Seven Dwarfs, that I had recently visited Disneyland. "You know," he said, "it was very hard to sell the idea in the beginning. Anyway, now we get four adults to every child. There were eighteen thousand people at our New Year's Eve party, four thousand more than last year. Since it opened in July of 1955, there's been twenty-five million people there. Isn't that something?"

On the wall behind us was a huge blowup of a page from *Variety*, with a list of the hundred top moneymaking pictures of all time. Several Disney features were checked off in heavy black ink. I asked the producer which was the favorite among his films. "Oh," he answered, smiling whimsically, "I guess *Snow White*. Maybe because I'm sentimental, and it was our first."

At the time I talked with him, Richard Brooks, director-writer (*Sweet Bird of Youth*, *Elmer Gantry*), had not won an Academy Award. "If I ever won one it'd probably ruin me," he told me in his office at Metro-Goldwyn-Mayer. "I'd start to believe that crap. Take Humphrey Bogart. He could never equate the money he was making with what he was doing. He was constantly mocking himself. And that's a good thing, you know what I mean?" Brooks paused and nodded his head. "He was quite a man, Bogart. He was genuinely tough and he was honest. I remember a couple of weeks before he died he was still having guests and seeing friends in the afternoon. I went out to see him one day and found him sitting there as usual, drink in hand. After a while, he had a terrible coughing fit and he started vomiting blood. It was an awful thing to see. I got up and started to leave the room till it was over. And Bogie looked up at me and said, 'What's a matter, Dick, can't you take it?' "

In his office at the 20th Century-Fox studios, Jerry Wald, producer (*Peyton Place*, *Return to Peyton Place*), proudly pointed out "a Picasso original" on his wall, sat on a long foam-rubber couch, and told me about his production of *Sons and Lovers.*

"It's a long story," he said with a smile. "The novel was published in 1913, the year after I was born. The first time I read it was in 1928, and in 1929 I was in a class that Thomas Wolfe was teaching and he praised the book. Irwin Shaw and Garson Kanin were in the class too. I thought at that time that *Sons and Lovers* would make a great motion picture. In 1931, I met Columbia vice-president Jack Cohn and told him about it. The next year, 1932, I went to Warner's and wrote some of their musicals. Then in 1934 I went to Mr. Mayer's dinner party and I met Thalberg on the beach and he said the book reminded him of his mother. I think Mayer said the same thing. In 1936, I became friendly with Leslie Howard; I told him about the book and that he'd be great for the part of the son. In 1940, I suggested the book to Warner's again, but they didn't want to do it because they thought *How Green Was My Valley* couldn't be topped. But in 1944, they bought another Welsh story, *The Corn is Green,* 'cause Bette Davis wanted to do it. In 1946, I came across the *Rebel Without A Cause* script and saw *A Flag is Born* on Broadway with Marlon Brando in it. I talked to him about *Rebel* and about *Sons and Lovers,* but nothing materialized. Then in 1948, at RKO, I talked to them about the property and around that time I was thinking of James Dean for the part. Anyway, RKO wasn't interested. In 1953 I went to Columbia as head of production. That's when Monty Clift did *From Here to Eternity,* and I thought he'd be great in the part of the son. I talked to Harry Cohn about it and he said, 'We'll see.' Then I talked to Dudley Nichols about writing the screenplay for *Sons and Lovers.* He was a good friend of Mrs. Lawrence. I wrote to Frieda and she said O.K., and I bought the rights to *Sons and Lovers* and *Lady Chatterley* for $50,000. They didn't want to try it then, though, 'cause *Lady Chatterley* had been a flop in Europe. Well, to make a long story short, in 1953, we were all set. We had Alec Guinness and Monty Clift for the father and son, and Peter Glenville to direct. Then Cohn called and said, 'I don't wanta do Lawrence,' he said. 'Shelve it,' he said. I said if I can't do it, I'll quit. So I quit Columbia. I came here to Fox. Here's where we finally got it going. Gavin Lambert'd never written a screenplay before, but he was enthusiastic and so was Jack Cardiff, who'd never directed before, and that's what really counts, I think, enthusiasm. We had Joan Collins all set, but she called two days before shooting and said she didn't wanta do it 'cause the part wasn't big enough." By this time, Wald was pacing the room and gesturing as he talked. "Well," he continued, "Mary Ure was a friend of Cardiff's, so we signed her up. Cardiff was in Europe by this time. He called me one day and said it was snowing for the spring sequence. Everything was going wrong, he said. So I called T. B. Clarke in to do a rewrite. So that's about it. Thirty years on the same story." He paused. "Oh, yeah, I almost forgot," he said, suddenly. "Right after *Goodbye, Mr. Chips*, I wanted Robert Donat for the picture. That didn't work out though. I wanted Raymond Massey once too."

A couple of men came into the office and told the producer he just had to come now because he was holding up a screening of rushes. Wald quickly slipped on his suit jacket and adjusted his tie. As he left, he said, "Listen, if there's anything else I can tell you about *Sons and Lovers*, let me know, huh?"*

Also at 20th Century-Fox, Mark Robson, director (*Bright*

---

* I discovered later, much to my surprise that in 1948, James Dean was only 17 and quite unknown; that Gavin Lambert had not only written a screenplay (*Bitter Victory*, 1958) before, but had also directed and a feature film, *Another Sky*, before doing *Sons and Lovers*; that Jack Cardiff, director of photography on such movies as *The Red Shoes*, *Black Narcissus* (for which he won an Oscar), and the *African Queen*, had directed *William Tell* in 1953; and that Thomas Wolfe had some precocious students in his New York University class of 1929; Wald (seventeen), Kanin (seventeen), Shaw (fifteen).

Victory, The Inn of the Sixth Happiness), who started in films at RKO, where he was an assistant cutter on Orson Welles' *The Magnificent Ambersons*, and later directed a series of unusual horror pictures for the late Val Lewton, spoke warmly of those early days: "Everyone who was associated with Orson at RKO," he said, smiling, "was involved in a kind of purge. We were all in trouble because of Orson. So a lot of us, Robert Wise and myself anyway, were kind of demoted to Val's low-budget B unit. The only thing is, Val was an artist, and all his pictures were carefully worked out, even though many of them started out simply as 'Let's make a picture about. . . .' For instance, we saw a painting by Böcklin in the *Book of Knowledge* called 'The Island of the Dead,' and someone said, 'Let's make a picture about something that happened on that island.' So we did." Robson paused and smiled sadly. "We only had a budget of about $125,000 a picture then," he continued, "and we had to make do with what we could find. We were always looking through art books and at photographs. It was a new way of making pictures. We had a lot of fun. I remember what Val said about that picture. He said the film was about a man who is driven insane by the natural process of premature burial." He chuckled. Then, speaking of the changes in film making since that time, he said, musingly. "Some of the spontaneity has gone out of it. It's not as much fun. I don't know how to put it really. Well, it's like. . . . People no longer get together and say, 'Let's get together and make a picture about. . . .' That doesn't happen anymore."

Angie Dickinson, actress, in the publicity offices of Warner Brothers, on Hollywood: "I love Hollywood. I love everything about Hollywood. Including the people."

George Stevens, director-producer (*The Greatest Story Ever Told, Shane*): "I find the Hollywood community tremendously related to the American scene. The boy next door and the girl next door have become the movie queens and directors. They've replaced the glamor queens. They're not 'Hollywood' people any longer; they're us." He paused. "But I have always thought," he said, "that the American demand for frivolous films is greater than the frivolousness with which they're turned out. Sure, I don't think it's ever good enough. If we don't criticize, nothing would ever get done. Still, it seems to me," he went on, seriously, "that pictures in America suffer from that uneasy label, 'Hollywood.' All American films are immediately labeled that way, 'Hollywood.' That's just as frivolous as labeling all the novels from America. Personally, I think films have progressed strangely to a greater degree than the novel or theatre in the last fifty years. There are more important films, three to one, than novels or theatre. I truly believe that American films would be put to better use if we could get rid of that frivolous label, 'Hollywood.' "

William Wyler has directed some of the most popular and successful of American films, including *The Best Years of Our Lives*, *Wuthering Heights*, *Mrs. Miniver*, and *Ben-Hur*. I met him in his office on the Goldwyn lot. "Hollywood is just like anyplace else," he said, defensively. "You find the best and the worst here. I don't like the way Hollywood is used as an adjective. I think things have changed for the better out here. We've progressed like everything else. Take a look at the old pictures sometimes, and you'll realize we've progressed just as much as the aviation industry." He paused to blow his nose. "Of course we are hurt by the amount of restriction imposed on us. The more freedom of expression, the more one can do. For example, twenty-five years ago I made an almost unrecognizable version of Lillian Hellman's play, *The Children's Hour*. It was called *These Three*, and we had to cut any reference or implication of the lesbian theme, which is crucial to the work. I've always wanted to do that play as it was written. Now we've done it. So you see, we've progressed."

Discussing *Ben-Hur*, Wyler said, quickly, "It was the greatest challenge to me because I'd done nothing like it. I know a lot of people said it was traitorish and disgraceful of me. The highbrow critics said so. But I don't care. Enormous popular appeal is what we were after. We weren't making a sophisticated story. It was not to be a New Wave picture," he added, a bit scornfully. "*Ben-Hur* presented dangers and pitfalls bigger than any I've ever encountered. We were on very touchy ground religiously, for instance. The result was the best thing for *all*. It was not intended as anything artistic. And it was terribly difficult to make." Wyler coughed twice and went on. "I think it's the best picture in its class that's ever been made. People who wouldn't care for this kind of picture shouldn't go see it. I got a tremendous satisfaction from it. DeMille was supposed to be the only one who could do that kind of picture. I didn't believe that."

Along a wall was a thin, rectangular table on which stood various packages, an Academy Award statuette, and other plaques, scrolls and statuettes. Wyler told me they were awards for *Ben-Hur*, from all over the world. Some of them hadn't been unpacked and were there on the table in their shipping boxes.

As I was leaving, Wyler said that he thought the standard of film criticism in America had not improved in relation to the films and was not as high as in Europe. As an example, he pointed out that his film, *The Big Country*, had had a wonderful reception in Europe, but had fared badly in America. "In Europe, you see," he said, "they're just as snobbish as they are in New York. They like foreign pictures."

Clifford Odets, playwright (*Awake and Sing!*, *The Big Knife*), film director (*None But the Lonely Heart*), and author of numerous screenplays (*Sweet Smell of Success*), lives in a comfortable, two-story house along the fashionable, tree-lined Beverly Drive. A tall, broad-shouldered man with wiry, white-streaked hair, powerful arms, and the hands of a pianist, he speaks with a kind of dangerously quiet, clipped intensity that gives one the feeling of imminent eruption. He met me at his front door in a light blue terrycloth coverall, made some coffee for us both, and sat on a couch in his living room, on the walls of which hung a couple of Klees.

"The main change in Hollywood," he said, carefully stirring his coffee, "is the decentralization. Hollywood started as something primitive, a done-at-home industry—like weaving, which started as a cottage industry, and developed into the factory system. It's the same with Hollywood. First it was a cottage industry, then a factory, and now it's gone back to being a cottage industry." He sipped his coffee and continued. "I think this speaks well for a more human expression in movies. But the people who are a part of this decentralization did this not for more human expression, but for a larger share of the money. One man, the single creator, is the key to this new establishment and that promises well for the future. In the last ten years, however, it hasn't shown any noteworthy results because the creator simply wanted more money. But if he will become interested in *how* to say something he wants to express, well, the form holds untold possibilities."

Had television been a contributor to the situation? "TV has nothing to do with it," he answered. "It simply drains the financial possibilities. And the bankers, you know, have no sentiment about the movies. As far as they're concerned, oil wells or buildings are as good. Studio owners have threatened more than once to break up the whole thing, but the sentiment of picture making has made them fight off the bankers."

He put a filter cigarette between his lips with a slow upswing of his whole arm, rolled it around for a moment, took it from his mouth, and regarded it abstractedly. "The general atmosphere in Hollywood is the same as in the rest of the country," he said, put the cigarette back in his mouth and, in a slow methodical manner, proceeded to strike a match, light the cigarette, and wave out the flame. "It's this new sort of pietism," he went on, scornfully. "I think it is the most stifling thing I have ever seen. But Hollywood itself is a company town. You have to be nice to the boss, you have to adhere to the ethics of the boss. I've often felt that Hollywood is like the teacher who wanted a job very badly. When he came up before the school board he was asked, 'What would you teach? Is the world round or flat?' There was silence while the teacher thought. Then he said, 'Well, I can teach it either way.' " Odets chuckled dispassionately, and took a drag on his cigarette.

"Hollywood is no better or worse than the rest of the country," he went on. "The whole country has become a cuddle-bunny. It's not just Hollywood. Maybe there'll be a new kind of moral vigor, a reversal of the so-called values by which the American people live today." He shook his head. "Everyone grabs at a healthy root, with food in hand, starts right in for college. In order to be a healthy, whole human being, you need several qualities which we lack in this country. You need bigger values. What are you for? What are you against?" The writer regarded his cigarette a moment and then put it out in an ashtray. "I don't mean everyone should be a Don Quixote," he said suddenly. "But I'd rather see that than see Don Quixote laughed at. In his *Civilization of the Renaissance in Italy*, Burckhardt said, 'Don Quixote gained his reason and lost his reason for being.' Americans have done similarly. We're such a *reasonable* people," he said ironically. "Still, if a man's got an ulcer, don't tell me *he's* an ulcer." He paused. "All of us should have the values of a St. George. But there is no St. George without a dragon. And we don't have a dragon."

August 1962

By the middle of *1964*, I'd moved to Hollywood. To Van Nuys, California, actually, which is in the San Fernando Valley, which is a suburb of Los Angeles, of which Hollywood is also a suburb.

With the money Harold paid me for an article he never ran, I bought a yellow *1951* Ford convertible and, with Polly Platt (whom I had married), her black dog, and a huge television set in the back seat, we drove all the way across the country.

Not long after we got settled, Harold called to ask me to write a very short piece on a then-popular discothèque, the Whisky à Go Go. It was an ephemeral phenomenon, but I have included it here since it describes a part of the Hollywood scene I have managed to stay away from since.

Go-Go Going

GOING IN, THE BACK WAY IS THE BEST. A huge, monolithic bouncer admits you (if you have or say the right name) and immediately countless bodies are pushing you off a balcony and down a narrow staircase. The noise is high and deafening, only semihuman: drums, electric guitars and voices magnified beyond recognition. Descending the stairs, there's a moment of panic when you realize you can't turn back from that raging sea of writhing bodies and screaming lungs before you. Countless men and women shake, wiggle, bounce, grind and bump in a massive orgy of movement. You wouldn't have thought it possible, but the noise actually gets louder. Your mind searches wildly for a good descriptive cliché: The lions' den? The Roman circus? The snake pit? No, more than anything, you decide, it reminds you of what they say it'll be like the day before the Bomb goes off.

Outside, the line runs all the way around the corner. People cluster next to it or meander aimlessly alongside. Cars piled up in front and on the side (Whisky à Go Go occupies the corner of Clark Street on Hollywood's Sunset Strip). The walls are plastered with French posters: lousy art films, l'opéra, Miró, Matisse, Rouault, Dufy, Klee, guys most of the people going in never heard of. There's also a big sign that reads: Johnny Rivers. He sings inside.

Now try it the front way. There's more of a jam because this way is for the slobs. Once you're in, there is nothing to see except a wall of bodies. No one around to show you a break in that wall, so you chip away at it until you crash through and are shoved into a place. No tables empty. Rarely are, unless you're somebody. The waitresses are cute, pretty and young, or tough, cheap and young. Their skirts are split on the side to stomach-level. French-style, you see.

"I finally got this crap," says one of the stags to another, both gazing glassy-eyed at the gyrating dance floor.

"Yeah?"

"Took me a couple of months to learn it."

"How'd ya do it?"

"I just threw myself onto the floor."

"No kiddin'."

"That's the only way."

"Yeah."

There goes Hedda Hopper, out the back way.

Above the dancers—a peninsula at the edge of the balcony—is a square, glass-walled room with a huge stereo hookup in the middle. Three girls in fringe-covered dresses with midriffs bare dance around inside. They also play the music. This booth is modern while the rest of the decor tries for a New Orleans' French Quarter atmosphere, a Montmartre quality, the Tennessee Williams look, baby. Because the girls look as untouchable and undesirable as newborn infants behind glass, the booth fails in its erotic idea: You may look, but don't touch. The French do it better: a huge, ornate, gold-plated birdcage with girls in skimpy feathers. But Kay Carson, Patti Bryton and Joanie Sannes don't care. All night they dance about up there, earnest and concentrated, sexy as insects in a bottle. Around and around they go, like automated dancing teachers in a school of the future. The Jerk, the Swim, the Watusi (New Yorkers call it the Frug), the Go Go, Mashed Potatoes, Walkin' the Dog, the Pony—all the dances look about the same, just as the songs sound identical. But, of course, that's the point. That's why it's popular. It's easy. Apart from all the psychological and sociological explanations of "release from anxiety," "getting rid of hostilities," the fact remains that a certain skill is required to do the Waltz, and a man must have style to Tango, while anyone can do the Go Go. Just throw your arms around by habit, move your pelvis by instinct, your feet by chance, and you're doing it. And if you're not, well, maybe somebody'll step back for a moment, look at what you're doing and put a name to it. Then there'll be a new dance: the Wince, the Twitch, the Broiled Lamp Chop, Walkin' the Bird.

The Whisky opened January 15, 1964, and is just now the hottest club in America. Jack Paar's program covered it and ABC-TV did a documentary about it, Johnny Rivers' records sell, and owners Shelly Davis, Phil Tanzini, Elmer Valentine and Ted Flier are doing fine. They have the furtive look of men who know they are riding a fad, their eyes darting about, nervous to make it now because they'll never get this kind of chance again.

But now, right now, everybody comes. There's Loretta Young over there. And Jack Palance and his wife. Shelley Winters, Laurence Harvey, Sal Mineo. Fred Astaire came around last week. So did Bob Hope and Dean Martin. And The Beatles. They caused a riot on top of the usual one. Pierre Salinger was in last night. That blonde dancing wildly in the middle of the floor, a big black bow in her hair, that's Mamie Van Doren. Johnny Rivers goes with her. And at the next booth are four of the Astronauts. That one in the middle is Scott, who may be going to the moon.

And the Beatniks from Venice come (under some new name), and the arty crowd from U.C.L.A. and the hippies from New York and the squares from all over and the has-beens who want to be in on the action, and the are-nows because they want to stay that way. There's a fellow with hair down to the middle of his back. And another with his hair cut like Shakespeare's. Quite a few mixed couples. Girls in the tightest possible Capri pants and high heels. Girls barefoot and covered with makeup. And boys covered with makeup. Men with beards and sunglasses. On the balcony, leaning against a pole, stands a surly young male prop in a goatee, staring down at the dance floor. He doesn't move all night. On the floor, if you are level with it, all you can see is heads bobbing up occasionally and movements that are vaguely spastic or openly orgiastic. Each dancer seems pre-occupied, self-absorbed, even bored. It is hot, very hot, and the air smells just a little like a gym, but no one seems to notice and the sweat makes them dance faster. There are three fellows in Beatle haircuts. That girl, over there, with the very large breasts smashing up and down, hasn't paused in ten minutes and her pace just increased. None of the partners ever touch except by accident. Some dance completely alone. One girl with brown hair and fat thighs wiggles as though in an orgasm but stops abruptly when someone accidentally bumps her from behind. She looks around and then peevishly shoves her bottom into the offender and is instantly back in her frenetic dance. When Johnny Rivers is announced, there is only a smattering of applause, and when he starts to sing, it could be another record for all anyone cares. The people at the ringside tables watch, a dull glaze over their eyes, drinks or cigarettes in their hands. All the moves and positions are frankly sexual, to the point of perversion perhaps, but the dancers' faces remain placid, the expressions blank. Like wind-up dolls gone berserk. Occasionally a flicker of pleasure flashes across a face, but soon it is gone in the sweat of physical strain, and the strange, subconscious threat of doom fills the place with an unspeakable depression.

That's how it goes, all night. The next evening, the crush at the front is still there, and the line of people is the same, all trying to get in the front way, while the people with faces go in the back. The noise seems louder and more inhuman and the movements on the floor resemble nothing so much as pseudoprimitives worshiping three young girls in a glass-walled room. And so it will go until that day (could be next month, next week, next day) when by some weird alchemy the herd instinct leads everyone up the Strip to Ciro's, where two fat girls in bikinis gyrate onstage, or maybe back to Cyrano's, where the thing is just to sit and talk heavy, or maybe to New York and a new, swinging, groovy place. Now the other clubs run only half-filled or empty while the walls of the Whisky à Go Go shake and swell from five times their comfortable capacity. Is it nicer? Better? Cheaper? No, man, it's in. Go. Go.   February 1965

2
ACTORS

*When I was a kid, there really was never a more mon-
strously loyal fan of Martin and Lewis: I kept a scrapbook,
for God's sake, saw their movies, listened to them on radio
(yes, they had a radio show for a while), watched them on
the* Colgate Comedy Hour *(had to go to friends' homes for
that because my father wouldn't have a TV in the house),
and prided myself in doing the best Martin and Lewis imitation on the block. (Still do, in fact.) By the time they
broke up, my fever for them had passed and their split only
increased my disinterest in them separately. But something
of the old passion must have remained—especially for Jerry
—and I think it shows through, albeit ambiguously, in that
little section on him in the* Talkies *piece. Harold must have
spotted that too, which is why I believe he asked me to do
a profile on Lewis as my second article for the magazine.*

*Afterwards, Jerry and I became friends and over the years,
through changes in his fortune and mine, he has been most
generous to me, but in the last five years I have only seen
him once. Frank Tashlin, the director who is featured
prominently in the following, also became a friend, though
we had a very touchy relationship. Before he died in 1972,
we hadn't spoken for well over a year, but he was instru-
mental in convincing me to move to California. He visited our
apartment in New York in 1964, a month or so after I'd
had a disastrous flop off-Broadway with a revival of Kaufman and Hart's* Once in a Lifetime, *and asked me what I
really wanted to do. I said I wanted to direct movies, and
he asked why the hell I didn't come to Los Angeles then,
since that was a far more likely place to get a break in pictures
than in New York—and I could continue to write for magazines just as easily from there—more easily, in fact, since
most of my subjects were in Hollywood. No one had put
it quite that simply before, and a couple of months later,
we moved, and less than two years after that, I was directing
movies.*

Mr. Lewis
Is a Pussycat

"LET ME TELL YOU about the Jewish Space Rabbi," said Jack Keller, who has been with Jerry Lewis for more than sixteen years. He was there in Atlantic City at the 500 Club on July 25, 1946, when Lewis and Dean Martin teamed up. Their press agent until they split, he has continued on with Jerry, and now handles all press relations for Jerry Lewis Productions, Inc. He is a man of medium build, sporty, in his midforties, tanned, rough-voiced and volatile. We sat in his office at the Paramount Studio in Hollywood.

"Before you meet him," Keller went on, "I better tell you there's a couple of things he's sensitive about. One of them is Dean Martin, though the antagonism is all on Dino's part. Jerry's always a little shocked, even now, when Dean lams into him. He's got a scrapbook called 'Dean Shoots His Mouth Off.' " Keller took a sip of his Scotch and lit another cigarette. "I was there the day they split up in 1956—July 25th, ten years to the day. They did their last show at the Copa and that was it. It was a traumatic experience for the kid, and to make it worse, he could never understand Dean's antagonism. But I say, when you divorce your wife, you don't speak to her. I can never understand these friendly divorces." Keller paused and sipped his drink. "But Dean's a tough one—I'll tell you a weird story." He took a drag on his cigarette. "A couple years ago, Jerry and Patti, his wife, were in a Las Vegas club. And Dean was filling in for somebody that night. They hadn't spoken, remember, for about four years, not a word. Suddenly Dean comes, sees Jerry sitting at a table, and comes over and sits down. He's very friendly, and they talk about old times. He tells Jerry he's got a train to catch, and asks him whether he'd fill in at the end of the show. Jerry says sure. Anyway, comes time for Dean to go on, he gets up there and announces, 'Ladies and gentlemen, there's a fella sitting in the audience I'd like you to meet, my partner, Jerry Lewis.' Not my former partner, 'my partner.' Well, it's a pretty moving scene—everybody's bawling. He and Jerry re-create some of their old routines; you know, they ask each other, 'Did we really do this shit,' they do a soft-shoe. Then Dean leaves to catch his train and Jerry finishes the show. Now get this. Not long afterward, in a U.P.I. interview, Dean slams into Jerry like crazy. So go figure." Keller put out his cigarette.

"But Jerry's a pussycat." He smiled. "Not that it's always waltz time. Like sometimes he'll call me up at two in the morning. 'Listen,' he says, 'I want you to hear something.' He wrote a new proverb maybe, and he wants me to hear it. Jesus! What do I want to hear at two in the morning!" He chuckled. "Jerry and me are like water and oil—we don't mix. I guess that's why we like each other." Keller finished his drink and got up to pour himself another.

Lying on his desk was a long yellow sticker reading, "Drive Carefully. Jerry Lewis May Be Watching." I asked him what it meant. "Well, Jerry has a phone in all his cars," Keller answered, "and one time he helped the police catch a drunk driver by following him and giving the cops a fix on the phone. The boys heard about it and had those signs printed up." Keller smiled. "I remember one time Jerry was in his car and I pulled up next to him at a red light. He's got the phone in his hand, he looks over at me, sticks the receiver out the window and says, 'Here, it's for you.' " He lit another cigarette. "Deedle-deedle-deedle," he said and grinned. "Let me tell you about Mr. Chips," Keller went on. "He's a springer spaniel, the first present Jerry ever gave Patti. This dog is a *pussy*cat. One of the horniest dogs that ever lived—he even ogles children. They got him a bride, Princess, and together they had ninety-eight puppies. Anyway, old Chipper was going deaf. You know what Jerry did?" Keller shook his head. "He went out and spent $15,000 on a hearing aid for him; it had to be specially developed for the dog." He laughed. "One time Israel's answer to King Farouk is playing at the Chez Paree in Chicago and he gets lonesome for Mr. Chips. So he calls me up and tells me to send him to Chicago. But not in the baggage car—oh, no. Jerry tells me to get him a first-class ticket. He says to me, 'The dog sits like anyone else!' So Mr. Chips goes first class to Chicago, and a chauffeured limousine takes him to a suite at the Ambassador East, overlooking the goddamn lake."

The phone rang, Keller answered it, spoke a few words, and hung up. "I'll tell you something," he said, turning back to me. "Something you people in New York don't realize about Jerry. He is the only star in the history of the industry who's never had a flop. That's a fact. Take any of your big stars—Cary Grant or Gary Cooper or Clark Gable, any of them—they've all had at least one picture in their careers that didn't make money. Jerry's made twenty-six films and not one has grossed less than five million dollars. Deedle-dee. You know what he gets for an hour on television? $400,000. For a week in a nightclub, his minimum is $40,000. And you can't even talk to him for less than that." Keller paused to let the facts sink in. "In 1960," he continued, "they had this picture, *CinderFella*, and they were a little worried about it. Jerry wanted to release it for Christmas—the fantasy angle and all that he thought would be good for the holidays. Well, Paramount wanted to release it in July, and Jerry said it'd die in the summer. See, they always release one Lewis picture for the summer holidays and one for Christmas vacation, the best timing for the pre-teenage audience. Only this time they didn't have any product for the July slot. Anyway, Jerry was on his way to Florida to appear at the Fontaine-bleau, and on his way he stopped in New York to see Barney Balaban, the head of Paramount. Jerry told him how he wanted *CinderFella* released in December, and Balaban said he needed a Lewis film for the summer. So right there Jerry stands up and says he'll make Balaban a picture while he's down in Florida; he says he's got the story and everything.

And right there he made up the basic outline for *The Bellboy*. On the spot. He had nothing when he walked in." Keller chuckled at the recollection. "Anyway, I'm sitting here in Hollywood, resting, when I get a call from Jerry. He says to me, 'Jake, you better come down here right away, we're starting a picture on Monday.' I said, 'Where *are* you?' He says, 'I'm in Florida.' I say, 'What picture? We ain't got no picture!' 'We do now,' he says. 'The trucks are already on their way.' So that's how he got to direct his first picture—he produced and wrote it as well. You shoulda seen that production. I asked him, 'Who's gonna be in it?' He says, 'What's the difference? We'll cast it from Celebrity Service.' Every scene was written the night before he shot it—for whomever was in town. That's Jerry. I gotta hand it to him, he's really got guts. The picture was made for $900,000. To date it's grossed eight million. Isn't *that* a pussycat!"

Frank Tashlin has directed Jerry Lewis in five films, including the last Martin-Lewis movie, and one of their best, *Hollywood or Bust*. ("They didn't speak to each other during the whole picture," he told me. "It was a bitch.") He has also directed, written and produced such rowdy satirical comedies as *Will Success Spoil Rock Hunter?* and *The Girl Can't Help It*. Starting as a cartoonist for Walt Disney, he now has several witty and caustic children's books to his credit, and was in the process of directing his sixth Lewis picture, *It's Only Money*, when I met him.

Lounging on a couch in an elegant, pink-marbled living-room set, in Victorian (mixed with Empire) furniture, Tashlin wore a beat-up faded-brown corduroy Norfolk jacket, white shirt with no tie, and a pair of wrinkled oxford-grey slacks. A large man in his late forties, about six-three and heavyset, and a kind, quiet, tanned and slightly fatigued-looking face; he has the air of a person with an infinite amount of patience who is duped by nothing. Around him, technicians were busily going about setting up the next shot.

"There's a side of Jerry Lewis you probably don't know

about," he said, his mouth moving a little to one side, less like a gangster than a cartoon character. "He's really an electronics genius. You see those television monitors over there?" He pointed at two TV sets near the camera. "That's really a marvelous thing Jerry made. At the side of the movie camera he mounted a small-size TV camera. It's lined up with the movie camera so that when you're shooting a scene you don't have to look through the viewfinder; you just look into one of the monitors and there's the shot just as it'll appear on the screen—it's like seeing your rushes as they happen. Jerry's used it since *The Bellboy*, and when he told me about it I said I didn't want to bother with it. He begged me to try it just one day on this picture. Well, the first day I didn't take my head out of that thing." The director put a stick of Juicy Fruit in his mouth; a technician asked him a question and he answered it briefly. "Another thing is the boom mike," he went on, frowning slightly. "This is a real horror—such an antiquated thing. For *Ladies' Man*, Jerry bugged his whole set with fifty or sixty mikes and cut his shooting time tremendously. You see, a director actually works maybe one hour out of eight—and four of those other seven hours are literally spent lighting for the boom—so there won't be shadows and so on. Jerry eliminated this problem. Paramount says that it worked and still they refuse to let us have it on this picture. It's ridiculous; this is 1929 sound."

After directing a short scene of a car driving up to the front of the house, Tashlin meandered back to the couch. "Jerry is my best friend," he told me. "I know if ever I were in any need, all I'd have to do is make a phone call. Sometimes, on a professional basis, he's exasperating—but anyone who's talented is. He has his high moods and they're very high—and his low moods are very low." The director pursed his lips and scratched under his nose. "But mainly, when you're working with Jerry, the occupational hazard is laughter. He can be terribly funny." Tashlin's secretary came over with a glass and a Thermos bottle, poured out a gin drink and retreated whence she had come.

"Jerry hates to do serious scenes," the director said and drank some of the gin. "I think he'd rather jump off a bridge to get a laugh. In *CinderFella* we had a scene where he's all alone and he sings a kind of serious little song. He was so nervous about doing that goddamn thing, he procrastinated one day from nine in the morning till four in the afternoon. Then at four he did it, one take, and it was beautiful." Tashlin looked at his drink reflectively. "He tried the serious thing on television a few years ago, doing *The Jazz Singer*. The critics tore him apart. That hurts, you know." He paused. "I really hate television. It's no experience. You sit at home, you don't get dressed up and go out. It's free—the audience doesn't participate—they sit there and turn the dial and be critical. I detest it."

Tashlin looked over his script for a few moments. "Jerry never rehearses," he said, looking up. "Just one take and that's it. You rehearse with Jerry and you'll die. So you can't really do anything interesting with the camera—his habits dictate your style. Sometimes when I have to repeat a scene, he'll change it around and do something completely different. And that's his charm, you see—you never know what he's going to do next. He doesn't look at his dialogue until he walks on the set, and then he never sticks to the lines anyway—usually he makes them better. I just tell him roughly what the scene is and he does it, kind of hit-and-run, and it's very successful. But you get no credit for doing a Lewis picture."

The director was called away to check a camera setup, and when he returned he had almost finished his drink. As he sat down again, his secretary reappeared with the Thermos and refilled the glass. "But there's no dreaming for Jerry," said Tashlin gently. "All he has to do is think of something and he can go out and buy it. Up in Vegas once he bought a hundred cashmere sweaters—he wears them a few times and gives them away." He sipped his drink. "Wait till you get out to his house—it's Louis B. Mayer's old mansion out in Bel-Air. Jerry left all the décor just as Mayer had it. All

he did was change the initials on the ashtrays." Tashlin smiled.
"When you drive up, you'll think there's a crowd there, but
it's all his cars. He's got something like fourteen of them. And
you've never seen so many leather-bound books in your
life—it's a complete record of everything he's ever done, like
the Pharaohs." The director paused and chuckled quietly.
"And you've gotta see the slave quarters—on warm nights
they come out and sing 'Swing Low.'" He sighed and
scratched the stubble on his upper lip he had missed when
shaving. "His wife, Patti, she's a rare woman," he continued.
"They've been married eighteen years. She's like a person in
a cyclone holding onto the kite—that's how strong she is."
    Tashlin took a long drink of the gin and looked around
him abstractedly. "Comedians always have an entourage," he
said. "It's the need for constant laughter, even though you're
paying for it. But don't misunderstand, Jerry's compassion
is as large as his extravagance. It often gets him in trouble,
too: I'll tell you a story. Somewhere, Jerry met this guy who
really needed a couple operations. Jerry felt sorry for him,
paid for his trip to the Coast, paid for the operations. And
then he gave the guy a job as a gagman. The stuff he turned
out was no good, but Jerry kept him on the payroll anyway.
One day he's on the set, kidding around, and this guy suddenly appears, rushes over to Jerry, puts his hands on Jerry's
throat and literally starts choking the kid—he's trying to kill
him. It took four guys to pull him off. Jerry was white; he
was shaking. And this guy is screaming, 'I'll get your kids,
I'll kill your kids.' Well, from then on there's been a police-
man guarding his home twenty-four hours a day. You know
what Jerry did? He paid this guy's plane fare back to his
hometown, and, I swear, to this day Jerry doesn't understand
why the man did that." Tashlin looked sadly about him, and
finished his drink.
    "You know, Chaplin personified the man of his time," the
director told me later. "He was lucky—he created a character
that people of his time could identify with. But no more. The

tramps today are wearing white shirts and ties. And what Jerry needs to do, I think, and I've told him this, is to find a character for himself that personifies his own time."

Jerry Lewis was born Joseph Levitch thirty-six years ago in Newark, New Jersey. He is a millionaire a few times over. On the door to his private office at Paramount the sign reads: "Jerry Lewis—The Chief." The office itself is spacious and simply furnished in modern style; on its oak-paneled walls hang hundreds of photographs of his wife, his five sons, himself with various friends and personalities, mementos, plaques, awards, and the Gold Record he received for 'Rock-A-Bye Your Baby with a Dixie Melody.' When I met him the first time, he was sitting behind a long, wide desk, surrounded by a typewriter, phones, dictaphone machine, and assorted gadgets, tanned and looking at least ten years younger than he is. He wore a powder-blue sweater, white shirt, grey slacks, white socks, heavy dark suede shoes, and a pair of black thin-rimmed glasses that he took off a few minutes after we began our conversation and never put on again. When he talks or listens he looks directly at you, and uses his professional high-pitched voice only rarely for an effect; his normal speaking voice, still nasal, is a good deal lower.

Jack Keller was sprawled on a couch nearby, and Lewis was discussing certain journalists with him. "Those guys have got *chutzpah*," he was saying. "You know what *chutzpah* is, don't you?" he asked me. "*Chutzpah* is a man who kills his mother and father and then pleads mercy to the court 'cause he's an orphan." He shook his head twice. "If I've been unkind and I know the other fella knows it, I wanta go bury my head in the sand." He paused to light a Kool, and I asked him why no one had thought of his TV-monitoring system before. "Too simple," he answered. "Same thing with the boom mike. On *Errand Boy* I used the boom very little. The sound department came in here—four very tall heads. 'We hear you're rebelling,' they said. 'When I'm through,' I said, 'you will too.'" Lewis tore a sheet of paper with his caricature on it from a memo pad and took a sharp pencil from one of the four glasses filled with them on his desk. He made a drawing to illustrate his points, explaining as he went along. "Now watch how sweet this is," he said. "If you're told not to open a door on the set twenty-five feet away from where we're shooting 'cause the boom'll pick it up— why shouldn't a mike, held eight feet away from the actor, out of camera range, be able to pick up the actor's voice as clearly as the boom over his head? We took a test and I showed them how well it worked—they still won't buy it. I use it on my own productions though, which *It's Only Money* ain't." He folded the piece of paper neatly in half, then tore it in half again, threw it in a wastebasket, and replaced the pencil in the glass.

"In order for people to justify their position," he continued seriously, "they have to complicate it. Comes from thirty or forty-five years of working one way. Whenever I'm ready to roll a scene, some poor guy will run on to put something in the scene that he could've put in before; it's quite sad. It's his way of calling attention to his little duty. People gotta learn." He took a deep drag on his cigarette and exhaled as he spoke. "I say if I pay you from Monday to Friday and if you can deliver in three days, you got the other two off. *They'll* stretch it out to five days." He shook his head. "One of my biggest peeves is fear. If everyone figures they can't do something, they'll never do it. You gotta try." He paused. "I know what you're thinkin'. You're thinkin' it's easy for somebody who's well-off like me to talk. But I was fired from every job when I really needed bread. And I feel this way: a person can tell me to go to hell, that's O.K., but he better know what he's talkin' about."

Keller sat up slowly on the couch, got up, and quietly left the office. Lewis glanced at him as he closed the door. "I think that in this day and age," he went on suddenly, "con-sidering all that's happened in the industry, what we need is peace of mind. I want people to leave my movies with a happy heart. I think when you depict the ticket buyer, it's sad.

Two-and-a-half hours of cold-water flat and then he leaves
and goes home to his cold-water flat—that's unfair, it's unjust,
it's a terrible rap." He paused to pour himself a glass of water
from a plastic pitcher nearby. "I have a dedication to the
people I make my pictures for. I make a picture without a
plot so the kids can come down the aisle with mommy or
uncle anytime. They don't have to worry about gettin'
there at the beginning. A thin plot, O.K., but otherwise it gets
in the way."

Keller returned and sprawled on the couch again. Lewis put
his feet up on the desk. "Did you ever read *The Catcher in the
Rye?*" he asked. I told him I had. "Well, you never saw a
more Holden Caulfield guy than you're sittin' with right
now." He grinned slightly. "And Salinger's sister told me she
used to call him 'Sonny.' That's what my grandmother used to
call me. It's frightening."

Keller stood up and began practicing golf strokes with an
imaginary club as Lewis went on to speak of Tashlin. "Tish,"
he said, smiling warmly. "Frank Tashlin made me understand
the use of the word 'friend.' I hear his name and I get tears
in my eyes. I hate him and he's a son of a bitch." He drank
the rest of the water. "Frank's my teacher," he continued,
pulling a loose-leaf binder from a shelf at the left of his desk.
"This is my Creed Book," he explained, leafing through it.
"I put things I believe in it, things I write that make me mad,
or nice things I receive. Here's a letter Frank sent me when
I started shooting *The Bellboy.*" Lewis read the letter, in
which Tashlin wished him good luck on his new venture,
saying he hoped Lewis found peace with himself through
directing, that he had a great talent and should depend on
himself and his own originality. As he finished, Lewis looked
up and said gently, "I've tried to get a price on this, and
there isn't one."

The comedian went on to discuss the duality in his own
mind between his screen personality and the man who plays
him; he spoke of the person on the screen as "him." "Sometimes I write a memo in the morning," he explained, "and

then later on the set when it's carried out, I rebel against it—
I've forgotten that it was me that asked for it." Keller took
another broad sweep on his imaginary golf club. The intercom buzzed, Lewis flicked a switch, and his secretary's voice
informed him that Mrs. Lewis was on Two. Quickly reaching
for the receiver, he fumbled it, dropped it on the desk, re-
trieved it, and said, "Did you hear Graceful pick up the
phone?" On the wall behind him I noticed an autographed
photo of President Kennedy. Jack looked at me, said happily,
"Deedle-deedle-deedle," and sat on the couch again.

After a few moments of quiet conversation, Lewis hung up
and smiled. "That's the third time today we've talked. She'll
probably call twice more." He lit a cigarette. "Patti calls me
the Jewish Sir Lancelot. I derive pleasure from giving happiness to people. She always asks me, 'Who'd you give an apple
to this morning?' " The comedian went on to say that when
he was busy he ignored people, even his friends, and that he
knew he was ignoring them. "If you turn your back on me
when I'm busy, don't come around when I'm havin' fun,"
he said. "And if a person ain't genuine, I know it. I can spot
a dirty, lying, phony rat—I can smell 'em." He smiled. "See
what I mean about Holden Caulfield?"

When I asked whether he ever thought he'd do a dramatic
picture, he said, "Why?" and paused. "Five thousand people
are far more capable of it than me," he explained rationally,
putting out his cigarette. "Why should I compete with them?
But there's only eight guys who do what I do. Ha-ha-ha,
that's my responsibility. Why should I do Sammy Glick or
something like that? For what? So dat four Park Avenue
dames can go see it and say, 'Didn't I tell you, John?' " he
mimicked effeminately. "I ain't turning my back on my
people. The Idiot has insurance values. The kids, they're
smilin' 'cause the Idiot's on his can. They built me a house in
Bel-Air, I ain't gonna forget that. When they come up to
the box office and their little hands reach up to the window
with their little money and they say, 'One child, please,' they
can't go inside and be disappointed. I mean that. They can

go see Charles Laughton belching at Elsa Lanchester if they want, but when they come to see me, they come to see the Idiot, and they're rootin' for me 'cause I'm the underdog." He paused and blew some ashes from a memo pad, tore off the top piece and threw it away. "I gotta lot of loyal people," he continued. "There's three-year-olds that grew up and now they bring their three-year-olds to see my pictures. There's this seven-year-old kid and his mother called me up this morning—he's deaf, but he reads me and he laughs. How can I take that away from him?" he asked rhetorically. "You're sayin' to yourself, 'Can this *shmuck* be genuine?' Well, if not, I'm foolin' myself."

"This is not a Closed Set. Come On In. You're Most Welcome," reads a sign on the entrance door to whatever sound stage Jerry Lewis works on. On the set every day is a man hired by Lewis to play electronic mood music or sound effects on a huge tape machine.

TUESDAY: An extended fanfare resounded through the set. "That's his music," said Frank Tashlin, and Lewis walked jauntily on, saying hello to everyone, wearing sky-blue pants (a hundred dollars a pair) and a tan windbreaker. Drums sounded and he walked to their beat. A bed had been placed on a waist-high platform for a close-up of Lewis underneath, snoring. Tashlin took him aside and quietly explained the shot to him: while he was under the bed, someone would sit on it, out of camera range; the someone was supposed to be an actress, but would actually be one of the heavier technicians so that the mattress springs would sag lower and hit Lewis. This explained, Tashlin attempted to get Lewis under the bed, but Jerry began imitating a monkey and jumping all over the director. "Did ya ever see a Jewish monkey?" he asked, a cigarette dangling from his lips. Tashlin coaxed him: "C'mon, Jerry. C'mon, little boy. Get under the bed and make your funny little faces. C'mon, be funny." Finally under the bed, Jerry suddenly yelled. "I'm hooked. Lift the bed up, ya ginney faggot!" A couple of technicians lumbered

over, lifted it, and Lewis unhooked himself from a spring.
The lighting man put a light meter near Lewis' face to gauge
the reading and Lewis bit his hand. "C'mon, Jerry," said
Tashlin quietly, "get your little arm out of the way so it
won't cover your little face." Lewis asked sarcastically
whether the bed would collapse on him: "If the whole goddamn thing comes down, I'm outta business." Tashlin
assured him it wouldn't. "From where you're standing you're
very confident," yelled Lewis. "Why don't you get under
here, you big giraffe!" Tashlin told him again to put his head
under the bed. Lewis made faces at him. "How far did you
read in the director's manual after it says 'Roll'?" "Page one,"
Tashlin replied and Lewis chortled. The director fixed
Lewis' hair so that it was more comical looking. "That's the
first affection I've had from you all day," said Lewis. Tashlin
called for the take to begin; Lewis started a symphony of
snores. Some onlookers laughed quietly. The technician was
poised to sit on the bed, but Tashlin held off giving the cue
and Lewis continued to snore. "You're going crazy waiting,
aren't you, you little bastard," said Tashlin. Lewis laughed
and continued his snoring. The director gave a hand cue, the
technician sat, Lewis reacted comically. "That's it, cut it,"
Tashlin said, and Lewis tried to scramble out from under the
bed, but some crew members had tied his shoelaces to the bed-
posts. "You shits! Who did that?" he screamed. "Who tied
my shoes to the bed? Chained! Like a goddamn Jew mouse!"
Someone untied the laces and Lewis crawled out. "You're
through for today," Tashlin told him, and Jerry imitated a
monkey again. "Put me on my bar," he said, climbing onto
Tashlin. "Do I have to play with those goddamn zebras again
today?" he complained. "You promised me orangutans."

WEDNESDAY: Wearing sunglasses, Lewis stood in a corner
conferring about script changes with Tashlin and Zachary
Scott. On the first take, the action was off its mark and the
camera missed some of it. A bald-headed makeup man applied
some tan to Lewis' nose. The second and third takes were
spoiled because the boom mike threw shadows. "Everything's

gonna be fine technically," said Lewis testily. "And the only thing that'll be no good will be the actors. I'm getting stale."

THURSDAY: "Jerry raised a big stink about the boom mike," Frank Tashlin told me. "So you'll notice there's no more boom mike."

FRIDAY: Paul Jones, producer of *It's Only Money,* was talking to Keller. A short, kind-looking man with a bulging stomach and an always-worried expression, Jones wore an outsize suit and a large felt hat. The fanfare sounded, and Lewis arrived dressed in an eggshell-white suit. "Hiya, Jerry," said Jones. Without a word, the comedian walked over to him, took off his hat, squashed it, and replaced it on his head sideways, then went on to untie the producer's bow tie and pull his jacket back over his shoulders by the lapels. This done, he gave away four baseball tickets to members of the crew, and then picked up two medium-sized boxes that were tied together and tossed them across the set to Tashlin. They landed at his feet. "That's your CARE package for the week," Lewis announced. "It's filled with one dirty sock, some rusty razor blades and a couple of broken shoelaces, and a lotta dirt." Tashlin grunted quietly; Lewis wheeled and left, three people in tow. "Yesterday he gave me a pair of sweat sox," the director told me later. "I'd never worn them before, and he told me they were very comfortable to wear on the set. First thing this morning he pulls up my pant leg to see if I've got them on. I did, and I made the mistake of telling him they really were comfortable. You know what's in those boxes? Ten or twelve dozen sweat sox he went out and bought. That's the way he is."

MONDAY: Lewis arrived wearing false buck teeth. "My mother," he said, "was scared by a beaver during the pregnancy." The comedian's father, Danny Lewis, who looks a bit like his son, came on the set wearing a blue blazer, white shirt, dark tie. He went over to Jerry, who sat in an armchair drinking a chocolate malted, told him that he had a spot on Ed Sullivan's television show next week, then asked advice on lighting and camera angles for the show while he stood in front of his son. Jerry slumped lower in the chair and answered the questions politely and quietly between sips of the malted.

"So how you been, Jerry?"

"All right."

"Everything all right?"

"Yeah, everything's swell."

"That's good."

Lewis sipped his malted.

"Watch me on the show," said his father.

"Yeah, dad."

"So everything's O.K., huh?"

"Sure."

"Well, I'll see you."

"Yeah, dad."

Danny Lewis walked away from his son and left by the nearest exit. Jerry sat silently drinking his malted. After a few minutes, Tashlin came over, smiled gently, and asked him what he knew about painters. Lewis' face brightened. "Everything," he said.

"What about Van Gogh," asked Tashlin. "Why'd he cut off his ear?"

"He didn't wanta hear all the crap on that side of the room." Two women and a little girl came on the set. "Hello, little missy," said Lewis, and immediately began to play with the child. He offered her some of his malted. "Can I give you a hug, huh?" he asked her. She nodded shyly and of the room." Two women and a little girl came on the set. "Hello, little missy," said Lewis, and immediately began to play with the child. He offered her some of his malted. "Can I give you a hug, huh?" he asked her. She nodded shyly and he put his arms around her. "Oh, God," he said. "So that's what they feel like. Boys are harder." The unit photographer came over and started snapping pictures of the comedian

with the little girl. "Hey, come on, cut it out," Lewis said
to him seriously. "You take pictures and all this looks like a
phony bit."

TUESDAY: The whole company moved out to the ocean
for some location sequences on a pier at Paradise Cove. The
sky didn't clear until after lunch, and Lewis amused himself playing football. At one o'clock the fanfare sounded and
he drove to the end of the pier in a little red golf car. "Hiya,
Tish," he called to Tashlin. "Another big day! Yes, sir, this
activity is drivin' me crazy. When I got loot involved, no
sun." He walked over to the director, who was sitting in a
canvas chair, patted him on the head and sat in his lap. "Kiss
me on the lips. Try it once. You never tried it." Tashlin
snorted, and called, "Hey, Carl, bring out the fish. You know,
the big one." Four technicians brought out a huge crate filled
with ice end a gigantic dead sea bass weighing 500 pounds;
they pulled the fish out onto the pier. Lewis was to put his
head into its mouth, and he walked over to look at it, leaned
over, pulled the fish's mouth open and looked inside. "John
L. Lewis says the strike is over," he yelled into it. "You men
can come out." He stood up and surveyed the fish critically.
"There's enough fish here to feed 300,000 Catholics," he said
and shook his head. "This poor *shmuck* had to get killed to
be in a picture." After two short takes, Lewis got into the
golf car and sped around the pier, chasing crew members
who jumped madly out of his way. "This all started," Tashlin
remarked, "because someone asked him to move that car out
of the way." Finally, Lewis stopped the car, jumped out,
picked up a broom and hurled it at a technician, who ducked;
Jerry ran after another, pulled off his cap and threw it over
the railing into the water. Running flat-footedly over to
Tashlin, he kissed him on the cheek. "Good night, Tish," he
said, walked bouncily back to the golf car and got in. The
crew was gathered around him, smiling. "Good night, Jerry,"
they said in unison. "There's too many good nights!" said
Lewis, jumping out of the car. "What'd you do, you bas-

tards? What'd you do to the car?" He got back in tentatively and turned on the ignition. The wheels began to turn, but the car didn't move—the men had put it up on blocks. After Jerry had driven away, zigzagging crazily down the pier, Tashlin meandered over to me. "How'd you like to have his energy?" he said. "This morning golf, then baseball, then football, then the car, and he's not through yet." All the way back to Hollywood in his Lincoln Continental, Lewis drove sixty to seventy miles an hour with one hand and spoke on the phone with the other. Passing through the Bel-Air shopping district, he pulled over to the curb. "I'm stoppin' at the florist's," he said, "to get Patti violets."

On the door of the Jerry Lewis home on St. Cloud Road is a *mezuza* on a gold plaque with an inscription: "Our House Is Open to Sunshine, Friends, Guests and God." A Negro maid opened the door (the butler was ill) and led me into the library. As Frank Tashlin had said, there were six or seven shelves of different-colored leather-bound volumes in the library, each with gold lettering, detailing the contents. The top shelf began with the scripts of Lewis' films, starting with *My Friend Irma* (1949) and continuing to the present. There were books of photographs, whole picture-stories of performances Lewis had given, with Martin and alone, as well as volumes devoted to his wife and children, a complete record of his life and career since around 1946. Behind the couch on which I sat were glass cabinets overflowing with awards, plaques and gold and silver cups that spilled out onto shelves in the room. On the wall opposite me was a framed painting of Lewis dressed as Emmett Kelly, the clown. One whole wall was a sliding glass door that looked out upon the pool, and further out was a recreation area with pinball machines, tennis, Ping-Pong, sun chairs; trees were everywhere. Facing each other, at opposite ends of this area, were statues of St. Anthony and of Moses. On a little table in front of the glass wall lay a silver-covered copy of the Old

Testament in Hebrew, a copy of the complete Bible, and a leather-bound autographed script of C. B. DeMille's *The Ten Commandments*.

"Jerry and Jack will be down in a couple of minutes," said Patti Lewis, coming into the room. A petite, effervescent woman, she wore a simple red dress, and her dark hair flecked with grey ("It started to grey when I was twenty") was casually combed; she sat in an armchair near the couch. "People always say I'm the rock of this marriage," she told me after a while. "Jerry says that too. But I don't feel that way at all. Jerry has provided everything for me and my family and I receive from him just as much as I give. Believe me." She smiled. "Jerry was playing at the Waldorf one time," she said, recalling the days before Lewis made it. "All I had to wear was this one brown maternity dress—that was when I was pregnant with Gary. I washed that thing so many times it was all shiny by the time Gary was born; there was no nap to the fabric anymore. I used to go down and watch Jerry do his act and I'd look around and envy the other women's clothes. The first present Jerry gave me was this secondhand fur coat—I think it was dyed squirrel. Well, I just thought it was the most elegant thing I'd ever seen and I wore it, you know, with great pride." She smiled warmly. "One night we went to a nightclub and I was wearing the coat and I caught some woman looking at it and kind of making a face. Well, I don't know, it just ruined the coat for me. Not because of her attitude or anything, but because it reflected on Jerry. It destroyed his gift."

Jack Keller came into the room, and Mrs. Lewis asked him if he wanted a drink; he said he certainly did and prepared one for himself. Coming back, he put a hand on Patti's shoulder. "Can a Polish-Italian, Catholic coal-miner's daughter," he said in mock soap-opera style, "find happiness with a Jewish movie star?" Patti laughed happily and Jack slouched low in an armchair opposite her. Soon afterward, Jerry came down wearing the same clothes he had worn on the set that day—a red sweater and blue slacks—and told his wife that Gary had definitely decided to go into comedy as a career, not baseball.

Dinner was served. During soup, Ronnie Lewis, twelve, came into the spacious dining room (also overlooking the pool), sat next to Jack and began talking with him about guns; Jack promised to take him duck shooting the next week. Jerry was on a phone that stood on a chair next to his place at the head of the table. Scotty Lewis, six, came down and shyly handed me a ball-point pen (with a Lewis caricature on it) wrapped in paper; Jerry kissed him for that. The governess appeared carrying Anthony Lewis, three, who wore fire-red pajamas, followed by a slightly bewildered-looking Christopher Lewis, soon-to-be-five, also in pajamas. Anthony was whimpering. He looked at Mrs. Lewis and said, heartbroken, "Mommy." Jerry jumped up. "Oh, God. When he says 'Mommy' like that I'm destroyed." He went over to the child and talked him out of his tears. Then the three younger children were taken to bed and, a little later, Ronnie finished his discussion with Jack, said goodnight and went quietly upstairs. During the roast beef, Gary Lewis, seventeen, came into the room and showed his father a comedy sketch he had just written. Jerry looked it over, laughed several times, and then asked us to listen to it; he and Gary read it. Jerry congratulated him and told him to retype it, double-spaced. Gary nodded and left. By this time everyone but Jerry had finished the main course, and the black maid came in to collect the plates. Jerry ran over to her and kissed her comically on the cheek. "She's so beautiful," he announced. "She does something to me." The woman laughed embarrassedly. "We'll kiss in the kitchen later," he said conspiratorially, "like before." Patti smiled and Jack said, "Deedle-deedle-deedle."

After the apple pie, Jerry took me on a tour of the house. The L-shaped (for best acoustics) stereo room had five professional tape recorders, complete 16mm movie-camera equipment, a hookup with the FM radio station he owns, tape and record albums (all neatly catalogued), three extremely powerful speakers and an intercom system that connected with every room in the house. Most of the equipment was specially designed and executed for the comedian. Behind a wall of the living room were two modern 35mm movie projectors (a CinemaScope screen could be lowered at the far end of the room by pressing a button) and an editing room where Lewis often cuts his own pictures. Next to the projectors were stacks of motion picture cans, each labeled. Among them was a print of Chaplin's *Modern Times;* Chaplin had sent it to him. The projection booth led into a soundproofed recording room containing at least a dozen shelves of tapes of performances he had given.

Later, in the stereo room ("The Jerry Lewis 'Loud' Sound Studios. If It's A Jerry Lewis Recording, We Dare You To Hear It"), Lewis spoke of his annoyance with visitors to the set who pretend not to be impressed when they are standing next to a movie star; he thought it hypocritical. "If John Wayne walked on my set, I'd shit!" he said. "I'd be impressed." Discussing money, he told me he always carried a thousand dollars with him in hundred-dollar bills, that he loved shopping and going through stores. Concerning his extravagance: "I discovered a few years ago that I can't buy what I really want, so I buy everything else."

And then, suddenly, he was speaking of Dean Martin: "The only contract we ever had," he said, "was a handshake. That was it. 'Cause I always say if I can't trust your handshake I can't trust you." He talked of the "complete emotional breakdown" between the singer and himself. "After the breakup, I asked Patti why she'd never said anything against Dean, and she told me that Dean was like a second wife to me and that she had no right to speak against him. Isn't that something?" And later: "I still love Dean, but I don't like him anymore."

Concerning his ego: "When I wake up in the morning," he remarked, "I think of *me* first and then my wife and then my children. I'd like to meet the guy that can honestly admit he does differently." He paused. "They say to me, I'm an egomaniac; what do I wanta do four things for? Why do I have to direct, produce and write too? D'ya think it's so easy? D'ya think it's such a pleasure? For each cap I wear, it's eight hours work. So I'm doing four things, that's thirty-two hours a day—there ain't that many. Why do I do it? 'Cause I'd rather work *that* way than work with incompetents. I'm gettin' the best people I know for the job. I can't get Frank all the time."

And much later, around three in the morning, over a can of beer, Lewis talked of his birth, his youth, his parents, his grandmother whom he adored and who died when he was eleven; his eyes watered when he spoke of her and how she had called him "Sonny," and how, when the hospital told him she had "expired," he asked if that meant she was going to be all right. He spoke of his reluctance to hate anyone ("I always say, do you love 'em enough to hate 'em"), of the various aunts he had lived with while his show business parents were on the road, of the way his grandfather had searched curiously for him behind the TV set the first time he was on, of his love for children, particularly his own ("they're nice people"), and of how he would always have a baby in the house. "When I'm ninety and in a wheelchair, we'll still have babies in the house. I'll adopt them." And finally: "If you're deprived of love when you're young," he said, "you can never have it given back to you. And that's what I don't want to happen to my kids."

It was after four-thirty in the morning, in front of his house, that Lewis said good night to Keller and me. And at six he was in his office at Paramount, ready for another big day.

One Saturday afternoon around four, Jerry Lewis was to go to a rehearsal at U.C.L.A. for a benefit he was to give that evening to raise money to send needy children to summer camp. I was to meet him at his house and shortly after I arrived he walked into the library in a black mood: he had a migraine. "I'm such a sucker," he grumbled about the benefit.

"I can't turn my back on anybody. And people know it."
Parked in front of the house was a brand-new maroon Lincoln Continental, with the dealer's invoice still taped to a
side window. Lewis surveyed it critically. He opened the
door and looked in. "Well, what the hell did they do," he
said, annoyed. "Nothing. No initials, no phone." He grunted
and pulled off the invoice. "They couldn't even take this
off." He walked around to the rear, opened the trunk and
gazed into it for a few minutes. "There's nothin' more
beautiful than a new car," he said. As we drove to the university, I asked whether the car had been custom-built for
him. "No," he answered. "Harry Ford Jr. is a good friend
of mine and he always sends me what I like."

The rehearsal in the two-thousand-seat auditorium con-
sisted of Terry Gibbs' seventeen-piece orchestra playing a
couple of numbers, and some halfhearted clowning. As Jerry
was leaving, Gibbs told him the band had to be at a recording date that night by nine-thirty. Lewis nodded and said
he would start exactly at eight and do forty-five minutes.
"If they ain't ready and if they don't like it," he said, "that's
tough."

That evening, at seven fifty-five, the auditorium was filled
to capacity, mainly with college students who had paid
$1.50 to get in. At eight sharp the curtains parted to the
tune of a loud song that Gibbs' band played with gusto;
there was a Lewis caricature on the bass drum. An offstage
voice came through the loudspeakers. "Ladies and Gentlemen," it announced, "Jerry Lewis." The band struck up
"When You're Smiling," a follow spot hit Stage Left and into
it stepped the performer, wearing a shiny black tuxedo with
a red handkerchief, a red bow tie on an eyelet lace button-
down dress shirt and black suede Romeos. The applause was
loud. He did impersonations of folk singers, boxers who
sing, made cracks at the audience ("How can you look so
clean and laugh so dirty"), sang "Rock-A-Bye Your Baby
With a Dixie Melody" in honor of Al Jolson, donned funny

hats and threw out one-liners, played a tiny trumpet, conducted the orchestra, sang "Come Rain or Come Shine," looking occasionally at Patti Lewis, who sat in the wings, did a tap dance, jumped in the air and fell on his side with a crash, threw ten or twelve twirling black canes in the air, missed them and, when he wanted to, caught them. Then the lights dimmed except for a pinshot on him sitting on a high stool, cigarette in one hand, microphone in the other, singing a melancholy song called "What Kind of Fool Am I." As he finished, he laid the mike down on the stool, the spot moved to it, and he walked off the blacked-out stage. The applause was thunderous. All the lights came up. Lewis returned, bowed twice and waved good-by. The applause continued as the curtains pulled slowly together. It was eight-fifty and he still had a migraine.

Lewis, Tashlin and I sat in the comedian's portable dressing room on the set of *It's Only Money:*
PB: What do you think of television, Jerry?
JL: Television is an infantile medium trying to do in eight years what we've done in fifty.
FT: Let's get the years right, Jerry, it's not eight years. It came in in '48 . . .
JL: . . . In fourteen years what we've done since 1920.
FT: Since 1910.
JL: You would remember. It was when you and McKinley were there. Go ahead, Mr. Bog-Bogavin . . .
PB: What do you think of psychoanalysis?
JL: For myself, I think it's dangerous: someone who has inner sad feelings about certain things which—instead of them burying him—can be put to better use. If I were to find out that these sad things are truly not sad, I think people would no longer find me funny, 'cause funny had better be sad somewhere.
PB: What do you think of newspapers?
JL: When they're honest, they're good. On the editorial page, they start out with a lovely premise: to report their

opinions. Now when you get to city side, they wanta sell papers and all of a sudden the man didn't hit the woman, the woman ate the man's foot, and then the dog died.

PB: What is comedy to you?

JL: Very serious business.

PB: What do you think of Hollywood?

JL: It has to be what it is. It's everything it's supposed to be. 'Cause if you had five thousand Abe Lincolns living in Hollywood, you'd have no lovely Hollywood—then you'd have Greensboro, North Carolina. But you gotta have a lotta phonies, and a lotta liars, and a lotta brownnosers, and a lotta yes-men, and a lotta the crap we hate, or you haven't got Hollywood. And it's the very crap that makes everyone wanta come here. 'Cause nobody wants to go to Greenland, where God built a beautiful substance—they wanta go to where all the crap is.

PB: What do you think of the Academy Awards?

JL: They're very nice statues.

PB: What is art to you?

JL: Art? A man with a brush, a man with a theme, a man with a song, a woman with a cry. I think a puppet, a puppy, anything tender. A woman is art. . . . A man's desire for her is even more arty. . . . And when they do it together is the most art!

FT: How do you feel about being a director as well as an actor?

JL: I love it. It's me, ain't it?

FT: Which end of the camera do you like most?

JL: Dependin' upon what end I'm at. When I'm in front of it, there's nothin' better. When I'm on the other end, the actor's a *shmuck*.

PB: Who've you been most influenced by in your direction?

JL: Mr. Tishman, spelled T-A-S-H-L-I-N. He's my teacher.

PB: What kind of pictures do you like, other than your own?

JL: I like good entertainment, nothin' sordid. I keep all the sordid things in the confines of a room with a broad; nobody sees that. I don't wanta go sit with two hundred people and watch someone do what I think I'd like to do sometime alone. Because it not only embarrasses me, but then I won't do it alone for fear that she saw that same movie. . . . And I ain't gonna sit in a theatre for heartache. I can go into my own room and close the door and look at myself and cry.

PB: What do you think of money?

JL: Money's a pain in the ass. And I can prove it if you stay with me a few days. You'll see how I love it.

FT: You love what it gives you.

JL: No, not really. Money completely disallows me to contribute and give what I have inside, 'cause the moment money's involved I'm being paid to deliver it.

PB: Why, for instance, do you have ten to fourteen cars?

JL: I don't know, it's just a lotta cars. I like to have a lot of anything, 'cause it's proof that you're doin' swell. I used to have two cars. Then I heard a lotta guys have two, then I hadda have four. Then, when I found out there were fellas that had four, I hadda have what they don't have. So now that I got it, they're enjoying their four and I'm stuck with ten.

FT: If you like having a lot of everything, how do you feel about having one wife?

JL: Because I have all of the wives in the world in the one. I picked the best. I have very good taste. I went into a store —you know where it says "Jewelry" in a store, this one said "Wives." I went to every counter, and then there was one that had guards around it, and you couldn't look into the case 'cause it was covered. And I asked the man, "Would you let me see?" and he unrolled this velvet and there she was, smiling. And there was a big price tag that said "Two Billion Dollars." And she took the tag off and she looked at me and she said, "You can have me for free if you'll love me." All the other wives lyin' around, they were all bulldogs.

PB: Why did you go into the restaurant business?

JL: Because I was hungry. I waited in line at Chasen's for two hours and I said, "I'll straighten this out," and we built it overnight; three chipmunks and a beaver put it up. I think it's a good business, and I can go there, and I get ptomaine and vomit. . . .

PB: If you could do anything you wanted, what would you do?

JL: Make the world better. I'd like to dip it in alcohol and cleanse it and have it come up pretty. I don't know how to do that, though, it's very heavy. But I'm doin' a hell of a job on the little globe I got around me. Got any other stupid questions, Mr. Bog-banovidan?

FT: What do you think when you read articles written about you?

JL: First of all, if it's written about me, I like it to start with, 'cause it beats the hell out of being written about another fella. 'Cause there ain't anything I like better than when it's about me. If it's a lie about me, I hate it. If it's nice about me, I love it a lot. If it ain't too good about me, I love it a little lot. But if it's about me and I can read it a lot and there's plenty of pictures, I have to get new hats and alla that. . . .

Jerry Lewis' restaurant on Sunset Boulevard has a simple white stone façade, on the side of which is the Lewis caricature and signature. The double-doored entrance is black with silver handles in the shape of "J" and "L"; inside there is another door, two-toned (lavender-purple); there are doormen for each. The restaurant itself is large and dimly lit, with a curved glass wall overlooking Los Angeles. The décor is dark purple, with silver trim and deep mahogany woodwork. The maitre d' wears tails, the waiters double-breasted maroon uniforms. The china is black and white, and at each place is an armchair. The menus are large (20" x 10" closed), covered in black felt, with huge JL's on them; there are twelve sections inside, with such selections as:

"Imported Caviar Malossol (per ounce) $6.50," and "Roast Baby Pheasant, Flamé on Canapé (Service for Two) $18." On the ceiling of the smaller dining room are six cupids pulling a cockleshell chandelier. "The restaurant reflects Jerry's thoughts," said Jack Keller, "about what he would like to be." But Lewis dropped in later, wearing a fisherman's straw hat and a sky-blue velvet coverall. He joked with the customers, had a quick drink, and left to pick up his new yacht, which was waiting for him in San Diego.

"You know, Jerry got a Gold Record for 'Rock-A-Bye Your Baby,' " said Keller after Lewis had gone. "It sold over a million copies. But the first time he ever sang that song publicly was *the* turning point in Jerry's career." Keller sipped his coffee. "Three weeks after his separation from Dean was final, Patti, Jerry, my wife, and I went to Las Vegas for no other reason than to get away from Los Angeles because, as I told you, the split was a traumatic thing for Jerry. He was floundering. He'd spent ten years with a partner. He was thinking what the hell would he do. Well, it was delightful in Vegas; we went to shows, kibbitzed, lay in the sun, had a ball. The last day we're all packed, ready to take the eight o'clock plane back, when Sid Luft, Judy Garland's husband, calls Jerry in the afternoon and says, 'Judy's got laryngitis; you gotta bail us out tonight.' Jerry says he'll call him back. He turns to me and says, 'What d'ya think?' I said, 'What d'ya mean, what do I think? You haven't got an act. You haven't done a single for over ten years.' Still, we talk about it and Jerry decides, against my better judgment, to help Garland out. He calls Luft and tells him he'll do it on one condition. 'I realize she can't sing,' he says, 'but people paid to see Garland. If she'll come out and sit on the stage—she doesn't have to say a word—I'll go on for her.' They agreed, and that night Jerry played the whole show to her." Keller lit a cigarette and went on. "I was pacing the aisles like a father in a maternity ward. Suddenly I stop. I realize we forgot one thing. You can have a great act, but you gotta have something to get off with.

Jerry was extremely funny for a whole hour. He was a real pussycat up there. Came the moment of truth: how's he gonna get off? Well, he leaned over to the bandleader and asked him Garland's repertoire. He looked through it and the only song he knew the lyrics to was *Rock-A-Bye*. So he sang it, and in her key yet. Well, he pulled out all the stops, he belted it out, got down on one knee, he was really flamboyant. It was the greatest thing I've ever seen. Even gave *me* the shivers, and you know what a cynical son-of-a-bitch I am. Well, when he was finished nine hundred people stood up and applauded like the Third World War had just been won." Keller paused. "And I'll tell you, that night when we were flying back home, you can't imagine how we all felt. We knew he'd made it. We knew he'd be all right."

November 1962

Sometime early in '63, I said to Harold, "You know who I'd really like to do a piece on? Bogart."

He said, "Humphrey Bogart?"

I said, "Yeah."

He said, "But he's dead."

I said, "O.K., forget it."

About a year later, there appeared in Time *magazine a one-column news item reporting the popularity of Bogart movies at Harvard and a kind of underground cult that was forming around the actor. That same week, Harold called me: "Hi, buddy! How'd you like to do a piece on Bogart?"*

I said, "You read the thing in Time."

He said, "Do you want to do it or not?"

After the article finally appeared in September '64, it was followed, over the next two or three years, by an avalanche of Bogart articles and Bogart books, Bogart posters, and Bogart film retrospectives on TV and at theatres and museums all over the country and abroad. There was even Woody Allen's Play It Again, Sam, *in which Bogart appeared as a kind of alter-ego. He has become, in death even more than he was in life, an authentic American Hero, which was my original title for the article. At that time in* Esquire, *however, Mr. Mailer was serializing his novel,* An American Dream, *so the present name was substituted by the editors.*

Bogie In Excelsis

USUALLY HE WORE THE TRENCH COAT UNBUTTONED, just tied with the belt, and a slouch hat, rarely tilted. Sometimes it was a captain's cap and a yachting jacket. Almost always his trousers were held up by a cowboy belt. You know the kind: one an Easterner waiting for a plane out of Phoenix buys just as a joke and then takes a liking to. Occasionally, he'd hitch up his slacks with it, and he often jabbed his thumbs behind it, his hands ready for a fight or a dame.

Whether it was Sirocco or Casablanca, Martinique or Sahara, he was the only American around (except maybe for the girl) and you didn't ask him how he got there, and he always worked alone—except for the fellow who thought he took care of him, the rummy, the piano player, the one *he* took care of, the one you didn't mess with. There was very little he couldn't do, and in a jam he could do anything: remove a slug from a guy's arm, fix a truck that wouldn't start. He was an excellent driver, knowing precisely how to take those curves or how to lose a guy that was tailing him. He could smell a piece of a broken glass and tell you right away if there'd been poison in it, or he could walk into a room and know just where the button was that opened the secret door. At the wheel of a boat, he was beautiful.

His expression was usually sour and when he smiled only the lower lip moved. There was a scar on his upper lip— maybe that's what gave him the faint lisp. He would tug meditatively at his earlobe when he was trying to figure something out and every so often he had a strange little twitch— a kind of backward jerk of the sides of his mouth coupled with a slight squinting of the eyes. He held his cigarette (a Chesterfield) cupped in his hand. He looked right holding a gun.

Unsentimental was a good word for him. "Leave 'im where he is," he might say to a woman whose husband has just been

wounded, "I don't want 'im bleeding all over my cushions."
And blunt: "I don't like you. I don't like your friends and
I don't like the idea of her bein' married to you." And
straight: "When a man's partner is killed he's supposed to do
something about it. It doesn't make any difference what you
thought of him. He was your partner and you're supposed
to do something about it."

He was tough; he could stop you with a look or a line.
"Go ahead, slap *me*," he'd say, or, "That's right, *go* for it,"
and there was in the way he said it just the right blend of
malice, gleeful anticipation and the promise of certain doom.
He didn't like taking orders. Or favors. It was smart not to
fool around with him too much.

As far as the ladies were concerned, he didn't have too
much trouble with them, except maybe keeping them away.
It was the girl who said if he needed anything, all he had to
do was whistle; he never said that to the girl. Most of the
time he'd call her "angel," and if he liked her he'd tell her
she was "good, awful good."

Whatever he was engaged in, whether it was being a reporter, a saloon-keeper, a gangster, a detective, a fishing-boat
owner, a D.A. or a lawyer, he was impeccably, if casually, a
complete professional. "You take chances," someone would
say. "I get paid to," was his answer. But he never took himself too seriously. What was his job, a girl would ask. Conspiratorially, he'd lean in and say with the slightest flicker of
a grin, "I'm a private dick on a case." He wasn't going to be
taken in by Art either; he'd been to college, but he was a bit
suspicious of the intellectuals. If someone mentioned Proust,
he'd ask, "Who's he?" even though he knew.

Finally, he was wary of Causes. He liked to get paid for
taking chances. He was a man who tried very hard to be
Bad because he knew it was easier to get along in the world
that way. He always failed because of an innate goodness
which surely nauseated him. Almost always he went from
belligerent neutrality to reluctant commitment. From: "I
stick my neck out for nobody." To: "I'm no good at being

noble, but it doesn't take much to see that the problems of three little people don't amount to a hill o' beans in this crazy world." At the start, if the question was, "What are your sympathies?", the answer was invariably, "Minding my own business." But by the end, if asked why he was helping, risking his life, he might say, "Maybe 'cause I like you. Maybe 'cause I don't like them." Of course it was always "maybe" because he wasn't going to be that much of a sap, wasn't making any speeches, wasn't going to be a Good guy. Probably he rationalized it: "I'm just doing my job." But we felt good inside. We knew better.

Several months ago, the New Yorker Theatre in Manhattan ran a cycle of thirty Humphrey Bogart movies. A one-day double bill of *The Big Sleep* and *To Have and Have Not* broke all their attendance records. "I had two hundred people sitting on the floor," said Daniel Talbot, owner of the 830-seat revival house and one of the two producers of *Point of Order*. "It was wild. I had to turn away a couple of hundred people. And that audience! First time Bogie appeared they applauded, and that was just the beginning. Any number of scenes got hands. And the laughs! Bogart is very hot right now," Talbot explained. "It's more than a cult, it's something else too. He's not consciously hip, but hip by default. You get the feeling that he lives up to the Code. Anyone who screws up deserves the fate of being rubbed out by Bogart. He's also very American, and his popularity, I think, is a reaction to this currently chic craze for foreign films and things foreign in general. With Bogart you get a portrait of a patriot, a man interested in the landscape of America. I think he's an authentic American hero—more existential than, say, Cooper, but as much in the American vein, and more able to cope with the present." Talbot paused and grinned. "Frankly, I just like to watch him at work. He hits people beautifully."

The French have a more intellectual, if nonetheless affectionate, approach to Bogart and the legend he has left behind. As Belmondo stares mystically at a photo of Bogart in Godard's *Breathless*, slowly exhaling cigarette smoke and rubbing his lip with his thumb, he murmurs wistfully, "Bogie . . ." and you can almost hear his director's thoughts, echoed, for instance, in the words of the late André Bazin, probably France's finest film critic. "Bogart is the man with a past," he wrote in *Cahiers du Cinéma* in 1957, a month after Bogart died. "When he comes into a film, it is already 'the morning after'; sardonically victorious in his macabre combat with the angel, his face scared by what he has seen, and his step heavy from all he has learned, having ten times triumphed over his death, he will surely survive for us this one more time. . . . The Bogartian man is not defined by his contempt for bourgeois virtues, by his courage or cowardice, but first of all by his existential maturity which little by little transforms life into a tenacious irony at the expense of death." Of course, the French too can have a more basic approach. "Finally in full color," wrote Robert Lachenay in the same magazine, "we see Bogie as he was in real life—as he was to Betty Bacall every night on his pillow. . . . I loved Bogart even better then. . . ."

The Bogart cult has been perpetuated for the last several years in colleges all over the United States. "I met a Harvard fellow recently," said writer Nathaniel Benchley, "who believed in only two things: the superiority of Harvard and the immortality of Humphrey Bogart." During every exam period in Cambridge, it has become customary for the Brattle Theatre to run a Bogart film festival. Sometimes they don't even list the pictures; they just put a large photograph of him outside the theatre. It seems to be enough. Walk into the Club Casablanca (in the same building) and ask one of the undergraduates. "Bogart has a coolness you can't get away from," he might tell you. "It's a wryness, a freedom," he'll say, at the same time denying that there is a real cult and that it's just that he's so refreshing, so pleasantly removed from their academic world. "There's no crap about Bogart," another student may observe. "He's also kind of anti-European and pro-American. Like he dumps on the European, you know what I mean?" By this time his date won't be able to control herself any longer. "He's so masculine!" she'll blurt out. "He's so fantastically tough!"

Was he? "He satirized himself a great deal," said writer Betty Comden. Raymond Massey recalled an incident during the shooting of *Action in the North Atlantic* (1943): "The scene called for our doubles to jump from the bridge of a burning tanker into the water below, which was aflame with oil. Bogie turned to me and said, '*My* double is braver than yours.' I said that wasn't so, that *my* double was the braver man. Then Bogie looked at me and he said, 'The fact is I'm braver than you are.' I said that was nonsense. And the next thing I knew we did the damn stunt ourselves." Massey chuckled. "I burned my pants off and Bogie singed his eyebrows."

To Joseph L. Mankiewicz, who directed him in *The Barefoot Contessa* (1954), Bogart's toughness was a façade. "You'd be having dinner with him," he said, "and someone would come over and you could just see the tough guy coming on." And to Chester Morris: "He had a protective shell of seeming indifference. He wasn't, but he did a lotta acting offstage. He liked to act tough, liked to talk out of the side of his mouth." Writer Nunnally Johnson said Bogart was convinced that people would have been disappointed if he didn't act tough with them. "A fan came over during dinner one time," said Johnson, "and Bogie told him to beat it. When the guy got back to his table I heard his companion say, quite happily. 'See, I told ya he'd insult you.' " Johnson reflected a moment. "But he was a lot tougher than I would be and a lot tougher than most people I know. I remember one time Judy Garland and her husband, Sid Luft, were at his home. Now Luft was a big alley fighter and a good deal broader than Bogart. But Bogie got annoyed about something or other and he walked right over to Luft, who also was a good head taller, and nodded at Judy. 'Would you take that dame out of this house,' he said, 'and never come back.' Luft

kind of looked at him a moment and then he took her out."
Johnson smiled. "Bogie took big risks."

Adlai Stevenson didn't find him that way. "He wasn't
tough, not really," said the Ambassador. "He was, to me, a
nonconformist. He had a cynicism without being unhealthy.
He had great curiosity and an arch kind of skepticism." And
still another opinion: "He was a pushover," said Lauren
Bacall.

"I never broke through his barrier," critic John McClain
said. "I don't think anyone really got underneath. Bogart
didn't unburden himself to men. He loved to be in love and
with a woman. I think he came closer to leveling with them
than with anybody." Bogart married four women during his
fifty-seven years, each of them an actress: Helen Mencken
(1926), Mary Phillips (1928), the late Mayo Methot (1938),
and in 1945, Lauren Bacall. "I think once a person was out,
they were really out," said Truman Capote, discussing the
divorces. "He had emotional attachments."

The Bogart-Methot marriage was a stormy one. "Their
neighbors were lulled to sleep," Dorothy Parker once said,
"by the sounds of breaking china and crashing glass." Johnson recalled that Methot once had Bogart followed. "She was
very jealous and positive that he was playing around. But
Bogie never had a weakness for dames. The only weakness
he ever had was for a drink and a talk." Johnson smiled.
"Bogie soon found out a guy was tailing him, and he called
up the fellow's agency. 'Hello, this is Humphrey Bogart,' he
said. 'You got a man on my tail. Would you check with him
and find out where I am.' "

The first time Bogart met Betty Bacall was coming out of
director Howard Hawks' office. She had made a test for
Hawks, who had discovered her and first teamed the couple
in *To Have and Have Not* (1945). "I saw your test," Bogart
said to her. "We're gonna have a lotta fun together." It was
with Bacall that he had his only children, a boy named Steve,
which is what she called Bogart in that first movie, and a girl

named Leslie Howard, after the actor who had insisted that Bogart be cast in the film version of *The Petrified Forest* (1936), the movie that really sparked his picture career. "He missed her when they were apart," Capote said. "He loved her. He used to talk a terrific line, but he was monogamous. Although that isn't entirely true—he fell in love with Bacall while he was still married to Mayo."

Bogart put it this way: "I'm a one-woman man and I always have been. I guess I'm old-fashioned. Maybe that's why I like old-fashioned women, the kind who stay in the house playing 'Roamin' in the Gloamin'.' They make a man think he's a man and they're glad of it."

The stories go that Bogart was a heavy drinker, but Johnson thinks otherwise. "I don't think Bogie drank as much as he pretended to," he said. "Many's a time I was with him, the doorbell would ring, and he'd pick up his glass just to go answer the door. He couldn't have been as good at his job if he drank as much as he was supposed to have."

But Bogart did drink. "I think the world is three drinks behind," he used to say, "and it's high time it caught up." On one occasion he and a friend bought two enormous stuffed panda bears and took them as their dates to El Morocco. They sat them in chairs at a table for four and when an ambitious young lady came over and touched Bogart's bear, he shoved her away. "I'm a happily married man," he said, "and don't touch my panda." The woman brought assault charges against him, and when asked if he was drunk at four o'clock in the morning, he replied, "Sure, isn't everybody?" (The judge ruled that since the panda was Mr. Bogart's personal property, he could defend it.)

But Bogart didn't have to drink to start trouble. "He was an arrogant bastard," said Johnson, grinning. "It's kinda funny, this cult and everything. When he was alive, as many people hated him as loved him. I always thought of him as somewhat like Scaramouche." Johnson chuckled. "What was it? 'Born with the gift of laughter and the sense that the

world was mad. . . .' He'd start a skirmish and then sit back
and watch the consequences. Of course, there was nearly
always something phony about the guy he was needling.
Needle is the wrong word—howitzer would be more like it.
The other fellow could use deflating, but it didn't take all
that artillery."

The Holmby Hills Rat Pack, which Bogart initiated and
which died with him, sprang from this distaste for pretense.
"What is a rat?" he once explained. "We have no constitu-
tion, charter or bylaws yet, but we know a rat when we
see one. There are very few rats in this town. You might say
that rats are for staying up late and drinking lots of booze.
We're against squares and being bored and for lots of fun
and being real rats, which very few people are, but if you're
a real rat, boy! Our slogan is, 'Never rat on a rat.' A first
principle is that we don't care who likes us as long as we
like each other. We like each other very much."

John McClain tells of the yacht club Bogart belonged to
and of the people who rented the large house next door for
a summer. They were the Earls and they Dressed for Dinner.
The members of the club (who were never invited) used
to peer over their fence, watching the lush festivities. Mc-
Clain had been invited to a Sunday dinner and had asked
if he might bring Bogart along since they would be together
on his yacht over the weekend. As they docked, McClain reminded Bogart to dress for the occasion and went off to get
ready himself. Bogart went into the club for a drink or two.
"After a while," McClain recalled, "Bogie announced to
everyone in the club, 'My dear friends, the Earls,' he said,
'are having an open house and they want you all to come.'
And into the Earl house comes Bogie followed by about
thirty people, all wearing shorts and sport shirts and terrible
sneakers." McClain laughed. "It was pretty funny, actually,
but I was furious at the time."

"He could be very wrong too," said Benchley. "One time
at '21' I was standing at the bar with a couple of friends and
Bogie got up from his table and came over. 'Are you a homo-

sexual?' he said to one of them, just like that. The fellow
looked rather taken aback and said he didn't see that it was
any of his business. 'Well *are* you?' said Bogie. 'Come on,
we got a bet going at the table.' The fellow said, 'Since you
ask, no.' I think Bogie could feel he'd been wrong and he
turned to the other guy with us and asked him if *he* was a
homosexual. The guy said no. He asked me and I said no
and then he said, 'Well *I* am,' and kinda minced away. He
knew he'd been wrong."

A few weeks after Bogart's death, Peter Ustinov said, in
a speech: "Humphrey Bogart was an exceptional character
in a sphere where characters are not usually exceptional. To
a visitor hot from the cold shores of England, he would put
on an exaggerated Oxford accent and discuss the future of
the 'British Empah' as though he wrongheadedly cared for
nothing else in the wide world. His aim was to shake the
newcomer out of his assumed complacency by insults which
were as shrewdly observed as they were malicious. . . . The
way into his heart was an immediate counterattack in a broad
American accent, during which one assumed a complicity
between him and his *bête noire*, Senator McCarthy, in some
dark scheme. . . . It was in the character of the man that he
smiled with real pleasure only when he had been amply re-
paid in kind."

Capote would go along with that: "The turning point in
our friendship—the beginning really—was during *Beat the
Devil* (1954). Bogie and John Huston and some others, they
were playing that game—you know the one, what d'ya call
it?—you take each other's hand across a table and try to push
the other's arm down. Well, it just happens that I'm very
good at that game. So, anyway, Bogie called over, 'Hey,
Caposy.' That's what he called me, 'Caposy.' He said, 'C'mon,
Caposy, let's see you try this.' And I went over and I pushed
his arm down. Well, he looked at me. . . . He had such a
suspicious mind, he was sure that Huston had cut off my
head and sewed it onto someone else's body. 'Let's see you
do that again,' he said. And again I pushed his arm down.

So he said, once more, and I said I would only if we bet a hundred dollars, which we did. I won again and he paid me, but then he came over and he started sort of semi-wrestling with me. It was something they did. He was crushing me and I said, 'Cut that *owat*,' and he said, 'Cut that *owat*.' I said, 'Well, do,' and he said, 'Why?' I said, 'Because you're hurting me.' But he kept right on squeezing, so I got my leg around behind him and pushed and over he went. He was flat on his can looking up at me. And from then on we were very good friends."

"Bogie's needling tactics were quite calculated," Johnson explained. "I had lunch with him and Betty at Romanoff's one time and she was giving him hell about some row at a party. He'd provoked it, of course. 'Someday somebody's gonna belt you,' she said, and he said, 'No, that's the art of it—taking things up to that point and then escaping.'"

In 1947, Bogart led a march to Washington to protest the investigations of the Un-American Activities Committee. Some people labeled him a pinko. He didn't like that. "I am an American," he said. Bogart's political freethinking was considered dangerous in Hollywood. In 1952, however, he campaigned most actively for Stevenson for President. "He never seemed to give a damn what people thought or said," Mr. Stevenson recalled. "And it was quite perilous in those days to be a Democrat, especially one partisan to me. He was disdainful about anybody trying to muscle about in a free country."

"He wasn't an extremist in anything," said Miss Bacall, "except telling the truth. You had to admire Bogie. He always said what he thought. 'Goddamnit,' he used to say, 'if you don't want to hear the truth, don't ask me.'"

"That's true," Johnson said. "Everything he did was honest. He used to say, 'What's everybody whispering about? I've got cancer!' He'd say, 'For Christ's sake, it's not a venereal disease.'"

Bogart also said that the only point in making money is

"so you can tell some big shot to go to hell." And: "I have politeness and manners. I was brought up that way. But in this goldfish-bowl life, it is sometimes hard to use them."

His widow thinks it was more than just good manners Bogart had. Finally, she'll tell you. "He was an old-fashioned man, a great romantic. And very emotional. He would cry when a dog died. You should have seen him at our wedding, tears streaming down his face. He told me that he started thinking about the meaning of the words. He was tough about life and totally uncompromising, but I remember he went to see Steve at nursery school and when he saw him sitting at his little desk, he cried."

Alistair Cooke met the Bogarts on the Stevenson campaign train and he remembered sitting with them one afternoon and saying that, of course, Stevenson wouldn't win. " 'What!' said Bogie, astounded. 'Not a prayer, I'm afraid,' I said, 'Why you son of a bitch,' Betty said, 'that's a fine thing to say.' 'Look,' I said, 'I'm a reporter. You're the lieutenants.' We bet ten dollars on it and when Stevenson lost he paid it to me. But he didn't really think I'd take it. You know what he said? 'It's a hell of a guy who bets against his own principles.' "

Cooke commented on this Bogart trait in an article he wrote for *The Atlantic Monthly* (May, 1957). "A touchy man who found the world more corrupt than he had hoped . . . he invented the Bogart character and imposed it on a world impatient of men more obviously good. And it fitted his deceptive purpose like a glove. . . . From all . . . he was determined to keep his secret: the rather shameful secret, in the realistic world we inhabit, of being a gallant man and an idealist."

Other friends detected a similar quality in Bogart. Mankie-wicz called it, "A sadness about the human condition. He had a kind of eighteenth-century, Alexander Pope nature. I think he would have made a superb Gatsby. His life reflected Gatsby's sense of being an outsider." Stevenson found "a wistful note in him, as there often is in thinking people. He was much more profound than one might think." And Capote called him lost. "It was his outstanding single characteristic—that something almost pathetic. Not that he would ever ask for sympathy, far from it. It just always seemed to me as though he were permanently lonely. It gave him a rather poetic quality, don't you think?"

That secret inner world of Humphrey Bogart was reflected in his passion for sailing and his love for the Santana, his boat, on which he went off whenever he could, accompanied by a few friends. They used to drink Drambuies and play dominoes or just sail. He had learned early about the sea, having left school (at their request) at seventeen and joined the Navy. It was on the troopship Leviathan that he received the injury that permanently scarred his upper lip. "Sailing. That was the part of him no one could get at," Capote said. "It wasn't anything materialistic. It was some kind of inner soul, an almost mystical hideaway."

If the *Motion Picture Herald*'s annual Fame Poll of the Top Ten movie stars can be trusted, it appears that Bogart's peak years of popularity were 1943–1949, during and just after World War II. Cooke explained it this way: "He was . . . a romantic hero inconceivable in any time but ours. . . . When Hitler was acting out scripts more brutal and obscene than anything dreamed of by Chicago's North Side or the Warner Brothers, Bogart was the only possible antagonist likely to outwit him and survive. What was needed was no Ronald Colman, Leslie Howard or other knight of the boudoir, but a conniver as subtle as Goebbels. Bogart was the very tough gent required, and to his glory he was always, in the end, on our side."

He didn't get his Oscar, however, until 1952 (for *The African Queen*), and popped up on the Top Ten again in 1955, just a little more than a year before he died.

Betty Comden: "I don't think this cult is anything new. . . ."

Adolph Green: "No. . . ."

Comden: "Bogart never stopped being popular. . . ."
Green: "There are so few originals around. . . ."
Comden: "Bogart's style had an innate sophistication. . . ."
Green: "He was less an actor . . ."
Comden: ". . . than a personality."
Bogart agreed. "Sure I am. It took fifteen years to make us personalities. Gable and Cooper can do anything in a picture, and people would say, 'Oh, that's just good old Clark.' "

"His great basic quality," said Ustinov, "was a splendid roughness. Even when perfectly groomed, I felt I could have lit a match on his jaw. . . . He knew his job inside out, and yet it was impossible not to feel that his real soul was elsewhere, a mysterious searching instrument knocking at doors unknown even to himself. . . ."

Perhaps this is what Bogart's admirers sense. "There was something about him that came through in every part he played," said Miss Bacall. "I think he'll always be fascinating —to this generation and every succeeding one. There was something that made him able to be a man of his own and it showed through his work. There was also a purity, which is amazing considering the parts he played. Something solid too. I think as time goes by we all believe less and less. Here was someone who believed in something."

"Like all really great stars," said director George Cukor, "he had a secret. You never really know him altogether. He also had boldness of mind, freedom of thought—a buccaneer. I think these young people haven't seen him," he went on, trying to explain the cult. "They're simply rediscovering him. After all, Bogie had class."

"The average college student would sooner identify with Bogart than, say, Sinatra, don't you think?" said Mankiewicz. "He had that rather intellectual disrepect for authority. Also I don't think anyone ever really believed that Bogart was a gangster—that's what fascinated people. Bogart never frightened them."

"It's angry youth," Chester Morris said. "They're cheering for the heavy today. Everything must be nonconformist.

They'd also like to do the kind of things he did. He was a forerunner of James Bond." Benchley: "He's a hero without being a pretty boy."

"Could it be anything as simple as sex appeal?" Cooke wondered. "He had an image of sophisticated virility and he projected it remarkably well. And with such humor. At last, he had such style that it doesn't wither, it doesn't age, it doesn't date. Like Billie Holiday."

"I think Robin Hood has always been attractive," said Adlai Stevenson.

Before the adulation, there must be something to adulate. And this must be created. "If a face like Ingrid Bergman's looks at you as though you're adorable," Bogart once said, "everybody does. You don't have to act very much." The late Raymond Chandler thought otherwise: "All Bogart has to do to dominate a scene is to enter it." Evidently it wasn't always that way. In 1922, playing one of his first stage roles, he was reviewed by Alexander Woollcott: "His performance could be mercifully described as inadequate." But two years later, of another performance, Woollcott again: "Mr. Bogart is a young actor whose last appearance was recorded by your correspondent in words so disparaging that it is surprising to find him still acting. Those words are hereby eaten." It would figure that Bogart often used to quote the first review but never the second.

" 'Why, I'm a National Institution,' he used to say," Capote recalled. "He was very proud of his success and fame. But he was most serious about his acting. He thought of it as a profession, one that he was curious about, knew something about. After all, it was almost the sum total of his life. In the end, Bogart really was an artist. And a very selective one. All the gestures and expressions were pruned down and pruned down. One time I watched *The Maltese Falcon* with him and he sat there, muttering in that hoarse way, criticizing himself in the third person. 'Now he's gonna come in,' he'd say. 'Then he's gonna do this and that's where he does the wrong thing.' I gathered during the silences that he liked it. It was braggadocio through silence."

Howard Hawks directed Bogart in his two most archetypal roles, as Harry (Steve) Morgan in *To Have and Have Not* and as Philip Marlow in *The Big Sleep* (1946). "He was extremely easy to work with," Hawks said. "Really underrated as an actor. Without his help I couldn't have done what I did with Bacall. Not too many actors would sit around and wait while a girl steals a scene. But he fell in love with the girl and the girl with him, and that made it easy."

Bogart used to say that an audience was always a little ahead of the actor. "If a guy points a gun at you," he explained, "the audience knows you're afraid. You don't have to make faces. You just have to believe that you are the person you're playing and that what is happening is happening to you."

Ustinov acted with Bogart once, in a comedy called *We're No Angels* (1955). "Bogart had an enormous presence," he said, "and he carried the light of battle in his eye. He wished to be matched, to be challenged, to be teased. I could see a jocular and quarrelsome eye staring out of the character he was playing into the character I was playing—rather as an experienced bullfighter might stare a hotheaded bull to precipitate action."

"When the heavy, full of crime and bitterness," said Bogart, "grabs his wounds and talks about death and taxes in a husky voice, the audience is his and his alone."

This emotion, elicited so consciously from his movie audiences, ironically became a reality. His death was horribly, heartbreakingly in character. He died on January 14, 1957, of a cancer of the esophagus, and it had taken well over a year to kill him. "These days," he said, "I just sit around and talk to my friends, the people I like." Which is what he did.

"I went to see him toward the end," said Ambassador Stevenson. "He was very ill and very weak, but he made a most gallant effort to keep gay. He had an intolerance for weakness, an impatience with illness."

"I went a few times," Capote said. "Most of his friends went, some almost every day, like Sinatra. Some were very loyal. He seemed to bring out the best in them all. He looked so awful, so terribly thin. His eyes were huge and they looked so frightened. They got bigger and bigger. It was real fear and yet there was always that gay, brave self. He'd have to be brought downstairs on the dumbwaiter and he'd sit and wait and wait for his Martini. He was only allowed one, I think, or two. And that's how we used to find him, smoking and sipping that Martini."

During that time, his wife rarely left the house, though her friends and even Bogart urged her to go out more often. When someone asked why she had only been out six or seven times in ten months, Bogart replied: "She's my wife and my nurse. So she stays home. Maybe that's the way you tell the ladies from the broads in this town."

"He went through the worst and most agonizing pain any human can take," said Dr. Maynard Brandsma. "I knew this and when I'd see him I'd ask, 'How is it?' Bogie would always answer simply, 'Pretty rough.' He never complained and he never whimpered. I knew he was dying and during the last weeks I knew he knew it too."

"I saw him twenty-three days before he died," said Cukor. "He couldn't come downstairs anymore and he was heavily sedated. He kept closing his eyes. Still he'd be telling jokes and asking to hear the gossip. But his voice was the wonder. That marvelous voice. It was absolutely alive. It was the last thing that died."

His death came in the early morning and that day the papers carried the news to the world. Most of the reports were similar. Quite a few of them told it this way: "Usually he kissed his wife Lauren Bacall and said, 'Good night.' But according to Dr. Michael Flynn, this time he put his hand on her arm and murmured in his familiar brusque fashion, 'Good-bye, kid.' "

Whether it really happened that way or not is beside the

point. Bogart the man and Bogart the hero had merged until now one couldn't tell the difference between the two, if indeed there had ever been any. He had walked through seventy-five movie nights for his public and it was too late now to change the image, too late to alter a legend that had really just begun.

September 1964

In late 1971, around the time The Last Picture Show *was opening in America (which was after my father had died and my marriage had broken up), Harold called from New York to ask if I'd be interested in doing a monthly column for the magazine. "About what?" I said.*

"Hollywood."

"What about it?"

"Anything you want—except movie reviews. Don't you have anything you want to say about Hollywood, for Pete's sake?"

Well, I did, actually, and the following appeared as my fourth column (which was called, not surprisingly, but a little ironically I think considering the nature of the magazine, Hollywood). *Its subject, Cary Grant, phoned me a couple of weeks after it came out. "Well," he said, "all I can say is I hope you'll read that at my funeral." About a year later, though, he gave me a nice finish to the piece, so consider the following a P.S.*

We were at the Beverly Wilshire Hotel for a gala honoring John Ford. Cary looked as marvelous as ever and was in high spirits—but then I've rarely heard or seen him low. Cybill Shepherd was with me. "Hel—lo, you beau—ti—ful girl!" he said as only he can, and she was lost to me for the evening. At the reservation desk, Cary leaned in toward one of the middle-aged ladies checking off names and said "Hel—lo! I've forgotten my tick—et—I'm awfully sorry—can I go in, please?"

She looked at him skeptically. "What's your name?"

"Cary Grant."

She said, inscrutibly, "You don't look like Cary Grant."

Without a pause, Cary said cheerfully, "I know—nobody does."

Cary Grant

CARY GRANT WAS THE FIRST SUPERSTAR I ever met. It was an odd experience, walking into an office at Universal—this was in 1961—and confronting a man who didn't know me but whom I'd known for as long as I could remember. He'd just come out of a long story conference, his hair was messy, he hadn't shaved for a day or so, and his dark slacks and white shirt looked as though he'd slept in them. Clifford Odets was a mutual friend—he was still alive then—and he had asked Cary to see me, so we talked about Clifford for a while, and I don't remember a word of what was said. My mind was flooded with images from all the Cary Grant movies I'd seen —and I had this uncanny desire to be terribly honest and open with the man, at the same time realizing this might easily put him off. It's a feeling I've had with several movie stars I've met—knowing them so much better than they could ever know me—and finding it impossible to satisfactorily bridge the gap. All I could think about was how like his movie self he was—the same charm, humor, the totally uncalculated yet unmistakable air of mystery. I kept thinking, "He's just like Cary Grant." The only difference I noticed was that I'd never seen him laugh on the screen as he did in life—because in person he really *laughs*, his eyes tear, and he looks joyous.

It must have been a thrilling conversation from his point of view—this kid staring at him and trying not to be completely moronic. If he noticed, I certainly never did—he was graciousness itself. I guess he was used to the reaction he was getting from me—he'd been a star by then for about twenty-five years—and must have encountered a lot of gawking. (He told me some years later that people often come up and ask him to say something—anything—they just want to hear him speak.)

Of course, it wasn't his celebrity that impressed me; I can think of several stars who wouldn't have affected me one way or another, but Cary Grant has always been among my three or four favorite actors, and certainly one of a handful of the great movie personalities. What sets him apart from all the rest, however—something especially pertinent in this time when the studio system has all but disappeared—is that Cary was the first movie star to go free-lance. From the time his Paramount contract ended in 1936, Grant was never again signed exclusively with any studio. Therefore, unlike any other film star (until the early Fifties), he himself picked the scripts and the directors he cared to work with; no executive assigned him to pictures, he was not forced to do anything he didn't want to do. Grant was responsible for his material, and formed the arc of his career, shaped his movie persona through his own choices as men like Bogart or Cagney or Tracy or Cooper were not as free to do. It's significant, in fact, that his unique characteristics did not begin to be seen till after his Paramount tenure was over. Until then, he was little more than a likable, slightly awkward, perhaps too good-looking, and fairly conventional leading man in a string of largely forgettable pictures. If some remember him opposite Mae West in *She Done Him Wrong* or Marlene Dietrich in Josef von Sternberg's *Blonde Venus* (a couple of the good Paramount assignments), it is because he is so surprisingly *unlike* the Cary Grant that was to evolve.

We begin to notice the difference first in George Cukor's *Sylvia Scarlett* in 1935, and two years later, already almost perfected, in Leo McCarey's *The Awful Truth*. By 1938, with Cukor's *Holiday* and Howard Hawks' *Bringing Up Baby*, the name Cary Grant became synonymous with a certain character—a kind of cockney brashness combined with impeccable taste and a detached and subtle wit. What made him so desirable as a player and so inimitable (and there've been many counterfeits through the years) was a striking mixture of farceur's talents and matinee idol's looks. Which other star could express anger by whinnying like a horse (as he did first in *Bringing Up Baby*) and still retain his masculinity? Who else could do a cartwheel to express a love of life (as in *Holiday*) and make it seem so utterly right? He had a way of saying the most lackluster line that would make it *seem* witty (see something like *Dream Wife* sometime).

He became such an accomplished master at comedy, both high and low, that his dramatic talents have been generally overlooked. However, the emotional depth and range of his work in films like Hawks' *Only Angels Have Wings* or George Stevens' *Penny Serenade* or Clifford Odets' *None But the Lonely Heart* should dispel any doubts. Even a minor but likable melodrama like Richard Brooks' first film, *Crisis*, is heightened considerably by the sense of truth and the professional skill he brings to his role; he plays a surgeon—watch him in the operation scenes and you will believe he has done it a thousand times. Given the right script and even an indifferent director, Grant's personality can transform a film like *Mr. Lucky* into something altogether memorable and affecting. When all the elements are right, his presence becomes an indispensable part of a masterpiece: Hawks' *Only Angels Have Wings*, *His Girl Friday*, Hitchcock's *North by Northwest*, *Notorious*.

The ideal leading man, the perfect zany, the most admirable dandy and the most charming rogue: except perhaps in his earliest years at Paramount, he was never allowed to die at the end of a film and with good reason—who would believe it? Cary was indestructible.

Yet, by 1965, he had never won an Academy Award. That year, accepting the Oscar for co-writing a Grant vehicle called *Father Goose*, Peter Stone was perfectly succinct: "My thanks to Cary Grant," he said, "who keeps winning these things for other people." Five years later, when the Academy finally gave him an honorary award for his whole career (it was the evening's highlight and the only TV appearance he's ever made), Grant gave an especially gracious and spirited thank you speech, prominently mentioning several of the best directors he's worked with. It was quite a list, and no accident either, but rather a monument to his good taste as well as his ability—for he has worked with more good directors than any other star in pictures: Hawks (5 times), Hitchcock (4), Stanley Donen (4), Cukor (3), McCarey (3), Stevens (3), Raoul Walsh, Frank Capra, Joseph L. Mankiewicz, Blake Edwards, Garson Kanin.

Each man brought out different facets of Grant's fascinating personality; I have asked several of them about certain particularly delightful moments in their Grant films, often getting the same reply: "That was Cary's." Hitchcock, whose reputation at least (though I know it's not true) is of a director who cares little for actors, told me, "One doesn't direct Cary Grant, one just puts him in front of a camera."

Cary hasn't made a film since 1966, when he did *Walk Don't Run*, in which he let Jim Hutton and Samantha Eggar have the love interest, while he played their matchmaker, a role that had been done originally by Charles Coburn in the first version of that story, *The More the Merrier*. It was not an unlikable movie, but audiences didn't care to see him in that sort of part. There is a moment in the movie when Cary gives Miss Eggar a glass of champagne and a kiss on the hand that must have made everyone yearn to see him go further—it was certainly the most romantic bit in the picture. But Cary had decided he was too old to play opposite young women, and, in fact, I would guess the relative failure of *Walk Don't Run* prompted his unannounced exit from the movies. If people only wanted him as a romantic figure and he felt he was too old, the only thing to do was quit. How does one convince him he's wrong?

I told Cary recently that I'd love to get him into a movie again, and he answered jokingly that if there was a role for an old fellow in a wheelchair, maybe he'd do it. No matter that he only looks about fifty years old, and that most women I know (young or old) become slightly moony at the mention of his name. Nothing to be done—he is off in the international business world and fascinated by it, he claims. Perhaps he is happy, but the movies have lost someone quite irreplaceable. Too soon. He can argue that he's done everything in pictures, and of course he has, but I do wish he were still at it. Personally, I'd give anything to have him in a movie, as I know many directors would, and I'm sure audiences would not be unhappy to have that special style and unique sophistication before them again. He must be to them, as he was to me that first time I met him, an old and dear friend. We miss him.

April 1972

The best stories James Cagney told me the one time I met him are either unprintable or depend for their effectiveness on being acted out—something I haven't figured a way to do on paper. In fact, for that very reason, I've been better doing Cagney on talk shows than I was in this column. The spirit and brilliance of the man is something largely visual and verbal, so please consider the following a failed attempt to capture some of that and also as an inadequate tribute to one of the greatest of movie actors.

James Cagney

I FINALLY MET JAMES CAGNEY the other day—the real one. There's a bearded fellow going around lately passing himself off as the actor. I was in Miami when this guy was there—they made him honorary mayor of Hollywood, Florida—and a paper printed pictures of him. Didn't look like Cagney to *me*. When Barbra Streisand was singing in Las Vegas around Christmas, they told her Cagney was in the audience so she introduced him from the stage and when this same bearded chap stood up, she thought, "Doesn't look like Cagney to *me*." Cagney himself seemed rather amused at this; he told several similar incidents that have occurred over the years—people pretending to be his son and his daughter—and him. I guess it's the Hughes-Irving syndrome again—Cagney hasn't made a new movie in over a decade and is rarely if ever seen in public—so the impostor must have assumed no one would know the difference.

An incredible impudence. Cagney is the most imitated and one of the most inimitable actors who ever appeared on the screen. I don't think anyone in pictures ever had his energy or his theatricality. A year ago, I ran Raoul Walsh's brilliant gangster film, *White Heat*, for Orson Welles; he'd never seen it and is a fan of Cagney's and Walsh's, so we looked at it together one night, and afterward Orson got to musing about the absurdity of all the theoretical writings about the difference between movie acting and stage acting. "Look at Cagney—everything he does is *big*—and yet it's never for a moment unbelievable, because it's *real*. It's true. He's a great movie actor and his performances are in no way modulated for the camera—he never scaled anything down."

Even in a likable early programmer like Mervyn LeRoy's *Hard to Handle*, with a plot that spins dizzily from one maniacally contrived situation to another, Cagney's break-neck delivery and his elaborately embroidered gestures never

for a moment seem anything but convincing. His performances were always like that—walking that most dangerously
narrow line between gimmicky caricature and a unique
eccentricity with the sureness of a ballet dancer; he never fell
on the wrong side—he was always true.

During the course of a small dinner party in Brentwood,
he also proved to be an extraordinary raconteur. He doesn't
just tell a story, he acts it out, playing all the parts with remarkable precision and an economy of gesture that is as subtle
and revealing as most of his professional performances. He
gave us some memorable impressions that night of people
he'd worked with—a gentle Hungarian like director Charles
Vidor (Cagney had the accent down perfectly, and pantomimed holding a cigarette thoughtfully from below with
thumb and forefinger which immediately caught the flavor of
the man), a not-so-gentle Hungarian director like Michael
Curtiz (two hilariously unprintable stories here), and the
absolute essence of John Ford (in this context, he gave a great
with the belt, and a slouchy hat, rarely tilted. Sometimes it
one-word description of the Irish, of whom Cagney is one:
"Malice"). He did several others for us, including a "hop-
headed" pimp he observed in his Hell's Kitchen childhood
standing on a corner, nervously cracking his knuckles and
jacking his pants up with his arms—a mannerism he remembered and immortalized in *Angels with Dirty Faces*. One
of the guests asked him how he had developed his habit of
physically drawn-out death scenes, and Cagney told of a film
of Frank Buck's he'd once seen, in which the hunter was
forced to kill a giant gorilla. The animal died in a slow,
amazed way that gave the actor his inspiration, and which he
played out for us in a few riveting moments of mime.

It was a little frustrating to watch him and realize how
good he still is and to know that he has given up acting. I
asked him finally what it would take to get him into a movie
again. He leaned back on the couch, smiled gently, said, with
a tiny shake of his head, "I have no interest." He sat up and
leaned forward. "That's not a line either—I really mean it." So

Cagney and his wife divide their time between Los Angeles, where they have a house, and Martha's Vineyard, where they have a ranch; he owns a lot of land and cattle and seems contented. As the evening went along, I became less and less so. He is, after all, an artist, and I have never believed in retirement for artists. I don't blame it on Cagney, really, and I'm not sure the system is to blame. There are many people who'd love to have him in a picture, I know that, but he is wealthy and if, as he says, the desire has left him, what motivation can he find? After eighty pictures, I guess there are few things to challenge him but I can't help feeling a deep sense of waste—he's just too good to be idle. Yet perhaps there are reasons Cagney can't, and wouldn't want to, put into words; so many of his pals have passed away and certainly Hollywood is no longer the great gay place it once was. If I have a feeling of loss for those better times, how to calculate the ache felt by those who experienced them. Cagney gave a hint of this late in the evening: "When I drove through the studio gate, and the thrill was gone," he said, "I knew it was time to quit."

There have been many superb Cagney performances—not always in very good films (he says they'd shoot three pictures at the same time in his early Warner days)—but I am particularly fond of his reckless race driver in Howard Hawks' *The Crowd Roars*, his daredevil flyer in Hawks' *Ceiling Zero*, his ebullient dentist in Raoul Walsh's *The Strawberry Blonde*, his doomed "big-shot" gangster in Walsh's *The Roaring Twenties*, and his psychopathic mama's-boy killer in the same director's *White Heat*, which features two of my favorite Cagney scenes. In the first, set in the prison mess, he is told that his mother has died on the outside, and Cagney slowly builds his reaction from disbelief through sorrow, grief and, finally, complete hysteria, in one of the most chilling sequences in movies. At the end of the picture, fatally wounded, and trapped by the law on top of a huge globular gas tank, he grins malevolently, laughs, then fires his pistol into the tank itself, and, as the flames shoot up around him just before the blinding explosions begin, he screams happily, "Top of the world, Ma! Top of the world!" One critic wrote of this film that only a hard-boiled director like Walsh could get away with having Cagney sit on his mother's lap. But I do believe Cagney himself could get away with almost anything—such was the intensity of his conviction as a performer. Whether it was shoving a grapefruit in his girl friend's face (in the overrated *Public Enemy*) or doing a little dance step down the stairs of the White House after meeting F.D.R. (in *Yankee Doodle Dandy*), Cagney's indisputable authority as a film personality and his flawless sense of truth as an actor could transform even the most improbable material into something basically honest.

He was different from most of the great stars in that he often played villains—even late in his career—comically in *Mister Roberts*, with pathos in *Love Me or Leave Me*, as a psychopath in *White Heat*; the point is that his personality was as fixed in the audience's consciousness as Bogart's or Cooper's or Gable's—but he was also a far more resourceful and gifted actor. He could express ambiguities in a character even if they were not written into the script or featured by the direction. He was also innately sympathetic, which is what gave his heavies such an intriguing tension. *White Heat*, particularly, has a decidedly subversive duality because of this—the advanced, somewhat inhuman technology of the police and the undercover-informer cop (Edmond O'Brien) become morally reprehensible in the glare of Cagney's personality, though his character is in no way sentimentalized. (Nonetheless, Orson and I were hissing the law and rooting for Cagney like schoolboys.) He was that rarest of players—an actor who could transcend his vehicles. Like most of the other stars of the golden age of movies—which I would guess ended sometime in the early Fifties—he was one of a kind.

Cagney told us he was only tempted once these last ten years to break his retirement—when George Cukor offered him the Stanley Holloway part in *My Fair Lady*. "That was inviting," he said, "but I'd made up my mind." Interesting that it was a song-and-dance role because, although he won his only Oscar for playing George M. Cohan in *Yankee Doodle Dandy*, Cagney is remembered by most movie fans for his gangster parts. But someone asked him at dinner which of his movies he liked best, and he answered without hesitation, "I guess it'd have to be the Cohan picture."

Of course he was like no other dancer; his straight-legged, cocky and constantly surprising style of hoofing was only seen in a few other films—not very good ones, really, except for camp buffs. *Footlight Parade* is probably the best—but his manner as an actor and his grace as a performer no doubt owe quite a lot to his dancing days. There is no other way to put it, I'm afraid, but he *moved* eloquently. He could easily have been a great silent star, but he arrived with the talkies—and gave even the least of them a measure of his boundless panache.

July 1972

I'd been planning for quite a while to write something about John Wayne and when I finally did a column on him, it was both to get it off my mind and also to tell him in print what I genuinely thought since I was trying to talk him into doing a Western that Larry McMurtry and I had conceived for him. He liked the piece, but he didn't like the script, so the movie has still to be made. Frankly, the script is better than the column (though we're currently reworking it) and since I still have hopes of persuading him, the following has not been amended to include my personal opinion of his taste in screenplays. After all, it may yet prove to be exemplary.

John Wayne

I FIRST MET JOHN WAYNE six years ago while he was on location in Old Tucson for Howard Hawks' *El Dorado*. We spent over an hour talking about movies and directors and, when he was finally called away for a shot, he said, "Geez, it was good talkin' about pictures—Christ, the only thing anybody ever talks to me about these days is politics and cancer!"

It's true that too many people either endorse or deplore Wayne because of his political views, and it strikes me equally as silly as those people in charge of the gold stars on Hollywood Boulevard refusing to let Charlie Chaplin's name in because of *his* politics (at least they finally relented). You may agree with Chaplin's leftist leanings as you may oppose Wayne's right-wing attitudes, but neither of them matters a damn in terms of their work or what they will leave behind. Chaplin will not be remembered because he lost a paternity suit and espoused liberal causes any more than Wayne will be for winning a bout with lung cancer, endorsing some political candidates, or even for acting in a few easily forgettable anti-Communist movies of the Fifties.

Wayne will be remembered, I would guess, as an extraordinarily effective character actor whose unique qualities and talents have been explored and mined by at least two great directors and have enriched the works of a host of others of varying degrees of ability (from Henry Hathaway and Cecil B. DeMille to Nicholas Ray and John Farrow). After over twenty years of being a top box-office attraction (plus twenty before that as a not unpopular star), Wayne's persona has, in fact, attained mythic proportions which even the most myopic of our reviewers have finally noted. He brings to each new movie—good or bad—a resonance and a sense of the past—his own and ours—that fills it with reverberations above and beyond its own perhaps limited qualities. That is the true measure of what makes a great movie star, and the very longevity of his career is an incalculably important part of the impact. If the star system is not dead, it has certainly been gravely injured by the fact that so few movies are made anymore, and the audience is not allowed the familiarity of repeated exposure that stars used to have. A star today is lucky to do a picture a year, while one could see Cagney or Bogart or Gable or Tracy three or even four times a year. Wayne had already made close to a hundred Westerns in the ten years before John Ford saved him from the Republic treadmill in 1939 with *Stagecoach*. Of course Ford had first put him in pictures over ten years before that. Wayne was going to U.S.C., playing football—Marion Morrison was his name—and he went to the studios in the summer looking for work. Ford gave him a job as a propman and a gooseherder on *Mother Machree* in 1927, then bits and small roles in several other silent and early sound films. Raoul Walsh liked the way Wayne walked (who doesn't?) and cast him as the romantic lead in a 1931 Fox talkie called *The Big Trail*, which was also a giant dud at the box office, though quite a pleasant movie really. In fact, I saw it recently at the same time as I ran two critically acclaimed Oscar winners of similar vintage, *In Old Arizona* and *Cimarron*, and the Walsh-Wayne film is infinitely superior. (The other two are almost unwatchable.) From the start, Wayne had an engaging natural quality and it kept him going through the endless pictures he turned out until *Stagecoach* finally made him respectable. Even then, it took almost ten years for him to really find the character that has immortalized him—the gruff, tough, often mean, often bad-tempered, sometimes sentimental but certainly unregenerate older man he first played while still young in Howard Hawks' *Red River*.

All his best movies until then had been for Ford (*They Were Expendable, Fort Apache*), but his roles had been likable, decent leading men—not without color, but definitely without the later spirit. After *Red River*, Ford, not to be outdone, cast Wayne as an even older man in *She Wore a Yellow Ribbon*; the Wayne prototype had been established and this was the first of many variations on the theme, the character aging and deepening as Wayne and his two favorite directors aged and deepened their art. A remarkable series of films followed: from Hawks, *Rio Bravo, Hatari!, El Dorado*; from Ford, the more diverse and increasingly complex beauties of *Rio Grande, The Quiet Man, The Searchers, The Wings of Eagles, The Man Who Shot Liberty Valance.*

His performances in these pictures rate with the finest examples of movie acting, and his value to each film is immeasurable, yet none of them was recognized at the time as anything much more than "and John Wayne does his usual solid job," if that (more often he was panned). The Academy only nominated him once, for Allan Dwan's excellent *Sands of Iwo Jima*, an archetypal Wayne movie of non-Ford-Hawks dimension, but of course it was not until he put on an eye patch, played drunk and parodied himself in *True Grit* that anyone thought he was acting. The quality in a star which makes audiences immediately suspend their disbelief—something that men like Wayne or Stewart or Fonda bring with them naturally when they walk into a scene—is unfortunately an achievement that normally goes so unnoticed that most people don't think of it as acting at all. Too many believe acting means fake accents and false noses. Paul Muni gave his best movie performance in *Scarface*, but he became *Mr.* Paul Muni with the theatrical posturing of the *Pasteur-Zola-Juarez* series. Bogart was inimitably Bogart and often quite a bit more in any number of films from *High Sierra* through *The Harder They Fall*, but the academicians insist on remembering his three weakest—because most obvious—performances in *The Treasure of the Sierra Madre, The African Queen* and *The Caine Mutiny*. If he'd made a career of roles like that, there would have been more awards perhaps, but no Bogart cult. Seeing an actor at work, it seems to me, is as bad as being conscious of a director manipulating you. When the artifice shines through, much of the artistry disappears. John Wayne, therefore, is at his best precisely when he is being what we have come to call "John Wayne."

There is a splendid moment in *Rio Bravo*—which features I think his most endearing performance—when Wayne walks down the steps of the sheriff's office and toward some men who are riding up to meet him. Hawks frames the shot from behind—Wayne striding slowly, casually away from camera in that slightly rocking, graceful way of his—and the image is held for quite a long while as if to give us plenty of time to enjoy the sight: a classic, familiar figure—unmistakable from any angle—moving across a world of illusion he has more than conquered.

One of the most charming things about Wayne on a set is to see how much he himself still relishes that world. I've seen him play around with his six-shooter off camera, or with the rifle he often carries in pictures, with as much enthusiasm as a kid with a new toy—and certainly they're not a novelty to him now. Yet after forty years in films, he still has more excitement about the job than most people just starting out. He likes working with newcomers too and is generous with advice; those who don't let ego stand in their way can learn a few pretty good tricks from the old man. (For all that, there is not a note of pomposity or pretentiousness about him; indeed, he always seems genuinely surprised, even slightly embarrassed, by praise.) Hawks has said to me that "when you have someone as good as Duke around" it becomes "awfully easy to do good scenes" because he helps and inspires everyone about him.

It's been reported that Wayne also has a tendency to be generous with advice to some of the younger directors he hires, but they don't really seem to mind too much either since at least two I can think of continually do pictures with him. Perhaps they realize that his interference comes from exuberance and a passion for the work rather than from a desire to bully. (Nevertheless, the two movies he signed as a director are better left unmentioned.)

A couple of years ago, I went out to his house at Newport Beach to film an interview for a documentary I was making on John Ford. While the crew was setting up on the terrace overlooking the bay, I chatted with Wayne inside, and asked him if it was true that he was always directing Andrew McLaglen's direction on their films together. (Of course, McLaglen, the son of Victor, a great Ford regular, grew up on Ford-Wayne sets and was given his first feature-directing job by Wayne.) Duke answered it was true that he occasionally made suggestions to Andy, but that he felt there could be only one boss on a picture. I let it go, and went to check the setup. When it was ready, Wayne came out and, looking around, immediately began issuing orders excitedly. "Move that light over a little bit," he said, "and take that one to the side. Better give me a higher chair to sit on—bring that stone elephant over—that'll do—" After several moments of this—my tiny crew had jumped into action on his first word—he glanced over at me. I'd been watching him and I guess I looked amused. Our eyes met, held a second, then he grinned broadly. "Oh," he said, "sorry, Andy."

May 1972

For some reason, this is the only piece *I've ever done on an actress. I really don't know why, since any number of favorites spring to mind, as dissimilar as Carole Lombard and Katharine Hepburn. Perhaps it's because part of my affection for film stars lies in wishing I were like them and it therefore follows that my interest would be more in the men. Also—and it's one of the great and tragic inequities of our society and of the movie game—male stars generally have a longer and therefore more fruitful life span. They have more often been able to create an image and a unified character. When asked once if he had it to do all over again, would he have been in pictures, John Wayne answered, "Sure—as long as I wasn't a dame."*

Miss Dietrich
Goes to Denver

"MARLENE DIETRICH'S TAKEN YOUR SEATS," the assistant director was a little out of breath. "You don't care, do you? She likes to sit in the first two on the right. They moved you guys behind her." Ryan O'Neal and I were at Los Angeles International Airport with a few others of the cast and crew of *Paper Moon*, which we were flying to Kansas to shoot. I said we didn't mind.

Ryan said, "Marlene Dietrich is on our plane going to *Kansas?*"

No, it turned out she was flying to Denver (we had to switch planes there) to give six concert performances at the Denver Auditorium. Hard to believe, but sure enough, there she was, sitting across from us at the gate, all in white—wide-brimmed hat, pants, shirt, jacket—looking great and also bored and a little suspicious of the noisy good spirits around our group.

We went over to say hello. I introduced myself. Ryan said, "Hello, Miss Dietrich, I'm Ryan O'Neal. *Love Story?*" He grinned.

"Yes," she said. "I didn't see it—I liked the book too much. I won't see *The Godfather* for the same reason—Brando is too slow for it anyway—why didn't they use Eddie Robinson?"

There were several people I knew who had worked with and loved her, and I mentioned a few of them, trying to get a conversation going, but she was a little frosty, so we slipped away after a few moments. Ryan said, "I think we did great," but I didn't.

She was right behind us as we waited to have our hand baggage searched. We tried again; she was nicer this time.

"I saw *The Last Picture Show*," she said to me. "I thought if one more person stripped slowly, I would go crazy."

"Did you see *What's Up, Doc?*" Ryan said. "We did that together."

"Yes, I saw it," she said and nothing more. I changed the subject—told her I'd recently run a couple of her old pictures —Lubitsch's *Angel* and Von Sternberg's *Morocco*. She made a face at the first and said the second was "so slow now." I said I assumed Von Sternberg wanted it that way—he'd told me he had. "No, he wanted *me* slow," she said. "On *The Blue Angel*, he had such trouble with Jannings—he was so *slow*." The luggage inspector was especially thorough on her bag—and she looked disgusted. "I haven't been through anything like this since the war."

On the plane she sat in front of us, with her blonde girl friday, and by now, she'd obviously decided we weren't so bad; she spent almost the whole flight leaning backward over the top of her seat, on her knees, talking to us. And she was just swell. Animated, girlish, candid, funny, sexy, baby-talk "r" and everything.

I told her I was trying to stop smoking again. "Oh, don't," she said. "I stopped ten years ago and I've been miserable ever since. I never drank before—and now I drink. I never had a cough when was smoking—now I cough. *Don't* stop— you'll get fat and you don't want to do that."

We talked about movies she'd been in and directors she'd worked for. After a while, it became apparent to her that I'd seen an awful lot of her pictures. "Why do you know so much about my films?"

"Because I think you're wonderful, and you've worked for a lot of great directors."

"No," she said it dubiously. "No, I only worked for two great directors—Von Sternberg and Billy Wilder."

"And what about Orson?"

"Oh, well, yes, Orson—of course."

I guess she wasn't so impressed with Lubitsch or Hitchcock or Fritz Lang, Raoul Walsh or Tay Garnett or René Clair.

or Frank Borzage. She looked amazed when I told her I liked Lang's *Rancho Notorious*, amused that I enjoyed Walsh's *Manpower*, confused that I was fond of *Angel*. I had read somewhere that her own favorite performance was in Welles' *Touch of Evil*.

"You still feel that way?" I said.

"Yes. I was terrific in that. I think I never said a line as well as the last line in that movie—'What does it *matter* what you say about people . . . ?' Wasn't I good there? I don't know why I said it so well. And I *looked* so good in that dark wig. It was Elizabeth Taylor's. My part wasn't in the script, you know, but Orson called and said he wanted me to play a kind of gypsy madam in a border town, so I went over to Paramount and found that wig. It was very funny, you know, because I had been crazy about Orson—in the Forties when he was married to Rita Hayworth and when we toured doing his magic act—I was just crazy about him—we were great friends, you know, but nothing. . . . Because Orson doesn't like blond women. He only likes dark women. And suddenly when he saw me in this dark wig, he looked at me with new eyes. Was this Marlene?"

"Well, he certainly photographed you lovingly."

"Yes, I never looked that good."

"You had great legs," Ryan said.

"Yah—great!" she grinned. "Great thighs!" She slapped one of them behind the seat.

"I dream about your legs and I wake up screaming," said Ryan.

"Me too," she said.

I asked her if she'd been upset about the late Josef Von Sternberg's acerbic autobiography, *Fun in a Chinese Laundry*, in which he'd said that he had created her, and implied that she would have been nothing without him. (He'd once said to me, "*I* am Miss Dietrich—Miss Dietrich is *me*.")

She pursed her lips, lifted her eyebrows slightly. "No—because it was true. I didn't know what I was doing— I just tried to do what he told me. I remember in *Morocco*, I had a scene with Cooper—and I was supposed to go to the door, turn and say a line like, 'Wait for me,' and then leave. And Von Sternberg said, 'Walk to the door, turn, count to ten, say your line and leave.' So I did and he got very angry. 'If you're so stupid that you can't count slowly, then count to twenty-five.' And we did it again. I think we did it forty times, until finally I was counting probably to fifty. And I didn't know why. I was annoyed. But at the premiere of *Morocco*—at Grauman's Chinese Theatre—" she said the name with just the lightest touch of mockery—"when this moment came and I paused and then said, 'Wait for me,' the audience burst into applause. Von Sternberg knew they were waiting for this—and he made them wait and they loved it."

I asked if he had gotten along with Cooper. "No—they didn't like each other. You know, he couldn't stand it if I looked up at any man in a movie—he always staged it so that they were looking up at me. It would infuriate him—and Cooper was very tall. And you know, Jo was not. I was stupid—I didn't understand it then—that kind of jealousy." She shook her head lightly, but at her own folly.

Which of her seven films with Von Sternberg was her favorite? "*The Devil Is a Woman* was the best—he photographed it himself—wasn't it beautiful? It was not successful and it was the last one we did together—I love it."

Ryan said, "I hear you're a good cook."

"I'm a *great* cook."

"When'd you have time to learn?"

"Well, when I came to America, they told me the food was awful—and it was true. Whenever you hear someone in America say they had a great meal, it turns out they had a steak. So I learned. Mr. Von Sternberg loved good food, you know. So I would go to the studio every day and do what he told me, and then I'd come home and cook."

I mentioned *Song of Songs*—the first American picture she'd done without Von Sternberg—and said I didn't like it very much. She agreed. "That was when Paramount was trying to break us up. So they insisted I do a picture with another director. Jo picked him—Mamoulian—because he'd made *Applause*—which was quite good. But this one was lousy. Every day, before each shot, I had the soundman lower the boom mike and I said into it so the Paramount brass could hear it when they saw the rushes, I said, "Oh, Jo—why hast thou forsaken me?' "

The next day—in my Hays, Kansas motel room—the phone rang. It was Marlene. "I *found* you." She said it silkily and low. It was lovely and a little unnerving. We hadn't told her where we were going so she must have done some tracing. "I got to my hotel last night," she said, "and I *missed* you."

"Me too. How're you doing?"

She told me about a press conference she'd been through at the airport after we'd left. "I don't think I made them very happy—but they ask such stupid questions. One old woman there—*old*—older than *me*—asked, 'What do you plan to do with the rest of your life?' I said to her, 'What do you plan to do with the rest of yours?' "

We talked several times during the week, and she sent me a couple of warm and funny notes thanking me for the opening-night telegram and flowers and supplying anecdotes about the Denver performances: "I sang fine last night," she wrote, "but I don't think it was necessary. . . . Lights are bad! They have no equipment. Poor country, you know!"

"How were the reviews?" I asked her on the phone.

"Oh, the usual—'the legend' and all that—you know—fine."

On Saturday, Ryan and I and six others from our company flew to Denver for the night to see her show. I've never seen as mesmerizing a solo performance. She sang twenty songs and each was like a one-act play, a different story with a different character telling it, each phrased uniquely and done with the most extraordinary command. No one has ever teased and controlled an audience better. "I'm an optimist," she told them, "that's why I'm here in Denver." They loved her. How could they not. How could anyone not?

Everything she does is done completely—there are no half-gestures or unfinished thoughts in her performance. When she says Von Sternberg's name, you know she is really thinking of him. And she never repeats an effect, doesn't move much, just stands there and performs for you. Meticulously rehearsed, everything appears spontaneous, as though it were the first time she'd done it: a great showman—very theatrical—but subtle beyond praise.

She also transcends her material. Whether it's a flighty old tune like "I Can't Give You Anything But Love, Baby" or "My Blue Heaven," a schmaltzy German love song, "Das Lied ist Aus," or a French one, "La Vie en Rose," she lends each an air of the aristocrat, yet she never patronizes. She transforms Charles Trenet's "I Wish You Love" by calling it "a love song sung to a child" and then singing it that way. No one else now can sing Cole Porter's "The Laziest Gal in Town"—it belongs to her. As much as "Lola" and "Falling in Love Again" always have. She kids "The Boys in the Back Room" from *Destry Rides Again*, but with great charm. Singing in German, "Jonny" becomes frankly erotic. A folk song, "Go 'Way from My Window," has never been done with such passion, and in her hands, "Where Have All the Flowers Gone" is not just an anti-war lament, but a tragic accusation against us all. Another pacifist song, written by an Australian, has in it a recurring lyric—"The war is over—seems we won"—and each time she sings it a deeper nuance is revealed.

Of course, she saw World War II at close range, entertaining the troops for three years, and it's all brought back in her touching introduction to "Lili Marlene" which consists mainly of the names of all the countries in which she sang that song during the war. It called to mind what Hemingway had written in *A Farewell to Arms:* "There were many words that you could not stand to hear and finally only the names of places had dignity. Certain numbers were the same way and certain dates and these with the names of the places were all you could say and have them mean anything. Abstract words such as glory, honor, courage, or hallow were obscene beside the concrete names of villages, the numbers of roads, the names of rivers, the numbers of regiments and the dates." And that's what Marlene conveyed; as she said, "Africa, Sicily, Italy, Greenland, Iceland, France, Belgium and Holland—Germany—Czechoslovakia," her inflection carried with each a different untold story of what she'd seen, what the soldiers she'd sung for had seen. It was there in the way she did the song too. And suddenly you understood another thing Hemingway had written—this time about her—and you knew the soldiers must have understood it too when she sang to them those three long years: "If she had nothing more than her voice she could break your heart with it. But she has that beautiful body and that timeless loveliness of her face. It makes no difference how she breaks your heart if she is there to mend it."

After the show, still onstage, she saw that all the musicians and technicians got a drink, and thanked each one personally. She was particularly effusive about the local soundman. A short, middle-aged fellow, he came up shyly to say good-bye, and she embraced and kissed him lovingly, not the way I would guess it's usually done in Colorado, or anywhere. The guy looked bewildered, thrilled, overwhelmed all at once; speechless as Marlene Dietrich hugged him to her and told him it was the best sound she'd ever had on the road. He wandered away with glazed eyes, a foolish grin—the happiest man in Denver.

In the dingy dressing room, her helpers were packing up. "Closing night is my favorite," she said, "because I can call and cancel the insurance." She sipped champagne, then picked up the only photo on her makeup table—a framed picture of Hemingway, the glass cracked, an inscription on it that read, "For my favorite Kraut." She spoke to the photo. "Come on, Papa," she said, "time to pack up again, huh? Okay, here we go." And she kissed it. Proudly, she showed off a pair of ballet slippers she'd been given by the Bolshoi troupe, a sentiment in Russian carved on one sole, and some Scotch heather in a plastic bag—for good luck. "If you carry this with you, it means you will come back." And a stuffed black doll she picked up gingerly. "Remember this—from *The Blue Angel?*"

We all ate at Trader Vic's and she told stories and unwound from the show. She called Ryan her "blond dreamfriend" and said she'd have to look at *Love Story* now. The next morning she came downstairs to see us off, stood at the hotel entrance in her slacks and shirt and cap watching us pull away.

She gave me an envelope as we left. In it were two pieces of hotel stationery—on one she'd written out a quote from Goethe: "Ach, Du warst in längst vergangenen Zeiten— meine Schwester oder meine Frau." On the other her own "literal" translation: "Oh, you were in long passed times my sister or my woman." You too, dear Marlene, for all of us.

January 1973

The following was my last article for Esquire until the column started six years later. The title of the piece is not mine (I called it Speaking of Jimmy), *but the opening, done without even an apology to Mr. Dos Passos, is. And, in case there is any doubt, it was meant with respect to both the author of* U.S.A. *and to my subject, who is, along with Orson Welles and James Cagney, the best storyteller I've ever met.*

Th' Respawnsibility of Bein' J...
Jimmy Stewart

WILLIAM SMITH Jefferson Smith Ben McKenna Jeff McNeal
was bornandraised
   in LansingMichigan Muncie MiddletownOhio FortDodge
   grew to sixfootfour but had a way (which wasn't easy)
of keeping his head down and looking up at you; stuttered,
stammered; was great at basketball, better at baseball; a Boy
Scout leader; wore his hair slicked down ("Jus' like a kid
goin' t' Sund'y School"); hemmed, hawed; had a nasal stuffed-
jaw voice that shook when he whispered, that you could
tell a block away ("I don't s'pose you'd . . . m'by . . . shlow
down on your way through Fort Dawdge an' m'by . . . drawp
by?"); took his hat off coming into your house.
   Reticent ("Never been much of a talker"), bashful ("Always took a team just to drag him to a dance"), innocent
("Jus' a country boy"), easily hurt ("Ya gotta put some
pants on that guy"), awkward (kept his fingers together
when tolding a girl, as though if he opened them, she might
slip away), he
   became a lawyer, doctor, reporter, shop clerk, flier, sheriff,
teacher, was appointed to the Senate, never left the hometown.
   His Dad used to tell him: "The only causes worth fighting for are lost causes. . . ."
   That sank in—deep.
   But the bigguys—fat pokerplaying moneygrubbing graft-
taking guys with bigcigars—they didn't think he looked like

much: "The simpleton of all time—a big-eyed patriot—knows
Washington and Lincoln by heart . . . collects stray boys and
cats. . . ."

"This boy's honest, not stupid."

"Dreamer!"

"He'll be good—when his voice stops changing."

"Don Quixote!"

"He wants to go it alone—but we'll get him."

Thought because he was too shy to look at the marriage
bed, this sap was a pushover, a twentyfourkarat sucker.

They didn't know Willie Johnny Scottie Jeff. Didn't
know you could fool him just so long. Didn't know what his
Dad used to tell him.

"Dope!"

"Idealist!"

That he could go from: "*Who!* Miss—! Is that—? Why
didn't you—? Holy smoke. H-hello. . . . Yes, Miss Paine. . . .
How—how are you, Miss Paine . . . ? What. . . . Escort you
—gee—I mean—*sure—yes!* I'd be—Reception for a *princess!*
Gawsh!"

to a twentyfourhour filibuster culminating in: "You think
I'm licked. You *all* think I'm licked. Well, I'm *not* licked and
I'm going to stay right here and fight for this lost cause even
if this room gets *filled* with lies like these."

At his lowest ebb, he wished he'd never been born till a
fellow showed him what his town'd be like if that were so
—all those people he'd helped, all those lives he'd saved.
Always fairandsquare never belowthebelt where the bigguys
hit.

The kids knew about him—no matter what anyone said or
what lies they printed. Not fooled. Knew about this dreamer-
dope. Knew what his Dad had told him.

Then the war came.

And it changed Slim Mac Joe Skinny. No longer the
wideeyed boy in the bigcity, shocked by corruption, outraged
by deceit. Knows now that the world stinks; what men are

capable of; that fighting fair doesn't always win. Had seen his fellows fall with the flag; knows it takes more than ideals and a stoutheart to win.

No more the simplesucker the easytouch the fallguy; tough now, skeptical, worldly, cynical ("I'm only a reporter—I just *write* the story").

"The only causes worth fighting for—"

"That an' a dime'll buy me a cup a coffee!"

But the kids know, can see beneath the hard shell. Just convince him. Make him believe. Show 'im it ain't phony. The kids know, without knowing. . . .

". . . are lost causes."

that the toughness hides a view of the way the world oughta be but never is but—*oughta be.*

Better fighter now, stronger, can tell the fatguy's move, more stubborn, knows about bending the rules of the game;

would use his fists now (though he still looks even in the midst of fury saddened at the violence sick because of it); let them kick his insides up, drag him through the fire, shoot him in the hand—they could not equal what he'd seen *before* he

fought this battle.

Though settleddown with wifeandkids; sourly ridingthe-range; bitterly coveringthestory arguingthecase drawingfaster --aging—the old words and the hometown come back to haunt him still

THEmuncieONLYdodgeCAUSESlansingWORTHmid-dletownFIGHTING. . . .

Still wears his hair slicked down; still stammers near the girl; still takes his hat off in the house;

Still the American.

"That's just the way Jimmy was," said Henry Fonda. "It was all part of his character—his way of talking, everything." (*They met in 1932—Fonda was doing stock on the Cape—and Stewart, just out of Princeton, came up for the summer to do bits and play the accordion. They became friends.*) "You know, he just kinda *fell* into acting. When we got back to New York, he took the part in *Carry Nation* just for a lark. An' when that was over he was set to go home but something else came along—he took that—an' then when *it* was over he was goin' home—an' something just kept *happening*. Till, finally, it started dawning on him that he was getting good at this. An' he *was*. He'd had no training, no background. I'd been at it ten years an'. . . . I saw him in *Divided by Three* with Judith Anderson, 1934, and as far as I was concerned— this *punk*! this sonofa*bitch*! what right did he have to be so *good*! And he just fell into it really. . . ."

" 'S true," Jimmy Stewart said. " 'Cause if I hadn't become an actor, I think I'd a been mixed up in flying . . . I took my B.S. in architecture, but I was always wrapped up in flying. It was. . . . Acting was getting bit by a malaria mosquito— but flying. . . . When I was about nine or ten, right after World War I, I was working in my fawther's store, just . . . just savin' up so's I could take a ride in one of those barnstorming planes used to come around. Fifteen dawllars for fifteen minutes. That was a *hell*ova lawta money. . . . It was . . . But I saved it up and finally . . . finally, I talked my fawther into it. Dad was good about things like that . . . he was. . . . And we gawt in the car . . . but on the way we stawpped so's he could pick up the family *dawctor*! I thought it was nice—the tremendous faith my Dad had in this new invention."

"He's one of the great guys I've ever known," Fonda said. (*When the two came to Hollywood, they shared a house for a time.*) "He was such fun company to be with—life was just too *much*—laughing all the time."

"We were both too skinny," said Stewart. "An' one time we d'cided to . . . to gain a little weight . . . a little . . . so a fella told us for breakfast every morning we should drink an eggnawg with brandy. But the thing was . . . we noticed that the eggnawg kept getting darker an' darker—and by eleven

a.m. we were both *pissed!* So we . . . we said, There's . . .
there's gawta be a better way. . . . I was always a big fan of
Garbo's, you know—we were at the same studio—at M-G-M
—and I never *saw* her . . . never. . . . Then she . . . she moved
in next door to us and I thought, waall, now I'll . . . now
m'by I'll—but she moved in and she built this eight-foot stone
wall around the place! Waaall, noow, we . . . gawt pretty
sore about that—and one night, we . . . one night, we gawt
drunk and we d'cided to . . . that if we dug a hole under
the wall . . . we could just . . . just dig right up into her front
yard! And we gawt just far 'nough down to hit a water main
. . . and. . . ."

"Seems to me we got drunk and *talked* about digging a
hole."

"And then . . . we had *cats!* When we moved into the
house there was a mother cat there and she'd just had a litter.
We said . . . waall, that's . . . that's *fine*. But they . . . these
weren't *ordinary* cats—they were *wild!* And they started to
attract other wild cats in the neighborhood until . . . we
had cats all . . . all around . . . in the trees, under the house,
on the . . . you'd hear them at night walking on the tile roof.
You'd come home in the dark and . . . and you'd go up the
walk to the front door . . . fumbling for the key . . . you'd
hear this *noise*—right under your feet . . . it was . . .
hhhhrrrrrrr!! ssssss! One time I came home . . . and I found
Fawnda in the front yard with a . . . he had a bow an' *arrow!*
He was . . . he said if he could just shoot an arrow through
the cat sideways—it would get stuck goin' through a narrow
place and he could *catch* it! He could. . . . Didn't work.
We called the A.S.P.C.A. They said, 'Sure, *sure*, we'd love
to take your cats. Just . . . just put 'em in a bawx and we'll
take 'em. . . .' Waaall, then, I had a cousin of mine—senior
at Princeton—came to visit one summer, and I said, 'I'll make
a deal with you, I'll . . . thirty dawllars to get rid of the
cats.' Nooow, he had an idea—it was a fine Princetonian idea—
he caught one of the cats and painted it *purple!* The idea was

—that when the other cats saw it, they'd all say, 'Look at that—purple—let's get outa here!' Didn't work . . . didn't. . . . We just had a purple cat around the place, that's all!"

"And the *fleas* they had," said Fonda.

"Yeah. . . . Wonderful days."

How'd you like being in pictures?

"I loved it. Right away—didn't miss the stage at all. Loved it. All that stuff ya hear 'bout how the big studio was nothing but an enormous factory—this just isn't true . . . it's nawt. . . . It was wonderful—you were doing something all the time— if you weren't shootin' a picture, you were working out in the gym or doing a test with someone or taking singing lessons or. . . . Picture-making was . . . it was more *exciting* in the old days . . . it was more fun. And the big studios had a lawt to do with generating that excitement. . . . An' this stuff 'bout no freedom! Nobody told Lubitsch what to do, or Frank Borzage, or John Stahl. An' you could . . . you could bargain about parts—you didn't have to take *everything* they offered—you could make deals."

"Well, Jim had it pretty good at M-G-M," Fonda said. "His experience was quite different from mine at Fox. He really enjoyed it."

"When I first gawt out there one o' the things they tested me for was a part in *The Good Earth* . . . it was . . . as a *Chinaman*! They gawt me all made up—took all morning— an' gawt me together with Paul Muni and . . . there was just . . . just one thing . . . wrong . . . I was too *tall*! So they dug a *trench* and I walked in it and Muni walked alongside . . . an' I . . . I didn't get the part. I didn't. . . . They gave the part to a Chinaman!"

"Jimmy had a kiiind of specific inarrticulation," said George Stevens. "This film we did was about inarrticulation. . . ." (*It was Stewart's fourteenth picture—and his first of any distinction—a 1938 comedy called* Vivacious Lady, *which Stevens directed, and in which he played a timid college professor who disrupts the staid atmosphere of the institution by getting engaged to a nifty nightclub singer acted by*

*Ginger Rogers. Stevens is an unhurried, thoughtful man, who
sounds as though he had gone to an Eastern prep school,
which he didn't, and who has since directed several extremely
likable pictures including* Penny Serenade, Gunga Din,
Woman of the Year, *and others, more famous, like* A Place
in the Sun, Shane *and* Giant.) "The boy and the girl had
no-o business getting together—so the movie was really
about the pleasant frustration of non-communication. This
was very *close* to Jimmy Stewart's vein of expression—this
struggle to get anything said. No-ow, to overcome disbelief
is the most *dif*ficult thing to do in films. And Jimmy, with this
extra*ooor*dinary earnestness he had, just walked in and ex⁀
tinguished disbelief."

"He had some of the same qualities that Cooper had," said
Frank Capra. "That indefinable personal integrity—awfully
hard to make Jimmy look bad." (*Mr. Capra—a small, sad-
eyed man who speaks in a clipped yet hesitant manner and
seems most at ease when he's laughing, which he does with
abandon—first directed Stewart in a supporting part in* You
Can't Take It With You, *which he made in 1938. The next
year, Capra gave him the title role in* Mr. Smith Goes to
Washington, *and in 1946, the lead in* It's A Wonderful Life,
*which remains Stewart's favorite among all his films. The
Capra hero—from his silent Harry Langdon comedies to such
great successes as* Mr. Smith, Mr. Deeds Goes to Town,
Meet John Doe—*is an innocent dreamer who comes up
against hard reality, yet manages not only to keep his illu-
sions but to triumph with them. Because this is the way
Mr. Capra would like it to be.*) "When *Mr. Smith* came
along, it was either Cooper or Stewart, and Jim was younger
and I knew he would make a hell of a Mr. Smith—he looked
like the country kid, the idealist—it was very close to him. I
think there's no question but that this picture shaped the
public image of him, of the real Jimmy Stewart."

"Yeah, that was the picture . . . that was the first time I
felt I was really getting across."

"Cyclically speaking," said Cary Grant, "Jimmy Stewart

had the same effect on pic-tures that Marlon Brando had some years la-ter. We did one picture together in 1940 called *The Philadelphia Story*. . . ."

"I never thought that much of my work in *The Philadelphia Story*." (*But the Academy awarded him an Oscar for it, though it's probably true, as the story goes, that they gave it to him that year because they had passed him up the year before on* Mr. Smith Goes to Washington. *The Academy has a way of doing that—giving their award to people who once deserved it—when it was given to someone who didn't.*)

"Jimmy had the ability to talk naturally," Grant said. "He knew that in conversations people *do* often interrupt one another and that it's not always so *easy* to get a thought out. It took a lit-tle while for the sound men to get used to him, but he had an *enormous* impact. And then, some years la-ter, Marlon came out and did the same thing all over again—but what people forget is that Jimmy did it first. And he affected *all* of us really."

"Isn't thaaat interesting!" said Stevens. "Of course, it's true. Jimmy did it with a kiind of emphasis and Brando did it with a kind of reticence."

"We did a scene together," Grant said, "in which he was drunk . . . and I got absolutely *fascinated* with him—watch-ing him—you can see it in the film—he was so *good*!"

"He was good in anything," said John Ford. "Played him-self but he played the character. . . . People just liked him."

Then the war came. And Stewart, who had had over four hundred hours of civilian flying time, joined the Air Force. He moved from second lieutenant to colonel, commanded twenty bombing missions over Germany, was awarded the Air Force Medal, the Croix de Guerre, the D.F.C. with Oak Leaf Cluster, came home when the war was over. His ex-perience of war is something he doesn't talk about. But once, in a conversation about the tragic, disastrous low-level bomb-ing raids on the Ploesti oil fields—in which he himself did not take part—Stewart remarked, "Everything's planned . . . it's

all set . . . it's all—and then you're over the target—and it's
. . . nothing's the way . . . it's all *different*! *Every*thing's different from the way you'd planned—everything's *wrong*. And
you're nawt supposed to—but everybody gets on the radio
and starts yelling!"

"After flying those B-29's," Capra said, "Jimmy didn't feel
quite right being back in pictures. In the middle of *It's A
Wonderful Life*, which was his first film after the war, he
told me—he said he thought maybe being an actor was not for
decent people. That acting had become silly, unimportant
next to what he'd seen. Said he thought he'd do this picture
and then quit. Lionel Barrymore was in the film, and he felt,
you know, that acting was one of the greatest professions ever
invented—very outspoken about it too. One day he said to
me, 'That Jimmy Stewart is good.' 'Yeah,' I said, 'but he's
thinking of quitting.' 'Really? Why?' So I told him what
Jimmy'd said. A few days later, Lionel Barrymore talked to
Jimmy. 'I understand you don't think acting is a *worthy*
enough profession,' he said, and then he gave Jimmy a pitch
on acting as I've never heard. 'Don't you *realize*,' he said,
'you're moving millions of people, shaping their lives, giving
them a sense of exaltation. . . . What other profession has that
power or can be so important? A bad actor is a bad actor.
But acting is among the oldest and noblest professions in the
world, young man.' Jimmy never said anything to me about
it, but I think it must've had an effect on him. He never *said*
it, but I think Jimmy decided if he was going to be an actor,
he was going to be the best there was."

"I realized after the war that I wasn't going across anymore—after a couple of pictures. I remember on *Magic
Town*, one critic wrote, 'If we have to sit through another
picture while that beanpole stumbles around, taking forever
to get things out.' *The New York Times* sent a guy out here
to do an article on me, and he said, 'Now, I'll tell ya right
off, the title of this thing is gonna be *The Rise and Fall of
Jimmy Stewart*!' I realized I'd better do *some*thing—I couldn't

just go on hemming and hawing—which I sometimes overdid too. . . . I looked at an old picture a mine—*Born to Dance*— I wanted to *vawmit*! I had t' . . . toughen it up. . . ."

"When he's doing those tough characters," Frank Capra said, "he's *not* playing himself—fundamentally, Jimmy is an idealist."

"I gawt . . . tougher—and I found that in Westerns I could do it an' still retain what I was. People would accept it."

People did. "You can't knock a Western," John Ford says, and he has made the best of them, "they have kept the industry going." If you don't believe him, look at Fame's *annual exhibitors' poll of the Top Ten Money-Making Stars: on the list for eighteen years, Gary Cooper; for sixteen years, John Wayne; for ten years, James Stewart. His initial appearance (fifth place) was in 1950, the year in which his first two postwar Westerns (he had made one other, in '39) were released, one of them, Anthony Mann's* Winchester 73, *a classic of its kind. He remained in the Top Ten throughout the Fifties (hitting first place in 1955): of the score of pictures he made in those ten years, a third were Westerns. Hitchcock's* Rear Window *and* The Man Who Knew Too Much *and Preminger's* Anatomy of a Murder—*three very popular Fifties' films—did not hurt his standing either. (In 1960-1964 he dropped out of the Top Ten but was back in eighth place last year: the picture that did it was called* Shenandoah.) *Besides the Westerner, Stewart also played two other distinctly American heroes in that decade: Glenn Miller ("Helen, I gawt . . . Helen, I gawt the sound!") and Charles Lindbergh ("I can make it all right . . ."). James Stewart was a star— the real kind—after sixteen years and almost forty movies. It takes time to get to know someone.*

"Casting the film star is, in many respects," said Alfred Hitchcock, "a compromise. Now, Stewart can play all the scenes, and in character, but what I mean is epitomized in those film reviews—you read the résumé they give of an adventure story: 'Well,' they say, 'Jimmy Stewart rides in on a horse and comes face to face with a hundred Indians.

But Stewart is very clever and he outwits them. . . .' You see, it's always 'Stewart,' never the name of the character he's playing." (*Hitchcock first cast Stewart in 1948 as the professor in* Rope, *and, most recently, as the retired police detective in his 1958 masterpiece,* Vertigo.) "But the *enormous* advantage in casting the star is because of familiarity. His *face* is familiar. . . ."

"I've always felt, from people, that it was a friendly attitude, which has been very *nice*. 'Geez, I *know* that fellow—' They're . . . you can feel the *concern*—the friendliness—they come up an' say, 'I feel like I *know* you.' Some of it has resulted from the kind of parts I've been in. But the important thing *is* that they should be concerned for your welfare up there on the screen. 'Cause I've always felt, through the years, although they're . . . they're always sure everything's going to come out all right—they're nawt *quite* sure in my case. . . ."

"You see, the moment he gets into jeopardy," Hitchcock said, "the audience reaction is much stronger than it would be if the actor were a character man, who might be more right for the part. So your story is helped enormously."

"People used to ask Spencer Tracy," said Stewart, " 'Don't you ever get tired of playing Spencer Tracy?' An' he'd say, 'Who the hell do you *want* me to play!?' I'm against people who yell the star system is dead. I've never agreed with that —ya talk to people an' they can't put it into words—but a star is just someone to root for. . . ."

"Stewart is a perfect Hitchcock hero," the director concluded, "because he is Everyman in bizarre situations. I mean, let's look at his private life—Princeton, Air Force colonel— he's not an uneducated oaf, you can believe him as a professor, a doctor, family man. . . ."

"I always wanted to live on a hill—I don't know why. An' I used to. But when I gawt married . . . and the kids . . ." (*married in 1949, two boys from his wife's first marriage, twin girls in 1951; large Tudor house at the foot of the Beverly Hills*) ". . . I thought m'by it'd be good to go back to the old way, where there was a *sidewalk* an' you could go 'round the corner to the grocery store. And the twins. . . . I think now that if they have pills to stawp babies, they oughta be able to have pills that make *twins*! Because . . . I think it's . . . the most wonderful. . . . They're never lonely . . . they're . . . and they have a bond between them that's. . . . They . . . they hold secret *meetings* in the cellar . . . and I can't go —no one's allowed down there—no one . . . but the *dog*! The only thing I wish . . . is . . . I think they've gawt too much work in cawllege . . . the boys are in cawllege and *I* never coulda gawtten through the stuff they've gawtta do. They . . . I guess the teachers would kill me, but I wish they were given a little more time to dream. . . ."

Coming out of a restaurant one evening, Stewart was approached by a man and his wife. "I don't guess it means anything to you," the man said, "but I just wanted to say we've seen your pictures many times and have enjoyed you very much." "Why," said Stewart, "it means everything to me."

Being a star?

"I take it as a sort of respawnsibility. . . . Ted Healy once told me, long time ago, he said, 'Treat the audience as a partner, nawt as a customer.' Good advice. You know, I gawt an awful lawtta letters after *Anatomy of a Murder*: 'Ya let us down, I'm nawt goin' t' your pictures anymore— I took m' family to see a Jimmy Stewart picture an' you're up there in court talkin' dirty and holdin' up women's panties . . .' An' . . . I have to take these things into consideration. Now, I didn't think *Anatomy* was offensive— or in bad taste. An' if anything like it came along again, I'd have to take it— parts like that just don't come along every day. . . . But, ya see, I think our business is to tell stories—that involve people emotionally—and if the story gets so far away from what people can understand, then you're nawt . . . you've lost your audience. . . . Now, I've seen actors 'n' actresses who do a realistic, technically beautiful jawb in a scene of, say, withdrawal from heroin addiction—it's frightening, very effective. Later on, the same person comes in an' says, 'Hello, were there any messages for me?' an' you don't *believe* it. . . . *That's* it . . . that's . . . *believability*! The withdrawal thing is a sort of an exercise in acting realism, but as far as believability is concerned, the audience doesn't know what the symptoms of withdrawal are—he could stand on his head —that . . . that might just as well be the way you do it. But *every*body knows about 'Hello, were there any messages.' Believability—so the audience can understand—so they can believe what you're doin' up there."

Just as the gods were for the Greeks—the stars form a twentieth-century mythology created by the movies. These are no longer actors playing a part—for all their roles have merged into one definitive character, one special folk hero, similar to but not necessarily identical with the original mortal. And this creation, this symbol becomes a valid dramaturgical element. (Robert Aldrich, director-producer of Stewart's most recent film, The Flight of the Phoenix, *admits that he and his scenarist decided to use for the picture "what Stewart seems to be.") One may admire a performance, say, by Guinness, but it remains a performance, one is conscious of the actor. Bogart is fine in* The Caine Mutiny *but he is Bogart in* The Big Sleep: *Queeg could have been played by Lloyd Nolan (as he was on the stage) but who else could be the kind of Bogart Bogart was? Objecting to a star in a picture (given that he fits the story) is like objecting to a film because it is shot on location: a star is authentic; you never doubt him; he is real—not an actor nor even, any longer, someone playing himself. He simply* is: *Cary Grant. John Wayne. James Cagney. James Stewart is seventy movies, a million magnified images combined to create one image called—whether you're from the Midwest or Europe— "Jimmy"—Stewart, even now, at fifty-eight, the name for a boy. . . .*

"Funny how it caught on. There w'd no pattern to it—my Mom called me *Jimsy*! And with my Fawther it was Jimbo, and my teacher called me Jamie. . . ."

"People just like him," said John Ford.

"This is the great thing that the movies have . . . the potential to really press things home *visually*—they come closer than anything else, the people can see your *eyes* . . . they can—I remember we were up in Canada, in 1954, in the mountains shooting a picture called *The Far Country*. We were havin' a bawx lunch—the usual terrible bawx lunch—and this old guy came into the camp . . . and looked around . . . he looked . . . and he came over t'me . . . nawdded at me. 'You Stewart?' 'Yeah. . . .' 'You did a thing in a picture once,' he said. 'Can't 'member the name of it—but you were in a room—and you said a poem or something 'bout fireflies. . . . That was good.' I knew right away what he meant—tha's all he said—he was talking about a scene in a picture called *Come Live with Me* that came out in 1941—and he couldn't remember the title, but that little . . . tiny thing—didn't last even a minute—he'd remembered all those years. . . . An' *that's* the thing—that's the great thing about the movies. . . . After you *learn*—and if you're good and Gawd helps ya and you're lucky enough to have a personality that comes across—then what you're doing is . . . you're giving people little . . . little, tiny pieces of *time* . . . that they never forget."

July 1966

3

PREFERENCES

I've been known in some circles as the only American film critic to become a director and, truth to tell, have always felt acutely uncomfortable with that description. Mainly because I don't think I was ever much of a critic. I only started writing about movies professionally so I could get my name on screening lists and get invited to see pictures free. To borrow Shaw's phrase, and without meaning to be pretentious, I was more a popularizer than a critic since I mainly enjoyed writing about things I liked rather than things I didn't (as should be clear from the bulk of this book).

I was also never much good at theorizing or at analyzing in depth the hidden symbolism or sociological significance of the pictures I liked. The best I've ever been able to do—and usually not at all as well as I'd hoped—has been to try to pass on my passions and enthusiasms with some semblance of intelligence. The next four columns fall in this dubious category and are not actually among my favorite prose turns.

The final piece in this section was actually my last "Hollywood" column for Esquire. Around that time, Harold Hayes quit the magazine and I frankly couldn't see any fun in being there without him, so I did too.

A Few Favorites

SEVERAL MONTHS AGO, the British film quarterly *Sight and Sound* wrote me (and a hundred others) asking us to name our ten favorite movies. Caught in a perverse mood, I rattled off (in chronological order) the first ten that came to mind: *Young Mr. Lincoln* (John Ford), *Only Angels Have Wings* (Howard Hawks), *The Magnificent Ambersons* (Orson Welles), *Red River* (Hawks), *She Wore a Yellow Ribbon* (Ford), *The Searchers* (Ford), *Touch of Evil* (Welles), *Vertigo* (Alfred Hitchcock), *Rio Bravo* (Hawks), *North by Northwest* (Hitchcock). I acknowledged the absurdity of the list in an accompanying note which explained that on a different day, in another mood, the list might be altogether changed, though the four directors represented would no doubt remain constant.

But I've been thinking about it since then, and I'm a little ashamed of the list now just because it is so impulsive and such a lack of a sense of history is evident. How can one have a ten-favorite list—which automatically, no matter how loud one's protestations to the contrary, translates into a "ten-best" list—and ignore D. W. Griffith or Buster Keaton or Jean Renoir or Ernst Lubitsch. Not to mention Fritz Lang, Charlie Chaplin, Josef von Sternberg, Kenji Mizoguchi, Max Ophuls, F. W. Murnau. Picking one's favorite directors is hard enough, but then figuring out their best films is almost impossible. How to choose, for example, between Hawks in his *Bringing Up Baby* mood or Hawks in his *Only Angels Have Wings* mood? A dumb charade, at best. Like researchers for *Guinness' Book of World Records*, however, people are always after superlatives.

Actually, I don't have favorite movies as much as favorite directors—men whose company I enjoy—and I can claim no consistency in those choices. Why does one feel like hearing Beethoven one day and Mozart the next, or Cole Porter in the afternoon and Hank Williams at night? I've seen about six thousand movies and I have a large fund of happy memories—many of which I like to recapture. Generally, my affection for a director goes through a very hot period, during which I try to see everything he's made—and, if I like the sum total, he joins a group of people to whom I return with affection.

I would admit to a preference for English-language films. First of all, I hate reading subtitles; their intrusion makes it awfully hard to achieve the sort of direct impact with which movies are at their greatest. I also prefer talkies to silents (except the silent comedies) because of the intrusion of titles which usually only reduce the meaning of the images rather than enhance them. This may seem philistine on my part, but it is a fact I'm afraid I have to live with. Nevertheless, since so much of everything in life is a contradiction, some of my most treasured memories are of silent films like *The Birth of a Nation* and Chaplin's *The Kid*, Keaton's *The Navigator* and *The General*, and Harold Lloyd's *The Freshman*. I remember seeing these and many others with my father, who took me often to the afternoon show at The Museum of Modern Art, where we sat with a wonderful feeling of seclusion—the subways that occasionally rattled by above us the only reminder of the outside world, which seemed so remote at those precious times. The world on the screen was more removed from reality than anything the talkies achieved —it was both more realistic and less too—a strange combination. I suppose the great silent films created a universe of their own that was more pervasive and haunting *because* of the missing element of talk.

They weren't really silent since Mr. Arthur Kleiner supplied wonderful piano accompaniment—originally the films had had orchestras or organs to go with them—but the impact of the work relied on the power of the image, and this created a universal language which was wiped out by the addition of sound in the late twenties. I don't remember ever feeling as much at peace with pictures as when I saw those silents

I grew to love. Perhaps it was the sense of innocence they preserved, but I think it has something to do with the medium —which was less bombastic and more profoundly poetic than the talkies. Still today the great sound films are remembered, with few exceptions, for those elements that recall the almost mystical power of the silent screen—when the image was the beginning and the end.

I was not a child of the silents, though, which may explain my acquired fondness for them as well as my impatience with all but the best. On the contrary, as a kid, I was more a fan of radio, though that medium died on me around the time I began my adolescence. But childhood memories are much more mixed up with *The Shadow* and *The Lone Ranger* and *Sky King* and Edgar Bergen and *Suspense* and Fred Allen and *The Great Gildersleeve* and *Gangbusters* than with the movies. Not that I didn't go to them a lot. In fact, I wanted very much to be a movie star. I think I evolved from wanting to be either Douglas Fairbanks Jr. or Errol Flynn when I was eight through Richard Widmark, William Holden, Gene Kelly, Jerry Lewis to Marlon Brando when I was thirteen. (I remember acting out, at home, in strenuous detail, the essence of *Sinbad the Sailor* and *The Adventures of Robin Hood* and *Kiss of Death* and *Take Me Out to the Ball Game*.) I know I always wanted to *look* like Holden, and wished my name were Jim—I don't think I could ever decide on a properly Anglo-Saxon last name, though I remember my dear father's distress when I announced around age twelve that I was going to shorten the one I've got to an ambiguous Bogdane. Can't recall whether it was to be James or Peter. That didn't really matter as much since in school everyone called me Bugs, because of a popular imitation I did of Bugs Bunny; as I grew older, the impersonations expanded and my nickname alternated between things like Dino, Jerry and Marlon. (My father's favorite name for me, when I was being particularly unpleasant, was Harry Fabian, a fairly scabrous character Widmark played in *Night and the City*.)

My favorite movies as a child had been *Red River, She Wore a Yellow Ribbon* and *The Ghost Goes West* (René Clair). I saw each of them numerous times, but never was really aware of who directed them, nor, in fact, that such a person was necessary. Orson Welles changed all that. I didn't see *Citizen Kane* until it was fourteen years old and I was sixteen, but it was the first time I remember consciously realizing that an overwhelming presence was possible to exist *behind* the camera. I'd thought vaguely about directing before that, but now it became a conscious ambition. I would guess Orson has been a similar inspiration to more people than any other director since D. W. Griffith.

Certainly he would have to be represented on any top-ten list of films, but I'd have a lot of trouble deciding exactly which pictures. I like several of them even better than *Kane* —*The Magnificent Ambersons*, flawed as it is by the recutting of the studio, is an even more daring and imaginative work; it is also much less self-conscious and, I believe, truer to Orson's real personality. *Touch of Evil* is a terrifying, Goyaesque vision of corruption, and probably the most original thriller ever made. His films of *Othello, Macbeth* and *Falstaff (Chimes at Midnight)* are, without question, the only original and valid pictures based on Shakespeare, and I am especially fond of them. One begins to see how hard it is to narrow the field just within Welles' career in order to find the representative choice as "best." If Welles is difficult, with about fifteen movies to choose from, how impossible does it become with Ford's 140-odd pictures, at least twenty of which are magnificent; all the other great directors have had almost equally long careers and the possibilities become totally unmanageable. Allow me, therefore, to get out of this gracefully and say that the following directors are the ones I most admire and place in parentheses after their names the titles of several of their films that are among my favorites.

—John Ford (*Young Mr. Lincoln, How Green Was My Valley, They Were Expendable, My Darling Clementine, Fort Apache, She Wore a Yellow Ribbon, Rio Grande,*

Wagon Master, The Searchers, The Wings of Eagles, The Man Who Shot Liberty Valance).

—Orson Welles (*Citzen Kane, The Magnificent Ambersons, Othello, Falstaff, Touch of Evil, The Lady from Shanghai, Mr. Arkadin, The Immortal Story*).

—Howard Hawks (*The Dawn Patrol, Scarface, Twentieth Century, Ceiling Zero, Bringing Up Baby, His Girl Friday, Only Angels Have Wings, To Have and Have Not, The Big Sleep, Air Force, I Was a Male War Bride, Red River, Rio Bravo*).

—Ernst Lubitsch (*The Student Prince, So This is Paris, Monte Carlo, The Smiling Lieutenant, The Merry Widow, The Love Parade, Trouble in Paradise, The Shop Around the Corner, Heaven Can Wait, Ninotchka, To Be or Not To Be, One Hour With You, Cluny Brown*).

—Alfred Hitchcock (*The 39 Steps, Shadow of a Doubt, Notorious, Rear Window, Strangers on a Train, I Confess, The Wrong Man, Vertigo, North by Northwest*).

—Buster Keaton (*Sherlock Jr., The Navigator, The General, Our Hospitality, Seven Chances, College*).

—D. W. Griffith (*The Birth of a Nation, Intolerance, Broken Blossoms, Orphans of the Storm, Way Down East, True Heart Susie, Hearts of the World, Isn't Life Wonderful, The Struggle*).

—Jean Renoir (*The Grand Illusion, Bondu Saved from Drowning, La Chienne, Rules of the Game, Swamp Water, The River, La Crime de M. Lange, Une Partie de Champagne, French Can Can, Diary of a Chambermaid, The Elusive Corporal*).

Other choices are really too hard to narrow down. I like a lot of Fritz Lang, Charlie Chaplin, Josef von Sternberg, Max Ophuls, George Cukor, Otto Preminger, King Vidor, Preston Sturges, Kenji Mizoguchi, F. W. Murnau, Erich von Stroheim . . .

The list is endless and keeps changing.

June 1972

B-Movies

THEY SAY TELEVISION HAS REPLACED THE B-MOVIE, but it's not true. The reason why the "second feature" was so often able to achieve such vigor and interest is that it was made, so to speak, while no one was looking. Never taken very seriously by critics, and even less so by the studios (as long as costs and schedules were closely observed), the B-movie director could many times work in a freer atmosphere than some of his higher-budgeted contemporaries. TV production is so closely supervised by networks, sponsors, advertising executives and producers that any sort of personal expression becomes almost impossible. Actually, the only relation between television films and the old B-movies lies in their similar budgets—whence the B-picture acquired its name in the first place.

However, even an exceptional TV film like Tom Gries' and Truman Capote's *The Glass House* was budgeted at over twice what the average B-movie director usually had to work with. That's one of the main reasons why they were required to be far more resourceful and imaginative in achieving their effects that the fellows with A-budgets. In need of an exotic location, they'd have to find a way to shoot it in Griffith Park. Want a city block, a small-town square, a western street? Check the back lot. Sam Fuller, making a New York story like *Pickup on South Street,* had to figure out a way of disguising downtown L.A. to look like Manhattan and Brooklyn. Allan Dwan once did a whole film in ten days on the sets left standing from Orson Welles' *The Magnificent Ambersons.* That was the other thing—they had to work fast. Ten, fifteen day schedules. I can't imagine how they did it and made the films look so good. One of the most absurd questions I've heard—and several producers, in discussing one or another man who has only worked under those circumstances, have asked it: "But do you think he can handle a big budget?" I never could figure out why time and money should be considered more difficult to deal with than speed and poverty. If you want a particular kind of sunset and you can afford to wait till it comes along—they say David Lean has been known to do that—where is the problem?

The fact that several of these directors not only did their films "at a price," but also made a series of movies that form a cohesive personal vision is nothing less than remarkable. Sam Fuller, Don Siegel, Budd Boetticher come to mind. Also men like Edgar G. Ulmer, Joseph H. Lewis, André de Toth, Phil Karlson, Allan Dwan (in his sound period). If they were sometimes defeated by their assignments or their casts—Siegel with *Spanish Affair* or *No Time for Flowers*, Fuller with *Hell and High Water*, Boetticher with almost everything before 1955—they nonetheless brought their considerable craft and distinctive styles to even the most lamentable material. Almost all the work falls into the action genre—westerns, gangster films, thrillers (though Dwan made a delightful group of low-budget comedies in the Forties: *Brewster's Millions, Up in Mabel's Room, Getting Gertie's Garter, Rendezvous with Annie*); these are things American directors have consistently distinguished through the years and for which little critical recognition is ever received.

Don Siegel, for example, has managed, often against stifling odds, to bring a disquieting ambiguity as well as a unified viewpoint to assignments which, in other hands, could easily have been routine. Schooled in the tough no-nonsense Warner Bros. tradition of Raoul Walsh and Howard Hawks, his films are unpretentious and as precisely executed as they are unconventional in their implications. (His recent escalation to sizable budgets has not dimmed his energy nor diminished his bite.) *Invasion of the Body Snatchers*, despite its pulp title and its tacked-on opening and close (studio cold feet) is, along with Hawks' *The Thing*, the best and most terrifying science-fiction movie ever made. A cautionary fable about the world's relentless movement toward a lack of feeling, it retains a special meaning today, even though it was made while

America was still reeling from the McCarthy era's assault on sensitivity. *Riot in Cell Block 11* is still the finest prison picture to come out of the U.S. (the best from Europe is probably Jacques Becker's eloquent and little-known *Le Trou*), just as *Hell Is for Heroes* remains one of the only war films to examine the inherent psychosis of a man who is brave in battle, whose most antisocial behavior actually becomes heroic in the abnormal circumstances of war. Siegel's best police movie, *Madigan* (he has made at least two others), is particularly interesting in its examination of the easy corruptibility of lawmen, at the same time as it reveals the squalor and misery of their daily life. On the other hand, he has looked at the underside of the underworld with chilling incisiveness in *Baby Face Nelson, The Lineup* and *The Killers* (1964 version); as Andrew Sarris has pointed out, his hero—whether within the law or not—has always been "the antisocial outcast" in a world of pervasive corruption. A bleak vision perhaps, but free of cant in its depiction and marked by a vigorous gift for visual storytelling.

Even a casual look at the final chase sequence in *The Lineup* puts to shame some of the more publicized recent examples of the form, and the fatal shootout at the end of *Madigan* is among the most brilliantly shot and cut pieces of action I've ever seen. It never fails to move me, not simply because of the poignancy of its outcome in the story, but even more for the excellence and clarity of its direction. Howard Hawks, a master of action, has summed it up: "That stuff's hard to do," and indeed it is something not to be taken for granted in a medium that has, for twenty years, been steadily losing its sense of craft.

Having himself been a bullfighter, it is not surprising that Budd Boetticher has made the best pictures on that subject: *The Bullfighter and the Lady, The Magnificent Matador* (he dislikes those B-movie titles as much as anyone would) and his latest, *Arruza*, which took him fourteen years to complete and an incredible series of disasters to overcome, at least two of which almost cost him his life. The story of the making of *Arruza* is, in fact, a testament to the dedication and indestructibility of the B-movie director at his best, often having little at his command but guts and determination. Between a disquieting little thriller called *The Killer Is Loose* in 1956 and an effectively perverse gangster film, *The Rise and Fall of Legs Diamond* in 1960, Boetticher made an extraordinarily consistent and evocative series of seven Randolph Scott westerns that forms one of the high points in the history of that much-maligned genre. Even less well known than the comparable, though higher-budgeted, series of five that Anthony Mann did with James Stewart during roughly the same period (*Winchester 73, Bend of the River, The Naked Spur, The Far Country, The Man from Laramie*), Boetticher's films were never noticed by critics—except in France and, later, in England—but taken separately, or as a whole, they are far more beautifully directed and considerably richer in their implications than Sam Peckinpah's much-acclaimed *Ride the High Country* (with Scott and Joel McCrea) which actually concluded the cycle, and which Boetticher was not free to do because of his involvement with *Arruza*.

Beginning with *Seven Men from Now* and ending with *Comanche Station*, the Boetticher-Scott westerns, all made very quickly and inexpensively, explore, without pretense but with considerable humor and energy, the often ambiguous relations between heroes and villains, as Scott is pitted against such imposing adversaries as Lee Marvin (*Seven Men from Now*), Pernell Roberts (*Ride Lonesome*), Richard Boone (*The Tall T*), Claude Akins (*Comanche Station*). If *Decision at Sundown, Buchanan Rides Alone* and *Westbound* are less memorable, it is mainly because the casting of the "heavies" was not on as interesting a level—just one of a B-film director's many limitations. That Boetticher was able to transcend these more often than not is just another indication of his ability.

Sam Fuller is probably the most explosive talent ever to blast its way through Poverty Row. Eccentric, iconoclastic and in the tradition of tabloid journalism (Fuller began as a reporter and one of his most personal films, *Park Row*, deals with early New York newspapering), his pictures all bear the same vibrant individualistic stamp. One of the only low-budget American directors who has consistently written and produced most of his films, he has had to compromise on his material less often than any of his contemporaries, though still having to be content frequently with inadequate actors or schedules. In Fuller's case, however, he has generally been able to turn even the most crippling restrictions into an amazingly consistent, exciting style. His films abound with meaningfully inventive camera work and unusual, complex cutting patterns that are nothing if not bold, as well as being uniquely his own. Several books have been written about his work in France, England and Germany, but American recognition is long overdue. His westerns—*I Shot Jesse James*, *Run of the Arrow*, *Forty Guns*—are as different and against the grain as they are filled with a kind of pugnacious authenticity. Similarly, he has made the only war films that look like they were made by a man who lived through a war, which he did as a member of the 1st Infantry ("The Big Red One") during World War II. *The Steel Helmet*, *Fixed Bayonets*, *China Gate*, *Merrill's Marauders*, *Verboten!* are completely free of the sentimentality or piousness that informs most films about men at war; you get the feeling that this is really the way it was—amoral, totally destructive, unbearably intense and claustrophobic.

Similarly unnerving are Fuller's crime pictures, the best of which, *Pickup on South Street* and *Underworld, U.S.A.*, are riveting classics in the genre, and reveal, along with the others, *The Crimson Kimono*, *Shock Corridor*, *The Naked Kiss*, a decidedly unglamorous, often scabrous side of modern American life. (*House of Bamboo* took his seamy Americans to Japan for a similarly relentless view.) Often extreme, his vision of the world is reflected in broad, expressionistic strokes, and belongs entirely to the movies; he has brought his feisty, uncompromising zest for pictures into every frame he has ever shot.

A good-sized book could be written chronicling the impressive accomplishments of these men and others in this largely unheralded tradition (and now just about defunct in the new boom-or-bust movie industry). Classics in the field like Fritz Lang's *The Big Heat,* Robert Aldrich's *Kiss Me Deadly*, Joseph Losey's *The Prowler*, Nicholas Ray's *On Dangerous Ground*, Phil Karlson's *99 River Street, The Phenix City Story* and *The Brothers Rico*, Joseph H. Lewis' *Gun Crazy* and *The Big Combo*, Gerd Oswald's *Crime of Passion*, Edgar G. Ulmer's *Detour* are only a fraction of the work that has been produced with little means and considerable talent in a style the French have named "le film noir." They conclusively prove that the quality of a picture can never be measured by its cost—that, in fact, some of the best work in Hollywood has been done without fanfare, encouragement or much hope for reward. The achievements themselves have most often been their makers' only real satisfaction. Television has a long way to go to measure up.

September 1972

The Best American Films of 1939

EVERYONE'S ALWAYS DOING ten-best lists at the end of each year when really the only way to do them right is twenty or thirty years later. Some perspective might be possible then, though it would help to see all the movies again, since outlooks change as much as the films themselves date or don't. Two months ago, I tried to deal with a list of the ten-best films ever made and found that an impossible task even to justify. On a yearly basis, it seems to me, the odds are even tougher. For example, Howard Hawks' *Bringing Up Baby* was soundly blasted in 1938 by the critic for The *New York Times* as well as by some other reviewers as a silly, insipid waste of time; Cary Grant and Katharine Hepburn were panned for their frivolous performances, and the picture was not even a financial success. Until 1961 when the New Yorker Theatre revived the movie (in a series called "The Forgotten Film") and, the following year, when The Museum of Modern Art included it in a three-month Howard Hawks retrospective, *Bringing Up Baby* had never received even the slightest degree of respectability, except in France, where Truffaut, Godard, Bazin and other revolutionary critics had "discovered" Hawks in the mid-Fifties.

This year, however, reviewing a movie I directed called *What's Up, Doc?*, a few critics compared it unfavorably to *Bringing Up Baby,* which they now referred to as an old comedy classic. (Of course, it serves me right since I had programmed both the New Yorker and Museum showings and then made the mistake of saying in interviews that Hawks' picture was the inspiration for mine; never offer critics ammunition. I should have said my movie was inspired by *Trader Horn* or just kept my mouth shut). Anyway, bearing in mind the history of *Bringing Up Baby*, I'm looking forward to 2006 for the definitive critical word on *What's Up, Doc?* As the man said, times change.

Take 1939, the year I was born. Like most of the great golden years of Hollywood—to my taste they turn slowly to some lesser metal toward the end of the Fifties—it is simply too rich to easily categorize or safely pigeonhole. The big movie news was a little something David Selznick put together called *Gone With the Wind*. It won eight Oscars, including one for director Victor Fleming, even though George Cukor, Sam Wood and Selznick himself had directed various lengthy sequences; but then Fleming had also guided Judy Garland through another of that year's favorites, *The Wizard of Oz*. Selznick also brought Ingrid Bergman to America that year in *Intermezzo* (Gregory Ratoff directing), and Wood directed Robert Donat's Oscar-winning performance in *Goodbye, Mr. Chips*. William Wyler, with the help of writers Ben Hecht and Charles MacArthur, producer Samuel Goldwyn, photographer Gregg Toland, Laurence Olivier and Merle Oberon, turned Miss Brontë's *Wuthering Heights* into a successful movie which the New York Film Critics voted the best of the year. Hecht and MacArthur also had a hand in reshaping Mr. Kipling for George Stevens' *Gunga Din*. Garbo laughed for Melvyn Douglas in Ernst Lubitsch's *Ninotchka* and Dietrich got shot for Jimmy Stewart in George Marshall's *Destry Rides Again*. Stewart also gave what most people—including the New York Film Critics but not the majority of those in the Academy—considered the best performance of the year in Frank Capra's *Mr. Smith Goes to Washington*. (As often happens, Academy members made up to Jimmy the following year by giving him an Oscar for a much less impressive job in *The Philadelphia Story*.)

For cultists of various sorts, the year may be memorable for other reasons: the first Henry Aldrich movie perhaps. (Remember the radio version? "Heeenry! Heenry Aldrich!" "Co-oming, Mother!") A quite nice little comedy it was too, called *What A Life*, directed by a gentleman named Jay Theodore Reed, and written by two now somewhat more famous names, Billy Wilder and Charles Brackett, who also worked on the divine *Ninotchka* that year, not to mention *Midnight*, a delightful semi-screwball comedy Mitchell Leisen directed. W.C. Fields' fans will remember 1939 as the year of *You Can't Cheat an Honest Man* (George Marshall directed), and Busby Berkeley buffs will think of *Babes in Arms* with Miss Garland and Mickey Rooney. For Bette Davis admirers it was, of course, a vintage four-handkerchief year, as Bette went gallantly blind in *Dark Victory*, sacrificed herself nobly for her daughter in *The Old Maid* (both under Edmund Goulding's tender hand) and had a fling with Errol Flynn in a bit of Warner Bros. historical research, *The Private Lives of Elizabeth and Essex* (directed by Michael Curtiz). About on the same level, and also for Warner's, Mr. Paul Muni (that was his billing) distinguished himself even more dubiously than ever in William Dieterle's *Juarez*, while the big "political" movie came from Burbank too with Anatole Litvak's *Confessions of a Nazi Spy*. John Cromwell directed Carole Lombard in two uncharacteristically teary vehicles she managed to transcend, with Jimmy Stewart's help in *Made for Each Other*, and Cary Grant's in *In Name Only*. Charles Laughton didn't live up to Lon Chaney in *The Hunchback of Notre Dame* (Dieterle again), nor did Zoltan Korda's remake of *Four Feathers* to memories of the original.

But what were really the best American films of 1939, now that we've had thirty-three years to live with them? Well, the New York Film Critics gave their Best Direction Award to John Ford for his first sound western, *Stagecoach* and, happily, they weren't far wrong. In fact, it is debatable whether he should have got it for that film or for another one of his released that year, *Young Mr. Lincoln*. I prefer the second myself, but I wouldn't want to live on the difference, since *Stagecoach* not only revitalized westerns, but actually revolutionized the genre. Inspired by de Maupassant's *Boule-de-*

suif, Stagecoach was the first "adult" western, made John Wayne a star in respectable pictures (as opposed to Republic programmers), gave us our first look at Monument Valley (Ford has since been back there for eight other movies, more memorably each time), and brought an almost expressionistic artistry to a form that had until then been likable but hardly profound.

Young Mr. Lincoln, seen now in the perspective of Ford's work since 1939, is a considerably more personal work, which is one of the main reasons I like it so much. Not only does Henry Fonda give a classic performance in the title role, distilling the very essence of the Lincoln myth, but it is as beautiful a piece of American folklore as has ever been made —a poetic vision of Lincoln's youth and destiny that is as simple in its telling as it is complex and poignant in its reverberations.

As if *Stagecoach* and *Young Mr. Lincoln* were not enough to make Mr. Ford the film maker of the year, he also directed *Drums Along the Mohawk,* his first color movie, and a much more potent piece of Americana than *Gone With the Wind,* though both are based on best sellers of small literary distinction. (Actually I also prefer to the Selznick landmark two other films of quasi-American history that came out that year: King Vidor's *Northwest Passage* and Cecil B. DeMille's *Union Pacific.*)

Another of my favorite movies, Howard Hawks' *Only Angels Have Wings,* was released in 1939; his first since *Bringing Up Baby,* it also starred Cary Grant. An evocative and richly dramatic picture about the flying of primitive planes through dangerous weather at a fogbound South American port, it brings to fruition most of the Hawksian themes of friendship among men which he'd been developing since *A Girl in Every Port* in 1928, and which he continued to explore in later films like *Air Force, To Have and Have Not* and *Rio Bravo.*

As we get to this ten-best list of 1939, bear in mind that the game is always a little suspect (even after thirty years), since the pictures are often too dissimilar to compare or rate beside one another, and that the films—particularly those at the top of the list—are all of such quality that the distinctions must be purely personal.

1. *Young Mr. Lincoln* (Ford's first masterpiece).

2. *Only Angels Have Wings* (Hawks' adventure story with Jean Arthur, Richard Barthelmess, Thomas Mitchell, Rita Hayworth).

3. *Ninotchka* (Lubitsch's hilarious and humane satire on cold-war machinations, advertised with the key phrase: "Garbo Laughs").

4. *Stagecoach* (Ford again, with Claire Trevor, John Carradine and Thomas Mitchell—he got a Supporting Actor Oscar for his performance of the drunken doctor).

5. *Mr. Smith Goes to Washington* (Capra's irresistible political fantasy with Jean Arthur, Thomas Mitchell again, Claude Rains, Edward Arnold).

6. *Love Affair* (Among Leo McCarey's most successful and characteristic mixtures of comedy and pathos—a touching affirmation of the picture's theme song, *Wishing Will Make It So*, with impeccable acting from Irene Dunne and Charles Boyer).

7. *Drums Along the Mohawk* (Ford yet again, with Henry Fonda and Claudette Colbert).

8. *The Roaring Twenties* (Raoul Walsh's terrific gangster picture about the rise and fall of a "big shot," featuring one of James Cagney's most memorable performances, and one of Bogart's least).

9. *The Women* (George Cukor's immaculately mounted version of Claire Luce's brittle, bitchy stage play, with a dazzling all-girl cast including Norma Shearer, Rosalind Russell, Joan Crawford, Joan Fontaine, Paulette Goddard).

10. A toss-up between *Gunga Din, Destry Rides Again, Midnight, Union Pacific, Northwest Passage* and, I guess there's no way around it, *Gone With the Wind*.

Besides the pictures I've already mentioned, there were several others that year worth remembering and seeing sometime, among them: Josef von Sternberg's *Sergeant Madden,* not much of a plot but damn good to look at; Walsh's *St. Louis Blues,* a likable programmer of some distinction; Alfred Hitchcock's *Jamaica Inn,* a period failure but consistently interesting; John Stahl's *When Tomorrow Comes,* a tearjerker with conviction; *Fifth Avenue Girl,* a minor Gregory La Cava comedy, but still La Cava; Allan Dwan's blunt, unadorned look at the Wyatt Earp story, *Frontier Marshal;* two little Garson Kanin comedies, *Bachelor Mother* and *The Great Man Votes,* the second starring John Barrymore toward the end of his decline, but still John Barrymore.

By any measure, it was an extraordinarily vigorous year for American movies, and not a little disheartening to contemplate in comparison to the meager pickings of the Seventies. Of course, there were four hundred seventy-six U.S. pictures released in 1939—as opposed to one hundred forty-three in 1971; nevertheless, imagine a director of Ford's caliber today —even if there was one—having three major films released the same year. And no one thought all that much of it in those mercifully unselfconscious days; as Ford would say, it was just "a job of work."

August 1972

Sex and Violence

THE COURTS ARE CLOSING DOWN *Deep Throat* across the country and I guess I'm supposed to be upset about it because I'm against censorship. The only trouble is I'm also against *Deep Throat*, which any idiot can see hasn't an ounce of "redeeming social value" (that Supreme Court fence under which all the hard-core fellows have been crawling); it's just a depressingly ugly piece of work that displays not a hint of talent in any department, isn't sexy and isn't funny (intentionally or not). The premise of the picture lies in the fantasy that the leading lady's clitoris is located in her throat and that in order to climax she must therefore perform fellatio with the penetration of a sword swallower (the theatre marquee in L.A. bills the film, "The 100% Gulp"). This lady, who calls herself Linda Lovelace, is among the three or four least attractive women I have seen in a pornographic film—hard-core or otherwise—though I have to admit that in the scenes illustrating the film's title, she does exhibit a certain flair. An almost touching awkwardness and passionate yearning to please comes out in those couple of elongated sequences of fellatio, and what Linda Lovelace lacks in finesse or beauty she certainly attempts to compensate for with energy.

The irony is that these two or three numbers—the only salvageable parts of the hour-long movie—could have been spliced together into the usual short 8 or 16mm stag reel bought under the table for years for between twenty-five and fifty dollars and not raised even an eyebrow, much less become the N.Y. cocktail party hit of last season (since replaced by *Last Tango in Paris*) and made more money than any pornographic film in history (something like six million so far). Perhaps it's the very insipidness of the rest of the movie that gives Camp followers their thrill, because there certainly aren't any in the erotic department. In truth, the only memorably sexy pornographic film I've ever seen was the famous Candy Barr short, and part of the charm of that one was Candy's reluctance, her air of inaccessibility, not to mention her physical attractiveness. By the way, she would have nothing to do with Miss Lovelace's specialty—in fact she got a little tough on her costar when he tried to assert his maleness into her face. The reel also looked remarkably candid, which added immeasureably to its voyeuristic impact and is perhaps a key to making screen pornography at all erotic.

What am I saying here? That Candy Barr was O.K. because she was sexy and Linda Lovelace isn't because she's not? Well, that's part of it—sexiness in a woman is certainly a redeeming social value—but I do also believe that a good deal of the effectiveness of pornography (to a degree like lovemaking itself) depends on its privacy and, more important, on its unspoken air of being forbidden. (Just for starters, it's simply more erotic to buy a dirty movie on the black market than to go to a theatre with a bunch of creeps.) Maybe what I'm getting at is the very reason I think the sexual freedom of the screen has led to so little art *or* eroticism. If the glory of a good movie is that it suspends one's sense of disbelief, that it makes you forget you're watching shadows on a wall and puts you instead into a world of illusion and magic, then the graphic portrayal of sexual intercourse on the screen will never work, since it is almost impossible to forget one is watching people doing something private publicly. I remember in a picture called *The Comedians* that when Richard Burton suddenly reached over and grabbed Elizabeth Taylor's breast, the audience I was with tittered. They were embarrassed, suddenly reminded that Taylor and Burton were married, that they must do things like that in private—whatever—it jarred them, took them out of the film. I felt the same way about most of the sex sequences in *Last Tango in Paris*. What was it like for Marlon Brando, the movie star, playing all those scenes with a naked woman? Any mood that may have been created went right out the window for me.

The only way I've ever really felt sex scenes work in a picture is when they are treated for comedy, or when the sexuality is implied or veiled. That's one of the main reasons I think we've actually managed to become less erotic and less artistic the more of sex we've shown over the years. Way back in the heavily Code-supervised Forties, you never doubted for a moment what Bogart and Bacall were talking about in *To Have and Have Not*—I mean, it was clear they wanted to sleep together, and we didn't need it discussed; in fact it was much sexier left unspoken. Of course, there were stupidities imposed on filmmakers then—no double beds, for instance, and the length of kisses was timed—but did it matter finally? There was a shorthand at work, and I don't mean panning over to the fireplace—it was more inventive than that. See Hitchcock's *Notorious* again sometime—it is quite apparent to anyone except a child (no ratings necessary) when Grant and Bergman have slept together and when she has gone off and slept with Claude Rains. Luckily, again, we didn't have to see it, as has become obligatory these days; the dramatic point was made with the action off-screen, since the fact, not the act, was important. Today, we're redundantly spelling everything out, leaving little to the imagination, and less to the human spirit.

The good directors also had something else beside the Code or ratings to guide them—they had taste. Not being shown what the child murderer (Peter Lorre) does to his poor victims in Fritz Lang's *M* is far more effective than the slow-motion pyrotechniques of Mr. Peckinpah's type of violence; so much more horrifying too, since our imagination, with some skillful assistance, can conjure up unspeakable and unspecific terrors no camera can equal. The blood and gore of the Peckinpah school only manages to reaffirm the skills of the makeup and special-effects departments, forcing us either to look away from the screen in disgust or to wonder clinically how some particular bit of exploding flesh or decapitation was achieved. In either case, the spell is broken.

Arthur Penn was the first to use slow-motion violence (at the end of *Bonnie and Clyde*) but the reason it worked there, and hasn't since, is because Penn only slowed the movements enough to give us a sickening illusion of nightmare-come-true; not being able to tell it was slow-motion, you weren't jarred into admiring technique and so remained involved. Peckinpah, however, is more interested in calling attention to what he is doing behind the camera than in telling a story. Now nobody has matched the vigor of the violence in Howard Hawks' *Scarface*, as one example, but it was terse, fast—before you had a chance to marvel, it was over. I asked Hawks once what he thought of Peckinpah's *The Wild Bunch* and he said, "Oh, hell, I can kill five guys and have 'em buried in the time it takes him to kill one."

In Robert Altman's new film, *The Long Goodbye*, Mark Rydell (who used to be an actor, but is better known as a director) smashes a Coke bottle in the face of his girl friend. It's a horrifying moment, completely unexpected and brilliantly gratuitous (the character is trying to impress detective Elliott Gould that he means business), and Altman barely shows us any blood at all. (A good idea too since blood rarely looks real in movies, particularly in color). The whole incident is over before we've quite recovered from the initial shock, which seems to me the nature of most real violence—chillingly sudden, decisively final.

Since I've brought it up, allow me to say that *The Long Goodbye* is one of the best new pictures I've seen in quite some time. A black and funny send-up of the detective genre (as *M*A*S*H* was of the service comedy), it is also an extremely moving evocation of contemporary decadence. Gould gives one of his best performances—he's in no way Raymond Chandler's Philip Marlowe but rather a fascinating modern jazz variation on it. Rydell is mesmerizing as a maniacal heavy who manages somehow to be frightening and amusing at the same time, and Sterling Hayden's portrayal of a drunk-drugged novelist at the end of his tether is the most convincing job of its kind I've ever seen. But then Altman keeps the screen alive as very few directors today can; he is idiosyncratic, perverse, contrary, daring, resourceful and exciting. You may disagree with him, but his talent is undeniable, and I say that because evidently some people are put off by what he has done to Chandler, and still others are being ill-prepared for his movie by the ad campaign, which implies that the picture is in the private-eye tradition, when the whole point is that it's emphatically—anarchistically even—an atonal dead-end explosion of that myth. This very irreverence, which makes the film so fresh (without being cute), is what the audience must be prepared for before they get into the theatre. But if they are led to believe that Elliott Gould is following in Bogart's footsteps, they are in for a shock they won't accept. *The Long Goodbye* has about as much to do with *The Big Sleep* as *M*A*S*H* did with *Mister Roberts*.

One would also have hoped the past seventy years have proved that movies owe to literature or any other art only what they choose to owe, and if a director as good as Altman decides to make of Chandler what he has made, he should only be judged on the merits of his work, and I think this version of *The Long Goodbye* needs no apologies. It is its own vindication—just as every individual treatment of sex or violence must be the very criterion by which to appraise it. Finally, that's why any form of censorship can't really work, because who is to be the judge? There are too many cases in history where time has changed our values, and I personally don't like the idea of anyone telling me what I can or can't see. Inevitably that leads to artists being told what they can or cannot do and, like Mr. Altman, they should be free to go where their talent takes them.

The intriguing thing is that *Deep Throat* is unwittingly a good example of the kind of moral decay Mr. Altman is talking about in *The Long Goodbye*. That grubby little porno film coupled with its incredible success could almost stand as evidence of the state of the country at this particular time of our lives. There is some deep self-revulsion at work that no amount of legislation is going to stop. Mr. Altman has given us a vivid glimpse of this in his new film, and a good work of art is a better cure for what ails us than any court decision.

June 1973

4

DIRECTORS

The morning after I arrived (accompanied by Polly Platt) on the Cheyenne Autumn *location in Monument Valley, the unit publicity man met us for breakfast to ask—it seems he hadn't been notified—what my assignment was. "John Ford," I said.*

He turned ashen. "Oh, no."

"Yes," I said.

"Oh, no, no," he said again, and looked around nervously as though to make sure we hadn't been overheard. I asked what was the matter and, shakily, he tried to explain that Mr. Ford never granted interviews, hated reporters, shunned publicity, loathed talking about his movies and was simply unapproachable by anyone. I got the rather clear impression that this aging and by now almost haggard fellow would rather be swallowed up by the earth than risk even the thought of mentioning to Mr. Ford that I was anywhere within a thousand-mile radius.

I countered by saying that his employer, Warner Bros., had just paid for our trip from New York to Arizona and that they'd been fully informed of my assignment when they issued the tickets. (Actually, it had taken more pressure on Harold to agree to the article than Warners; he wasn't terribly interested in the idea, but John Ford had for years been among my most cherished directors and I was very anxious both to meet him and to watch him at work, so after much badgering from my end, Harold capitulated.) Well, said the bedraggled p.r. man, we could watch from the sidelines for awhile but I wasn't to speak to Mr. Ford or even come under his gaze. At the moment, agreeing to that seemed the only way to even set foot on the set, so I did.

For two days, with the unit publicist hovering at my elbow every moment, I followed the rules he'd set down. Mr. Ford would, on frequent occasions, pull out a handkerchief and chew on it, which the publicist nervously informed me was a sign of his displeasure and irritation. I only discovered sometime later that this was nonsense since Mr. Ford, if he is not smoking or chewing a cigar, is always chewing on a handkerchief—it is not a signal of anything except probably that he's trying to cut down on smoking.

On the first Sunday afternoon—the only day they didn't shoot—I accidentally came upon Jack Garfein (the director), who was there visiting his then wife, Carroll Baker; they were going riding. Garfein and I had a mutual friend, Gene Archer, who was with The New York Times *then, and I used this as an excuse to introduce myself. When he asked what on earth I was doing there, I told him.*

"Does Jack Ford know you're here?" he said.

"No, that's my problem," and I told him the situation.

"Oh, for God's sake," he said, "that's ridiculous. He'd love to see you. I'll tell him you're here."

About four hours later, a jeep came roaring down from the hill where Ford and the stars bunked (the rest of the company stayed below in trailors, one of which we'd been allotted), and I heard Ray Kellogg, the second-unit director, loudly yelling out what I finally figured out was a rough approximation of my name. I ran over.

"You MacDonabitch?"

"Yup."

"The Old Man'd like you to join him for dinner—around six. O.K.?"

"O.K.!"

Everyone was already seated when we arrived but whoever was on Mr. Ford's right (I was too flustered to remember) was moved so that I could sit there. He nodded a pleasant hello, pronounced my name correctly and said, "Serbian?"

I said yes as casually as possible but I was impressed. All my life people had always assumed the name was Russian or Polish or Czech or Hungarian; sometimes they guessed Yugoslav, but no one had ever pinned it down precisely on the first try. At this point, the co-producer of the film, one

Bernard Smith (of whom there will be more shortly), made some remark to the director having to do with business. Ford scowled at him silently for a moment, then turned to me: "There's a word for what he just said."

I leaned in. "Yes?"

"Govno," Ford said. I broke up. The word is the Serbian equivalent for "shit."

For the next week or so, Mr. Ford was more than co-operative with me on the set; he was, in his own gruff way, actively friendly. It was often cold on the location and Polly took to wearing an Indian blanket wrapped around her, prompting Ford to name her "Teepee-that-Walks." I was sporting a British suede hat which he evidently disliked, so one day he yelled "Wardrobe" and instructed them to give me a cavalry hat. He then fitted it on me himself, adjusting the brim trooper-style until it pleased him. "That's better'n' that Goddamn thing you've been wearing."

Now, this attention he was lavishing on us was not making the producer happy, mainly I guess because there had arrived on the location a writer and a photographer from Life, *whom Ford quite blithely either ignored or insulted. He used to refer to the writer as "that guy from* Life, Death *and* Fortune." *Eventually, producer Smith (with whom I'd also made the tactical error of not interviewing) must have decided something had to be done so I was informed, with much trembling and stammering by the publicist, that we would have to leave —tomorrow; our trailer, went the excuse, had to be used for arriving members of the company. Since I'd told Warners originally I would need at least two weeks to get the piece right and they had agreed, I was not a little upset and annoyed to be thrown out after barely a week. I asked if Mr. Ford was aware of this request and got an evasive answer to the effect that Mr. Smith had sent down the order. Finally I had a reason to talk to the producer, which I did, with small effect. He smoothly explained the supposed problem of space, at the same time getting in several bows for his "contributions" to the production.*

That evening, as he was heading in for dinner, I told Mr. Ford we would have to be leaving tomorrow and thanked him for his patience.

"Where ya goin'?" he said. I explained the space problems we'd been informed of and that I didn't want to impose on his hospitality or make any waves. "Oh, c'mon in and let's eat," he said and we did that. Shortly after we were seated, the producer arrived. Ford called him over politely. "Listen, Bernie," he said very reasonably, "you give Bogdanovich here my room and I'll double up with someone down below."

The producer turned an odd color. "Oh, no, Jack, we can't do that."

"No, that's all right," said Ford, still very evenly, "you just give 'em my room if there's not enough space and I'll double up."

"Jack, don't be—I mean, that's ridiculous—we—we can—we can work something else out."

"Oh, can you, Bernie? You think you can find some space for them?"

"Sure, I can, Jack, don't worry about it."

"Oh, thanks, Bernie." The producer started away with relief. Ford called after him. "But, listen, if there's any trouble, they can just use my room, you know." Smith waved back with a pained grin. Ford's expression turned finally to a scowl and he leaned over to me. "Stay as long as you want," he said.

Over the years, since the article was published, my relations with Mr. Ford haven't always been as amicable or easy; it's impossible to be his friend or his admirer and not get some of that waspish Irish tongue or a touch of what Cagney referred to as "malice." But he is one of the great men of the movies and among the few really fascinating people I have met. The article that follows, the book I eventually did about him (which cannibalized some of this same material) and the feature-length documentary I directed about his career taken separately or together do not begin to do justice to who he is or to what he has achieved.

The Autumn
of John Ford

"HE'LL BE COMIN' UP OVER THAT RISE ANY SECOND NOW," said Danny Borzage, looking anxiously up the road. A bearded, youthful old man playing an accordion, Borzage was dressed in the yellow and blue of a trooper in the U.S. Cavalry, 1878. The song was "Greensleeves." It was a little past 8:30 A.M. in Monument Valley, the sun warm, the wind dry and chilly. "I always play for 'im when he comes on the set," Borzage was saying. "Always start with 'Bringing in the Sheaves.'" He glanced up the road again. The rest of the huge company was preparing for the first scenes of the day; a couple stood by, listening to the accordion. "Back in 1924, he was makin' a picture called *The Iron Horse*," said Borzage. "My brother Frank was directin' on the same lot. Well, anyway, I was sent out to audition for him. In those days, y'know, they a'ways had mood music on the set to help the actors. Well, I met 'im and he asked me if I knew 'My Buddy.' 'Yes, sir, I happen t'know that one.' He stopped me before I was through and I was kinda nervous, thought I didn't have the job." Borzage looked up the road again. "Then he asked m'name. 'Y'any relation to Frank Borzage?' An' I said, 'Yes,' an' he said, 'Well, why didn't cha say so?' An' I said, ' 'Cause I don't want the job on his account.' And he said, 'You go over an' tell Frank Borzage his brother has a job.'" Danny Borzage smiled. "An' he's used me ever since."

"Here he comes, Danny!" someone yelled, and just then, over the rise, came a white jeep station wagon. Borzage rose and walked quickly to the side of the road. As the car came nearer, he began to play "Bringing in the Sheaves," letting the notes swell and fall dramatically. The car came to a slow stop about thirty feet from where Borzage was playing. A hush had fallen over the company.

John Ford sat in the front seat, peering out his side window through thick glasses, the left eye covered with a black patch. He wore an old, broad-brimmed felt hat pulled low over the left side of his face; there was a tiny orange feather in the leather hatband. He chewed on a short, unlit cigar. Borzage was playing "My Darling Clementine."

The prop man came over and handed him a cup of coffee. The director of photography and the wardrobe man had gotten out of the car and stood next to Ford's window. The director sipped his coffee, quietly staring around the area. His son, Patrick Ford, who supervised the cavalry, had joined the group at the car window, along with Wingate Smith, Ford's brother-in-law and the first assistant director. Borzage played "She Wore A Yellow Ribbon" as a muted conversation went on at the window. Soon the little group broke up, one by one, carrying out instructions. Someone opened the door and the director got out of the car. Ford stood for a moment surveying the scene, one hand holding the cup, the other on the backside of his hip. He was a thin, almost frail figure, but as he started toward the camera the walk was jaunty, both arms swinging, his body moving slightly from side to side. Borzage glanced up and smiled shyly at him, stepping back a few feet.

Ford wore a faded tan campaign jacket and a pair of loose-fitting khaki pants. People moved out of his way as he approached. Borzage played "We Shall Gather At the River." The director had a stern Yankee face, almost mean, a small growth of white stubble on his sunken cheeks. His eyes were pale blue. There was an orange scarf tied around his neck, and the laces of his dark blue sneakers were untied. He passed a Navajo and moved his right hand in a kind of half wave, half salute. "Yat'hey, shi'kis," he said and the man answered, "Yat'hey."

Recently, in New York, James Stewart reminisced about John Ford, having just completed a cameo appearance as Wyatt Earp in the director's latest film, *Cheyenne Autumn*.

"I love 'im. That's . . . that's first of all," he began. "And that is, of course, intermixed with respect and. . . ." He pursed his lips and nodded twice. "Admiration." Stewart leaned forward in his chair. "He's just . . . he's a genius. The way he'll do a script. Gets it across visually. Hates *talk*. I just wish there were more people like him." Stewart shook his head and pursed his lips. "Everybody's always talkin' about the Ford stock company, y'know. . . . I think it's a helluva good *idea*! Wish everybody'd do it. The people know how to work together. They don't have to . . . each film doesn't have to be the first time. And a lotta directors . . . y'know . . . it's a barrel a laughs on the set and ya have fun and . . . and then you see the picture and you say, 'Where is it? Where's the. . . .' But Ford *gets* it on the screen. And he's a real leader. I think he is the best man doing the job." He nodded vehemently.

"I went up to his office to see 'im about costume," Stewart went on. "For this first picture we did, *Two Rode Together*. And, of course, he didn't talk about costume at all!" The actor mumbled in imitation of Ford. "He talked about the Navy . . . and about the war . . . then a little about . . . Navy and a little . . . war . . . and Navy. And I could only hear every tenth word. I can't hear very well, anyway, and he mumbled and . . . that handkerchief he's always chewing on. . . . I just nodded my head." Stewart opened and closed his mouth slightly as though eating. "Then, finally, he asked me what I thought I oughta wear in this picture." He paused. "I thought . . . and he said, 'Now before you say anything I'll *tell* you what you're going to wear!' And he sent the wardrobe man out, brought back a costume and this . . . this *hat*!" He paused. "Waall, the brim on this hat was . . . it was as big as this!" He indicated the top of the table at which we sat. "Waall, I put it on and it . . . I looked . . . it was something *horrible* to see. And he asked me what I *thought*!"

Stewart pantomimed looking at himself in a mirror. " 'Waaall, I don't know. . . .' He says, 'Do you have Hat-Approval in your contract?' I said, 'I don't know.' So he said, 'Get the contract' . . . and everybody looked for the contract and they couldn't find it 'cause I didn't *have* one!" He paused. "After a while I went out and I brought *my* old hat . . . hat I've worn on every Western . . . old when I got it. So . . . so I put it on. He kinda looked at it for a few moments, and then he says, 'You *have* Hat-Approval.' " Stewart laughed. "On the next picture, he said to me, 'You *still* have Hat-Approval,' and on that one he wouldn't let me wear a hat at *all*!"

Stewart left the room for a moment, returning with a glass of water. "I was very careful . . . I really watched my step on *The Man Who Shot Liberty Valance*," he said. "Besides, he was givin' it to Duke Wayne all the time. And we were in the last two weeks of shooting and hardly a murmur. . . . And then one day we're shooting the funeral scene . . . coffin there and Woody Strode," he explained, referring to the black actor who has played in several Ford films. "And Woody was in his old-age makeup and he had on overalls and a hat. Ford came over to me and nodded at Woody. 'What d'ya think of Woody's costume?' " Stewart paused. "I paused and said, 'Waall, s'a little Uncle Remus, isn't it?' Now . . . now why . . . why I . . . I wished I could've just taken those words and just . . . just. . . ." Stewart had his hand under his chin and with his fingers he gestured putting the words back until finally all his fingers were in his mouth. "He just looked at me . . . just looked and I knew what was . . . I knew. . . . He says, 'And what's *wrong* with Uncle Remus?' I said, 'Why, nothing.' He says, '*I* put that costume together. That's just what I *intended*!' 'Listen, Boss,' I said. . . . He says, 'Woody, Duke, everybody, c'mon over here.' An' everybody comes over. 'Look at Woody,' he says. 'Look at his costume,' he says. 'Looks like Uncle *Remus*, doesn't it?' 'Yes, Boss, yes, Coach, yes, sir,' they said like a bunch a parrots. 'One of the *players*,' he goes on, 'one of the *players* seems to have some objection! One of the *players* here doesn't seem to *like* Uncle Remus! As a matter a fact, I'm not at all sure he even likes *Negroes!*'" Stewart sat back in his chair. "Someone said to me later, 'Ya thought ya were gonna make it through, didn't you?'"

Monument Valley lies within the Navajo Indian Reservation, straddling the Arizona-Utah state line. The red cathedral-like buttes and mesas that form its landscape were created by erosion and are named for their shapes: The Mittens, The Big Hogan, Three Sisters; from minute to minute the shadows change their appearance. There is a timelessness to the country that makes it as remarkable a natural wonder as the Grand Canyon, but far more dramatic. John Ford has made several movies there, the most recent of which is *Cheyenne Autumn*, which tells a story of the heroic flight of three hundred Cheyenne men, women and children from an Oklahoma reservation (where, because of neglect, they faced death from starvation and disease) to their native Yellowstone country, some fifteen hundred miles away. Pursued all the way by the Cavalry, only eighty survived to see their homeland.

Acting in the picture were two generations of Ford players. Of the veterans, besides Danny Borzage, there was George O'Brien, the silent-film star, whose first leading role was in the 1924 Ford western, *The Iron Horse*. John Wayne's son, Patrick, was on the roster for the seventh time although his father, who has acted in more than seventeen of the director's films, was not; Pat can be seen at age ten in *Rio Grande*, age thirteen in *The Quiet Man*, seventeen in *The Searchers*, and twenty-four in *Cheyenne Autumn*. Harry ("Dobe") Carey, Jr. was introduced in Ford's *Three Godfathers* (1948), a film that was dedicated to the memory of his late father, Harry Carey, who played in over twenty-five Ford movies, beginning in 1917 with *Cheyenne's Pal*; Dobe has been in eight others, including a portrayal of the young Dwight Eisenhower in *The Long Gray Line*. Ben Johnson, a champion steer roper and rodeo star, was a stunt man for the director before being cast in featured and leading roles on six pictures. Jimmy O'Hara, whose sister Maureen has made four films with Ford since her first, *How Green Was My Valley*, has been in three himself. For Dolores Del Rio, Richard Widmark, Carroll Baker and Mike Mazurki, *Cheyenne Autumn* marks only their second time around with the director. It is the first film for Victor Jory ("I always tried to work for him at Fox in the Thirties. He says I didn't, but I did"), Ricardo Montalban, Sal Mineo and Gilbert Roland ("He knows me from the early days when I was an extra using my real name, Luis Antonio Alonso. He still calls me Luis").

Every one of the Ford players has his favorite John Ford story, and most of them have several. After eighteen days on a Ford set, the tales become almost legendary, but the veteran Ford player will insist all of them are true. Ford is said never to look at his rushes, for example, something even the most experienced director would not hazard. And he also never looks at the script. The only time he does look at it, someone will say, is when he's going to change dialogue.

Coming onto a set once, on a dreary and overcast day when everyone was sure there would be no shooting, he told them all to make ready for the funeral scene. They looked at each other: there was no funeral scene in the script. What funeral scene? they asked. The funeral scene, Ford had yelled, the funeral scene! He had looked at the day and decided it was perfect for a funeral, so he put one in the picture (*Wee Willie Winkie*).

And there was the time he and Henry Fonda (who has been in seven Ford films) had several heated arguments during the filming of *Mister Roberts*, until finally the air just had to be cleared and the producers called for a conference to iron out the differences. And when Fonda rose to recount his grievances, Ford suddenly stood up and socked him on the jaw.

But perhaps the most notorious Ford gesture is said to have occurred when the studio head sent a man down to tell Ford he was two days behind schedule. Ford asked the man how many pages he thought they shot a day. About five pages a day, the man approximated, and then Ford asked to see the script. He leafed through it, counted out ten pages, ripped them out, tossed them in the air, and told the man to tell his boss they were now back on schedule. And he never did shoot those ten pages.

But, some other Ford regular will say, what about the time. . . . And, of course, the stories never end.

Dinner for the director, his cast and crew was served in a small adobe structure, a part of Goulding's Lodge, which is set on the lowest rim of Rock Door Mesa, overlooking a magnificent view of Monument Valley. Attached to the porch is a dinner bell, never rung until John Ford has taken his place at the head of the third table from the door.

He arrived wearing a navy-blue jacket, khaki pants and his pajama top, the collar half up, a shapeless sweater over it. He wore no hat and his hair was white and wispy. Sitting, he took out his bone-handled jackknife and banged it down next to him. Soon after everyone had arrived and the food was being served, the co-producer mentioned something about the day's shooting. "Pat Wayne!" called Ford.

"Sir!" said Wayne.

"Where's the bowl?" Wayne rose and went to get a little wooden bowl (filled with several dollars and a good deal of loose change) that stood on the piano top. "How much does he owe now?" asked Ford.

"That last one makes two dollars, sir," Wayne said.

Carroll Baker turned to me. "There's a fifty-cent penalty for talking shop or about Mr. Ford's movies at the table." She cut a bite of steak. "The other day," she said quietly, "he was telling me something about *The Long Voyage Home*, and he stopped, paid his fifty cents and then finished the story."

The rest of the dinner that night was spent playing Twenty Questions. Ford led off with something that was animal and vegetable. No one could guess it and finally, with disgust, he informed the players that it was, of course, Sherlock Holmes' Moroccan slipper, the one he used as a tobacco pouch. "Probably one of the most famous props in literature," he growled. "It seems that none of you, including Jory, have read *Sherlock Holmes*."

After the meal, the director remained for a while, smoking a cigar he had first cut in half with his knife, and chatting with his actors. Then he walked over and nudged his son. "I'm going to call Mother," he said. The two Fords left together.

Twenty-five miles from the Lodge flows the San Juan River. Rising high above it are tall red cliffs and down at the bank are weeds, small trees and piles of silver driftwood. The water itself is the color of clay.

As "Bringing in the Sheaves" heralded the director's arrival, Navajo men and women (playing the Cheyenne) on horseback and pulling travois were assembled at the river's edge. Among them were several stunt men in Indian costume and makeup. On the cliff above, and several hundred yards back from the edge, was the Cavalry. The entire area was in a turmoil of activity. Lee and Frank Bradley (Navajo interpreters who have worked on eleven other Ford films) were shouting instructions to their people through bullhorns.

Ford stood looking out over the river and chewing on his cigar, which he held from underneath. "This river was designed by Remington," he said, sweeping his arm across the landscape. "It's the most typical Western river I know. Classic." He shook his head. "Y'know, the producer said to me, 'What d'ya wanta shoot out here for? What's so interesting about this?' I mean, y'know. He says, 'Why don'tcha go to the Adirondacks? The Catskills?' " Ford took the cigar from his mouth. "I said, 'You mean Grossinger's!' "

He walked off quickly and collared one of the wranglers. "Can Carroll go in the river with the wagon?" he asked.

"Well, where I went in . . ." the man began.

"Don't give me the story of your life!" Ford interrupted, throwing away his cigar. "Just answer the question."

The man said that she could.

Ford nodded sharply. "Good," he said, pulling a long white handkerchief from his back pocket. Someone was there to hand him a bullhorn. "Okay, Lee. Frank. Start your people across!" he called, chewing on one end of the handkerchief, the bulk of which hung down over his chest like a misplaced napkin. "Easy!" The interpreters relayed the instructions and slowly the Navajos moved into the water. Ford called to Chuck Hayward (stunt man), who was halfway across the river. "All right, hold 'em there, Chuck! That's *well*!" The Navajos were spread out in the river, holding in place. "Fill up those empty spaces and get those travois up there!" Turning to the Cavalry, Ford gave some instructions and then all was ready, the camera trained on the troops standing off in the distance.

"O.K., we're rolling," said Ford.

"Speed," said the camera operator.

"All right. *Dick!*" The Cavalry came riding forward at a steady clip. "All right. Lee! Frank! Start 'em moving!" The tribe moved slowly through the water. Widmark raised his arm. "Troooop. Haaaalt!" Pat Wayne echoed him. The Cavalry stopped and Widmark gazed down at the Indians. Slowly the camera panned from the troops, across the barren, rocky slopes, slowly around and down at the Navajos, some of whom had reached the other side, others still moving across the grey river, their horses leaping up and down. The only sounds were of horses whinnying and the movement of people through the water. The camera held for many moments on the scene. "That is *well*!"

Harry Goulding, the tall, aging Westerner who owns the lodge in Monument Valley, was standing nearby, watching. He shook his head once and spoke with a deep Western twang. "Certainly is somethin', isn't it," he said quietly. Goulding was the person who first introduced John Ford to the valley, in 1938 when the director was searching for a location on which to film *Stagecoach*. "I didn't know if I was goin' inta the studio or inta the jail," he said, grinning shyly. "The Navajos'd been hit pretty bad by the Depression an', by God, if an Indian'd walked into our store an' put a dollar on the counter, why Mrs. Goulding an' I'd a fainted." He shook his head. "So I got inta the studio and I showed a whole stack a pictures to Mr. Ford an' three days later there was a score a jobs for the Navajos and a lotta lives was saved." He took off his hat, ran his hand over his head, and replaced the hat. "Then you heard 'bout the Hay Lift," Goulding went on. "In 1949, just after Mr. Ford'd finished shootin' *She Wore A Yellow Ribbon* here, we had a blizzard that left the valley covered with 'bout twelve feet a snow. Army planes dropped food in. Thanks to that an' the hundred fifty-two hundred thousand dollars he'd left behind, why, another tragedy was prevented." Goulding looked off across the river. "An' this year, he heard his friends was gonna have too little t'eat, an' here he is again."

Ford was yelling through his bullhorn: "I've told fifty people to get those people outa there!" he said angrily. "Now get 'em the hell out. Dry 'em off. Give 'em some coffee or something!" Goulding turned to me again. "I tell ya," he said simply, "to the Navajos he's holy, sorta. Ev'ytime they've had a rough time, boy, this thing comes outa the blue." He lifted his hat again and ran his hand over his head. "He's been taken into the Navajo tribe," he said, replacing his hat and smiling faintly. "They have a special name for 'im, the Navajos," he went on, looking over at Ford. "Natani Nez. That's *his* name, an' only his. Natani Nez," Goulding repeated softly. "It means the Tall Leader," he said.

John Ford was born Sean Aloysius O'Fearna in Cape Elizabeth, Maine, on the first of February, 1895. His parents had come to America from Galway, Ireland. He directed his first movie in 1917. (It was a two-reeler called *The Tornado*, about a cowboy who rescues the banker's daughter from a gang of outlaws and uses the reward money to bring his Irish mother to the United States. He also played the lead.) The only director to have received six Academy Awards, he is also the only one who has been cited four times by the New York Film Critics. As a Commander in the Navy, he made America's first war documentary, *The Battle of Midway* (1942), as well as *December 7th* (1943), an account of the Pearl Harbor attack and its aftermath; both were awarded Oscars as the best documentaries of their years. Over forty-six years, Ford has made almost a hundred and forty pictures.

One evening he sat up in his bed in Room 19 of Goulding's Lodge. The place was in total disarray. Clothes lay everywhere: on the floor, on tables and chairs, even on the refrigerator. There were also piles of books on every conceivable subject scattered around the room and next to his bed. On it lay a copy of *Gods, Graves and Scholars*. The little night table was covered with cigars, matches, a watch, pills, glasses, a couple of knives and pencils, loose paper, scripts, and frayed handkerchiefs. Attached to the headboard of the bed was a lamp. The director was discussing movie-making, and you could hear a slight but distinct Maine accent in his speech.

"I love making pictures, but I don't like talking about them," he said, cutting a cigar in half with his jackknife. "I mean. Y'know. It's been my whole life. But people ask me which is my favorite—I always say the next one." Raising his arm in the air, he pulled his faded-silk pajama sleeve down. "Y'know. I make a picture and then move on to the next one." He shook his head. "I love Hollywood. I don't mean the higher echelons," he said sarcastically. "I mean the lower echelons, and the grips, the technicians."

After a while, Ford lit a cigar-half and spoke of the difficulty of finding decent stories to do. "My agent," he began, "was at a property conference at one of the studios. And they hold up this book, on the jacket of which was a rather simplified drawing of a nun. He jumped up," Ford said gesturing. " 'My client's a Roman Catholic and that property would interest him very much,' he says." Ford grimaced and chewed on one end of the handkerchief. "I read this thing. —was about a nun who's seduced by a pimp and then falls in love with him. Gets pregnant. She was supposed to run away with him and he told her to meet him at some bridge at one in the morning." He took the handkerchief and held the end a few inches from his mouth. "She went there. Bong! One o'clock. No pimp. You dissolve. Bong, bong. Two o'clock. No pimp. Dissolve again. Three o'clock. So she finally throws herself into the river." The director put the handkerchief back in his mouth. "My agent walked in the door, I threw the book at him," he said, imitating the movement. "I mean, Jeez. That's y'know, that's the kinda junk they give you these days." He shook his head.

"Now this thing," he said, nodding at the script of *Cheyenne Autumn* lying on the table, "I've wanted to make this for a long time. Y'know. I've killed more Indians than Custer, Beecher and Chivington put together." He raised his arm and pulled the sleeve down again. "People in Europe always wanta know about the Indians. They just see them ride by, or they're heavies. I wanted to show what they were like. I like Indians very much," he said warmly. "They're . . . they're a very moral people. They have a literature. Not written. But spoken. They're very kindhearted. They love their children and their animals. And I wanted to show their point of view for a change." Ford pulled down on his cheeks. "S'amazing. . . ." He paused. "It is amazing, working with them, how quickly they catch on despite the language barrier." He rubbed his mouth with the handkerchief.

"But y'know, there's no such thing as a good script. I've never seen one." He paused. "Yes, I have. I've seen *one*. This

O'Casey thing I'm gonna do next. Based on his autobiographies. It's the first script I've ever read that I can just go over and shoot." (It was *Young Cassidy*.) He waved his hand in the air. "Well, you know the old thing: one-picture's-worth-a-thousand-words. Scripts are dialogue. I don't like all that *talk*. I try to get things across visually. Y'know, get back to the old thing." He picked up the other half of the cigar and lit it. "I don't like to do books or plays. I prefer to take a short story and expand it rather than take a novel and try to condense." He pulled reflectively on his cheeks. "Producers don't know anything about making pictures," he said earnestly. "And that's why I shoot my films so they can only be cut *one* way." He puffed on his cigar. "They get to the cutting room and they say, 'Well, let's stick a close-up in here.' " Ford paused. "But there isn't one. I didn't shoot it."

The director commented that he'd always wanted to do a stage play. "I like the form," he said and picked up a glass of stale water from the night table. He took a pill from a little box. "B means it's a Bufferin, right?" he said and swallowed the pill. "I once got a letter from the Metropolitan Opera people," he said sardonically. "It was a flowery, purple prose thing. Inviting me to direct *The Girl of the Golden West*. 'Course, they made it very clear I was to have nothing to do with the sets or costumes or the music or. . . ." Ford took the cigar from his mouth, holding his arm up by the elbow. "I wrote back that, first of all, I thought *The Girl of the Golden West* was a *lousy* opera." He paused. "But that I was very interested in directing *La Bohème*." He put the cigar back and puffed on it. "Well, you can imagine, y'know, what they thought of *that*! This dirty old *cow*boy . . . this mangy old . . . wants to do *La Bohème!* Well, I certainly knew more about the Left Bank than the manager of the Metropolitan," he said with a wave of his arm. "They wrote back that they weren't interested in having me do *La Bohème*." He chuckled.

The location was a stretch of sandy ground enclosed on two sides by sheer walls of red rock—a narrow canyon at one end—and after the director had been piped aboard by Danny Borzage, he walked away up the sandy hill. A long line of men followed, single file, behind him. Also on the set today were two men from *Life* Magazine, a photographer and a writer.

A group of Cheyenne warriors were to come from over the hill, charging down toward the Cavalry; the camera would be at the bottom of the hill. Several stunt men were costumed as Indians, Ford attending to them individually. After giving instructions to Chuck Hayward, who was to lead the ambush, he asked for a feather for another stuntman's hat and sauntered by me. "If you don't think this shot takes organization . . ." he grumbled as he moved past.

After a half hour, Ford sat, crossed his leg and lifted the bullhorn. The camera was trained on the top of the hill where nothing was yet visible. "Okay. We're rolling," he said.

"Speed!" said the operator.

"All right. Chuck!" Ford called through the bullhorn. As he did a score of horsemen came galloping over the sandy hill, whooping and firing their rifles. The Cavalry at the bottom fired back and the shots reverberated loudly in the valley. The riders swooped down the hill, dust flying, and thundered by the camera so closely that Ford's bullhorn was knocked from his hand. He did not move. An Indian had fallen off his horse and lay midway down the hill. The camera panned as the Indians rode into the distance. "That's *well!*"

Several people ran out to see if the Navajo was hurt, but he was walking gingerly away before they got to him. Another group clustered near Ford. One man, displaying the crushed bullhorn, shook his head. "We damn near went home early today," he said.

Nearby, another technician was pointing out how close the horses' hooves had come to hitting Ford. "Horse wouldn't dare," said his partner.

The director had got up from his chair and now turned

to the company. "Tomorrow we'll do it with film," he announced with a straight face. "That was for *Life* Magazine!"

Carroll Baker, dressed in the costume of a Quaker schoolteacher, a brown shawl over her shoulders, walked toward the lunch table. "I told Mr. Ford that I wanted to wear my hair *down* for this picture," she was saying, "like the women in Ingmar Bergman's films. He said, 'Ingrid Bergman?' 'No,' I said, 'Ing*mar* Bergman.' 'Who's he?' I said, 'Bergman, you know, the great Swedish director.' He let it go and I saw fit to change the subject," said Miss Baker. "But as I was leaving, he said, 'Oh, Ingmar *Berg*man! He's the fella that called me the greatest director in the world.' And of course, you know, he has." She laughed, pulled the shawl over her hair, which was worn up, and sat at the table.

Richard Widmark was sitting at the far end, finishing his Jell-O and munching on a cookie. "Never had as much fun on a picture," he was saying, "as I did on *Two Rode Together*, film I did with Jimmy Stewart and the Old Man." He grinned. "I'm a little deaf in this ear," he said, "and Ford's a little deaf in the other, and Jimmy's hard of hearing in both!" Widmark cupped his ear. "So all through the picture, all three of us are goin', 'What? What? What?'"

Riding back from lunch, Ford talked about the Navajo medicine man. "The original one was a fella named Fat. This fella we have now is just one of his disciples." He nodded at Harry Goulding, who was driving. "Used to tell Harry what I wanted and get anything I ordered. Thunderclouds . . . One night I said to Harry, 'Tell 'im we need snow. Need the valley covered with snow.' Next morning, I stepped outa my room. A thin layer of snow covered the valley." A Navajo with a lined face and hair braided with red cloth came up behind the car. "This is the *new* medicine man," Ford explained. "Yat'hey," he called to the Navajo. "Yat'hey," answered the medicine man. "Hako," said the director and the man trotted up. Harry stopped the car. Ford raised his arm and waved at the sky. "Nijone," he said, nodding his head. The man smiled. "Ah sheh'eh," said Ford and waved again. "Nijone." The Navajo nodded and the jeep moved forward. "There's no word for fleecy clouds in Navajo, so it's a little difficult. The first time he did it, he got 'em just right." He paused. "But they were in the wrong place!"

The vast majority of the six hundred people involved in the making of the six-and-a-half-million-dollar movie called *Cheyenne Autumn* lived in trailers and tents that had been set up as a small town at the foot of Rock Door Mesa. It was Sunday and the blackboard next to the mess hall carried a notice in chalk: Low Mass At Noon. A priest had driven two hundred miles to say Mass. At 11:40 the cars began coming down from the lodge. The director arrived first, followed by Dolores Del Rio, who was accompanied by Ricardo Montalban. Mike Mazurki and Gilbert Roland came next and then Pat Wayne. George O'Brien followed. They all went inside, and Jimmy O'Hara hurried in a few seconds later. Ford sent someone back up the hill to get the little wooden bowl from the piano top; its contents were to be part of the collection. Inside, at the far end of the hall, an altar had been improvised. Gilbert Roland had contributed an old Spanish cross for the occasion and it was nailed on an upright table. Two candles were burning. The rest of the place was still set up as a dining room. About forty people attended the service. Pat Wayne and Jimmy O'Hara served as altar boys. Mike Mazurki took the collection.

On the other side of the canyon they had shot at before, Ford placed some of the mounted warriors in shadow and some in light. It was an argument scene between Montalban (a chief) and Sal Mineo (a young brave), who violently throws down his rifle, leaps onto his horse and rides off. Ford stood alone, rubbing his hands together. There was a good deal of noise going on: "Wingate!" called the director. "What is this? Strike? Mutiny?"

Smith spoke through his bullhorn. "All right. Let's keep it down now. Please!"

It was hot and Ford had removed his jacket and sweater; he wore a white shirt, the cuffs unbuttoned. He chewed on his handkerchief. "All right, has anybody else got a reason why we can't do this?" he barked. "If not, let's go." During the rehearsal Ford spied one of the young Navajos in the scene grinning into the camera. He called him over, made him bend down over his knee, and spanked him. The Navajo was giggling, and everyone laughed. As the young man backed off, Ford made a mock gesture as though to sock him.

The camera rolled and as Mineo ran to his horse it shied and his first jump missed. Angrily, he grabbed the horse and jumped onto its back, whipped it and rode off, followed by several other warriors. "That is *well*," said Ford. "Print it." Mineo rode back and asked the director if he could try it again. Ford stared at him for a moment, chewing on the handkerchief. "D'ya wanna do it again with an empty camera, Saul?" Mineo grinned and said he thought it looked sloppy. "You were very angry," Ford explained reasonably. "And you missed. I liked it. *Completely* in character. I don't *want* it to look perfect. Like a circus." Mineo dismounted and moved away. Ford called after him. "But you can do it again with an empty camera, Saul." Mineo laughed and waved back.

That evening, long after dinner, Ford and George O'Brien sat talking. At the opposite end of the dining room a television set, much to Ford's disgust, had been installed. The reception was flaky, but Nancy Hsueh, Carmen D'Antonio (actresses) and Pat Wayne sat watching a movie called *From Here to Eternity*. Ford was talking about his childhood in Maine, about his parents, who had grown up in the same Irish county but had met in America, and about some of the characters he had known in his youth.

On the television screen Montgomery Clift was playing taps. Ford turned around, made a telescope of his hand and peered darkly at the screen. "George," he said turning back, "did you ever see a picture of mine called *Christmas Eve at Pilot Butte?*" O'Brien said he didn't recall. "Nineteen Twenty-one. Harry Carey and Irene Rich were in it. First picture made with actual nighttime photography. It was based on a story by Courtney Riley Cooper called *Christmas Eve at Pilot Butte*. Like to remake it sometime. A nice story." (The film had actually been released with a different title, *Desperate Trails*.)

Taps was still playing and Ford turned in his seat again. "That man doesn't know taps," he muttered in amazement. "You're right, Jack," said O'Brien. Ford looked back angrily, peering over to see who was watching the film. "Pat [Ford's son] was born while we were makin' that picture," he said, turning back. "And so was Dobe [Carey's son]. Within about a week of each other." He chewed on his cigar.

From the television set came the sound of bombs going off, planes zooming by, and then a radio report: "This morning, planes from the Imperial Japanese Air Force attacked Pearl Harbor. . . ." Ford swung around in his chair. "Good God! What's that?" O'Brien laughed. "Oh," said Ford and scowled at the television set.

Part of a dried-out lake bed had been covered with sagebrush and tumbleweeds. The Cheyenne would set it aflame in an effort to stop the pursuing Cavalry. It was a windy October day, and Ford seemed uncertain of how to begin the sequence. He paced about restlessly, worrying about the dangers involved. Eventually, after many precautions, he decided how he wanted to start. Two cameras were readied, the main one on a truck so it could be moved back if the fire got out of control. Stunt men as well as several Navajos were readied for the first shot.

Ford gave explicit instructions: only a small portion of the field was to be ignited now and it was being sprayed down with a highly inflammable mixture. He turned to Chuck Hayward suddenly and told him to begin the shot by riding right in front of the main camera, making sure his lighted torch flashed directly across the lens. He rubbed his hands, pulled down on his hat brim, and looked to see if the water truck was in readiness. The torches were lit. Once again the director checked over his instructions, and then the cameras rolled. "Chuck!" The riders, their torches held low, rode into the area. The second camera jammed. "All right, hold it. Kill it!" Before the interpreters could translate, the Navajos had lit the sage in two places. "Let's do it anyway!" someone shouted, but Ford calmly said no. Men rushed in to put the fires out before they could spread. The torches were extinguished.

The director went to his chair next to the main camera, sat, and lifted his bullhorn. He asked if the second camera was ready yet. No answer. "F'God's sake, will ya answer me!" He was told it was not ready. "All right, the hell with it! Shoot it with one camera! Light your torches." The camera rolled, and the riders with their flaming torches galloped into the field, lighting the sage as they went. The brush leapt high into flame and spread rapidly as the players rode out, whooping and yelping. The heat from the fire was intense and the camera truck moved back several feet. The rest of the crew had cleared it by several yards. Ford sat in his place, his legs crossed. He yelled to the stunt men to ride whooping by the camera again. They did and Ford stood. "That's well!" The men rushed in to put out the blaze. Wingate Smith was standing nearby and someone commented that Ford hadn't moved back from the fire as everybody else had. "Well," Smith said smiling, "he always likes to be the last."

Pat Ford came by on horseback, a pipe in his mouth, his hat pulled down fore and aft, and I asked if there was any truth to the rumor that *Cheyenne Autumn* was to be his father's farewell to the Western. "Hell, no!" he exclaimed. "Why, he'll be makin' Westerns a couple a years after he's dead," he said gruffly. "He loves these cowboys and Indians and this valley." And with that he rode off after the Cavalry.

Saturday night, after dinner, the custom was to have a party. About thirty people assembled in the lodge dining room. Montalban and Miss Baker started it off, dancing to the tune of "Put Your Little Foot," which Danny Borzage played. They had rehearsed, but counted nonetheless. When they had finished, Borzage struck up the "Tennessee Waltz." John Ford stood suddenly, tore off his jacket, dropped it on the floor, stepped out of his sneakers and took Miss Del Rio as his partner. They danced alone on the floor for a few moments, and then were joined by several other couples. Carmen D'Antonio tried to do a flamenco to it.

The music changed and, at Ford's command, everyone who was up joined hands in the "Virginia Reel." The director called out when it was time to "Re*verse!*" Then Miss Baker said she knew a song, stood up and sang "Come Out And Play With Me," a children's song about a little girl who can't go out to play because her doll is ill. She was feigning sobs by the last verse. There was applause as she walked happily back to her seat.

Montalban rose with a guitar, sat on a table and sang several Spanish songs. Ford called out the traditional whoops of pleasure during each of them. When this was over, Borzage struck up a polka and the director, with Miss Baker as his partner, danced with grace and exuberance. Carmen D'Antonio tried to do a flamenco to it.

Soon after this, Jimmy O'Hara stepped forward to sing some Irish songs that Ford had requested. The first was "The Young May Moon," and then "Kevin Barry," a ballad about a young revolutionary who was hanged in 1920.

> *Just a lad of eighteen summers,*
> *Yet there's no one can deny*
> *As he went to death that mornin'*
> *Proud he held his head on high. . . .*

Ford leaned back in his chair, his head resting against the wall. He gazed at the ceiling.

> *Another martyr for old Ireland,*
> *Another murder for the crown,*
> *Whose brutal laws may kill the Irish,*
> *But can't keep their spirit down. . . .*

When the song was over, Ford did not applaud, but everyone else did.

Outside, all of a sudden, a chant was heard. Someone came in to say that the Navajos had arrived to sing for Ford. The entire company moved out onto the porch, at the foot of which six Navajos, dressed casually in Levis and sport shirts but with bandanas tied around their heads, were performing a ceremonial chant. They moved and sang together or in counterpoint, shuffling their feet as they did. The chants were in celebration of the harvest time, and the sounds were atonal and piercing, the movements staccato, yet graceful. They performed two chants and after each Ford led the applause. The Navajos were invited into the dining room and there they performed another two chants. Ford watched with deep concentration. When they had finished, he thanked them. "Ah'sheh'eh, shi'kis," he said to the leader. "A'ha'alani."

After they had left, Jimmy O'Hara was asked to sing again. Ford waved to him. "Sing the national anthem, Jimmy," he said. O'Hara knew what he meant and, to Borzage's accompaniment, he sang "The Wearing of the Green," a song traditionally sung during Easter Week in Ireland) the melody is the same as *The Rising of the Moon*). After the second refrain, Ford contributed a verse:

> *Oh, Paddy dear an' did you hear*
> *The news that's goin' 'round?*
> *The Shamrock is forbid by law*
> *To grow in Irish ground.*
> *St. Patrick's day no more we keep,*

> *His color can't be seen.*
> *For they're hangin' men and women*
> *For the wearin' of the green.*

Everyone joined in on the last refrain.

> *For the wearin' of the green, boys,*
> *The wearin' of the green.*
> *Oh, they're hangin' men and women*
> *For the wearin' of the green.*

A little later, Ford peered at his watch. "My God!" he said in mock amazement. "It's 9:28! Danny, play one more waltz." The accordion sounded the "Missouri Waltz" and the director danced with Miss Del Rio. Soon after that, he moved toward the door. As he did, the group started "Auld Lang Syne," and they sang it as he went out the door and on to his room. A few people stayed on and danced a while longer and sang a couple of songs, but the party was over.

April 1964

Leo McCarey

LEO MCCAREY DIRECTED *Going My Way* and *The Awful Truth*—he won Oscars for those—and the best Marx Brothers movie, *Duck Soup*, and *Love Affair* (which he later remade almost as well as *An Affair to Remember*); he also did *Ruggles of Red Gap* with Charles Laughton, and a lovely film about old age that no one ever heard of but which remained his personal favorite, *Make Way for Tomorrow*. He made pictures with Mae West and W. C. Fields and Harold Lloyd, and he was the man who teamed Stan Laurel and Oliver Hardy. Jean Renoir said once, "McCarey understands people—better perhaps than anyone else in Hollywood."

Like most of the men who became directors in the silent days, he had planned to be something else. A lawyer. He told me about it the first time I met him, three years ago, in a room at St. John's Hospital in Santa Monica, where he was suffering from a severe case of emphysema. "I was a very poor lawyer," he said. "In the first place, I started out very young, so they mistook me for the office boy. A client would come in and say, 'Where's the lawyer?' And I'd say, 'I'm the lawyer, sir.' And he'd say, 'Oh, no! I'm in trouble. Isn't there an older man around?' Well, it got so bad that I used to beat the office boy in in the morning to get some papers to serve. You got ten cents a mile for serving papers. And I made more money that way than I did trying to practice law. Another discouraging factor in my legal career is that I lost every case. One time an irate client literally chased me out of the courtroom, and as I was running down the street, a friend of mine saw me and yelled, 'What are you doing, Leo?' And I yelled back, 'Practicing law!' After about three blocks, I lost the client but I kept running out to Hollywood."

McCarey spoke to me very slowly, with long pauses between words, longer ones between sentences. "You ask me a question and then I start editing in my mind. That's why there's long intervals where I don't say anything."

"You're getting the sentences ready?"

"Yes. Consequently, I bore the hell out of myself." Actually, he had great trouble breathing.

McCarey got a job as a "script girl" with Tod Browning, who was making Lon Chaney movies at Universal, but quite soon he was given the chance to direct one himself. *Society Secrets*. When it was finished, the studio fired him. "So I took the picture to another studio to get another job. And as I was sitting on the projection-room steps waiting for the big boss to look at it, John Ford came along, and I told him what I was doing. He said, 'Is your picture any good?' I said, 'No.' So he said, 'Well, I just made a good picture at Universal. We'll send for that and put your name on it.' Well, in my rather wild career I've always regretted I didn't do it, because that's the perfect way to start—with a bit of larceny."

Eventually McCarey got a job as a gagman with Hal Roach, working on *Our Gang* shorts, eventually directing and writing Charley Chase comedies. Still with Roach, he then helped to invent Laurel and Hardy. "At that time, comics had a tendency to do too much. With Laurel and Hardy, we introduced nearly the opposite. We tried to direct them so that they showed nothing, expressed nothing—and the audience, waiting for the opposite, laughed because we remained serious. I came in one morning and I said, 'We're all working too fast. We've got to get away from these jerky movements and work at a normal speed.' I said, 'I'll give you an example of what I mean. There's a royal dinner. All the royalty is seated around the table and somebody lets out a fart. Now everybody exchanges a *glance*, that's *all*.' Everybody died laughing, but I got my point over."

I was with McCarey to tape an interview about his whole career for the American Film Institute's Oral History program but, though he was in good spirits, it was really difficult for him to speak. "You know, this is a damn shame," he said that first time. "Everything you've mentioned is a gold

mine and I don't feel up to it." I asked about a recurring
Laurel and Hardy routine—thorough destruction—beginning
small and building to epic proportions. In *Two Tars*, it was
a traffic jam in which all the cars were systematically wrecked;
in *Big Business*, a man's house and the team's car and stock of
Christmas trees; in *The Battle of the Century*, a pie fight that
eventually engulfed an entire city block—and so on—all ach-
ingly funny.

"If my breath will hold out," McCarey said after a while,
"I'll tell you the start of the whole thing. I was in New York
with Mabel Normand, Hal Roach, Charley Chase, and I
forget who else. I've always had trouble tying a bow tie—
comes out cockeyed. So we're all ready to leave and Mabel
says, 'Let's nobody tie his tie.' And they all went out and left
me. I'm all dressed, but my black tie is hanging down. I sat
on the bed with a highball bemoaning my fate. Suddenly I
remembered that out on the West Coast I was at a skating
rink one night with a cameraman named Lee Garmes and
Lee said *he* had trouble tying a bow tie but his wife was very
good at it. Now his wife was a professional skater, and I'd
read that she was skating somewhere in New York but I
didn't have the faintest idea of how to get ahold of her, so
I called Paramount on the West Coast and I couldn't get
Lee Garmes. No, they said, he was in New York, too. So
I called the Long Island studio—I called everywhere—and
finally got ahold of Lee and he said, 'You're in luck. My
wife's about to go out to work, but she'll stop by on her
way and tie your tie.' Well, sure enough, she came by and
tied a beautiful bow tie and I went out to this nightclub
and told the whole story to the gang, and no sooner had
I finished than Mabel grabbed my tie and pulled it. I said,
'You little son of a bitch!' Well, everybody laughed, so I
pulled Roach's tie. Somebody else laughed, so Roach pulled
his tie. It began to spread to other tables and everybody
started pulling each other's ties and, running out of ties to
pull—it was too much fun to stop—they started ripping col-
lars off—rrrriiiip—until everybody's collar was off. Then

somebody got an idea that if you took a knife you could start up the seam of a tuxedo, then grab ahold and tear it, and this was very effective. Pretty soon the nightclub was a shambles. Well, *that* was the basis for at least a dozen Laurel and Hardy pictures."

McCarey even managed to incorporate a mild version of the actual tie incident at the start of what was an otherwise pretty serious melodrama called *Wild Company*. It was early in his career (1930) and the picture is badly dated, but it is typical of the mature McCarey pictures that he would begin in a comical, even frivolous way and slowly darken the story into drama or even tragedy.

Make Way for Tomorrow is like that—so are *Love Affair* and *An Affair to Remember*. He instinctively understood the ridiculous and the absurd in people's behavior; rather than condemning it, however, he celebrated this particular quality, which led to exceptional comedies, but also, in his best work, to a sense of the darkening future that no amount of laughter or irresponsibility can brighten forever. And there was the man himself, dying of a lung disease, regularly inhaling cigarillos—a gesture of folly and defiance that seemed to me to epitomize the most enduring elements in his work. He made films that way. If he felt like it, he'd stop shooting and play the piano for a while until he got another idea. The crews didn't mind, the actors enjoyed it, the bosses may have worried, but as the Thirties and Forties went by, Leo McCarey became one of the three or four most successful film makers in Hollywood—his pictures made a lot of money. As his life continued, though, it began to read like one of his own scripts. A bright, happy first half that led to sadness, tragedy. A near-fatal auto accident. Drink. Drugs. During the Fifties and Sixties—twenty years—he made only four pictures, all of them interesting, only one of them (*An Affair to Remember*) a success both commercially and artistically.

I had eleven more sessions with him in the next six months, but even the second time he was a different person. His lapses were longer, the blank areas more and more frequent. I could see him slipping away. They wouldn't even let him have the cigarillos anymore.

The last three times I saw him, I ran one of his own films for him in his room, hoping to stir some memories of how he had achieved those often inspired moments of obviously improvised comedy. It helped very little, though he laughed abruptly several times during the runnings. In fact his humor was the one thing least diminished; it was extraordinarily alive, and when he smiled or laughed, his face was suddenly forty years younger, no longer ill, irrepressibly gay, incorrigibly mischievous. It was almost shocking, the change.

Of course, I didn't really know him. I never really met Leo McCarey. Only a pale shadow of the man who'd made the films. Perhaps that's why so few of his friends visited him at the hospital, and why he probably preferred it that way. Irene Dunne came regularly. Ingrid Bergman once or twice. Frank Capra. ("My hero," McCarey called him.) The agony of his slow death must have been too much to bear for those who'd known him well—the handsome, reckless, crazy Irishman who understood people.

February 1972

Capra vs. Selznick

CALLED TO ARBITRATE between a director and a producer, I suppose I would be inexcusably prejudiced against the latter —particularly inexcusable in my case because so far I have personally had very little trouble with producers or the studios they might be representing, most of our relations having been more than friendly. Nevertheless, that has by no means been the case with many other directors, the history of movies being fairly littered with unrealized or compromised projects done in by what is commonly referred to as "the front office." Therefore, whereas I approached Frank Capra's recent autobiography, *The Name Above the Title* (Macmillan hardcover, Bantam paperback) with considerable partiality, I opened the just published *Memo from David O. Selznick* (Viking)—as close to an autobiography as we shall ever get from the late producer—with an almost comparable degree of suspicion. If Capra's book is the voice of the director (and it's the most entertaining and honest memoir ever written by an American film maker), the Selznick collection is as clearly the producer's, and the two books read back to back throw a revealing light on the mysteries of these two often conflicting positions, the functions of which are so frequently confused in the public's mind.

To be fair about this, I've also had several delightful encounters with Mr. Capra, who is as disarming in person as he is in his book, whereas I never met David Selznick. On the evidence of S. N. Behrman's affectionate introduction to *Memo*, however, and from the testimony of men who were closely associated with Selznick, he was apparently a more than charming person himself. I am thinking particularly of George Cukor; he had directed seven pictures under Selznick's aegis, when, after two years of preparation and some weeks of shooting on their eighth, his old friend replaced him with another director (to keep an actor happy). The movie was *Gone With the Wind* and, though the two never worked together again, Cukor's affection for Selznick has not dimmed to this day. Similarly, King Vidor, who angrily quit Selznick's production of *Duel in the Sun*, has also remained a partisan. A man who could command loyalty even after such traumatic eruptions must surely have been a considerably more than negligible force.

This is abundantly confirmed by the memos and letters—some many pages long and for years now a Hollywood legend—which Mr. Rudy Behlmer has carefully selected, researched and edited into a most valuable book (included also are lengthy autobiographical sections intelligently pieced together from various sources). A man who, over the years, increasingly controlled all aspects of the films he produced —often to the chagrin of his associates, but, just as often, to their greater glory—Selznick epitomized what was best (and sometimes worst) in that much-maligned capacity.

Prior to *Gone With the Wind*, which was both his making and his undoing, Selznick had been an exemplary partner in the working process. He consulted closely with his directors and writers on casts and scripts, encouraging and advising them at every step of the way, but he also allowed the director to *make* the film. With the great financial responsibility of the Margaret Mitchell best seller, things began to change, and he started to insist on an even closer supervision; he wanted to observe and approve each scene before the camera turned. This ultimately became not just unnerving but deeply debilitating for his directors, and the source of many a disagreement. The director tended thus to become a valuable craftsman on a Selznick picture rather than a creator, and the quality of the work suffered from the lack of a cohesive style and personality: *Gone With the Wind*, finally, had four directors, *Duel in the Sun* had seven. That the films were as successful and as effective as they nonetheless were is Selznick's greatest vindication, but in the long run they were not as sound artistically as many of those films on which Selznick had functioned more conventionally:

Cukor's *Dinner at Eight, Little Women, What Price Holly-wood?* and *David Copperfield* are good examples.

After *Gone With the Wind*, too, Selznick fell into an old and dangerous trap: he felt it necessary to top himself. This he equated to a large extent with size and, increasingly, modest projects were inflated out of proportion until, at last, an intimate love story like *A Farewell to Arms* became a Selznick super-production, bloated beyond recognition. Of course, to his way of thinking, he never *did* top himself and he knew that. It was a part of his sadness.

It is not insignificant that the three films Alfred Hitch-cock directed for Selznick—*Rebecca, Spellbound, The Para-dine Case*—are also Hitchcock's least personal and least inter-esting American films. *Notorious*, which began as a Selznick project, but which he sold and was not involved with actively as producer, is, also significantly, by far the best of that series. During those same years, away from Selznick, Hitch-cock made *Shadow of a Doubt, Foreign Correspondent, Suspicion*, among others, all key films in his career. A strong director like Hitchcock simply could not function at his best under the kind of authority Selznick imposed. Vidor quit. So did John Huston (on *Farewell to Arms*). Others, less individualistic, did not. After *Gone With the Wind*, Selznick never again worked amicably with a major di-rector. In some way, the work was always either second-rate or a compromise between two opposed temperaments.

"One man. One film." This is precisely what Capra cham-pioned and made to work, often against heavy odds. Ulti-mately, Selznick probably believed this too, but he con-sidered *himself* the man, and the film *his*, though he never took the final plunge and actually directed the pictures. He had, therefore, always to rely on others to bring his visions to fruition and, unfortunately, there is simply no way to direct films by remote control; no matter how manipulable the director, one has to be out there, under fire, making the decisions as the problems arise, choosing the setups, directing the actors, molding the work through the force of one's personality. This, finally, Selznick never did.

No matter what the literary source, Capra's films are his. The same signature can be identified from *It Happened One Night* through *Mr. Deeds Goes to Town* and *Mr. Smith Goes to Washington* to *It's a Wonderful Life* and even the relative failure of *Pocketful of Miracles*. But who is the author of *Since You Went Away*, *I'll Be Seeing You*, *Portrait of Jennie*, the last *Farewell to Arms*? Selznick clearly predominates but where is his hand? Is it his camera work, his direction of actors, his cutting? In the final analysis, Selznick's productions were collaborative and they cannot possess either the same intensity or the same personal authority of those films on which the director was the final arbiter. Selznick wrote memos of instruction—often incisive and acute —but he was an armchair general. Capra wrote no memos— he did the work. He not only made the decisions, he carried them out. At its essence, that is the difference between a director and a producer, as well as the reason why the movies are not a writer's, not a producer's, but a director's medium. He makes the film. You cannot instruct someone to paint a picture—at some point he has to hold the brush.

Selznick's genius—and there can be little argument on this —was in his commercial sense, his showmanship, as well as in his basic good taste. He brought Hitchcock to America, as well as Ingrid Bergman; he discovered Vivien Leigh and Jennifer Jones, established Cukor as a major director, to various degrees guided their careers with intelligence and passion, as he did with Joan Fontaine and Joseph Cotten and many others. He encouraged Cukor's instincts about Katharine Hepburn and he promoted *Gone With the Wind*, *Rebecca* and *Duel in the Sun* into record-breaking successes. His contribution to American movies was important and, in its way, invaluable, but he was not an artist. He never went all the way.

Capra was and did. For better or worse, his pictures are undeniably his own. But the two careers—Capra's and Selznick's—are not really comparable after all, though both achieved their greatest successes during the Thirties and just before the Second World War, and both were to movie-goers recognizable names that assured them of a considerable degree of quality. Capra takes his book's title from this fact —*The Name Above the Title* was his—it was *Frank Capra's* picture, and the possessive was apt. David Selznick's similar billing was less so. Watching a Capra film, we are indeed in the presence of one man—his obsessions, fantasies, dreams; with a Selznick film, we are in the company of a talented executive, influencing others less—and sometimes more—talented than he. The two are not the same; but read both books—they are an education.

October 1972

That's All, Folks

"Disney, of course, has the best casting. If he doesn't like an actor, he just tears him up."

—Alfred Hitchcock

"Eh, what's up doc?" "Eh-b-thee, ee-b-thee, eh, that's all folks!" "Beep, Beep," "I taut I taw a puddy tat," "Thufferin' Thuccatath. . . ." These famous catchphrases came from a series of Warner Brothers cartoons made over three decades (from the early Thirties into the early Sixties) by a group of imaginative and brilliantly inventive men, chief among them Mr. Chuck Jones, Mr. Friz Freleng, and, briefly, Mr. Tex Avery. In the great American comedy tradition of Buster Keaton and the Marx Brothers and Laurel and Hardy, their work was fast and unpretentious, wacky, uninhibited and always unsentimental.

A few weeks ago, I met Chuck Jones, a very likable, self-effacing and dedicated man, who shares with other cartoonists I've met (Walt Disney, Frank Tashlin) a slightly pixilated, off-center quality. He sketched little drawings on a note pad all the time we talked. I asked him how Bugs Bunny had come into being. "Well, a fellow named Ben Hardaway did a rabbit picture, but it was a crazy rabbit more like Woody Woodpecker. When he was preparing it, since he didn't draw very well, he had a fellow by the name of Charlie Thorson make a drawing for him, and when Thorson sent it to him, he labeled it with Hardaway's nickname, which was Bugs—so back it came as 'Bugs's bunny.' That's where the name came from, but it was a completely different character because of the way he was drawn.

"You see, if you hire an actor, obviously there's something going for you in terms of personality. When you make a drawing, there's nothing there but the drawing. It's like hiring an actor solely on a photograph—so having the draw-

ing doesn't really mean much. You have to find out who
the character is, and how he walks, what his intentions are.
All this has to be built into him—you have to decide who
he is. He's not James Cagney when you get the drawing,
he's Cagney when he starts to move.

"Now, Hardaway's Bugs would stand in a crouched,
ready-to-leap fashion, as somebody who's afraid and prepared to get the hell out of there. The Bugs that evolved
stood upright, a guy who's not going to go anyplace—sure
of himself. Tex Avery was really the one who put the
spark into Bugs Bunny—that absolute certainty of himself.
He caught this peculiar spirit because Tex was sort of that
kind of man himself. We also always tried to put Bugs into
a natural rabbit situation even though he's not really a
rabbit. Well, he's an anthropomorphic rabbit. And then
someone would come along and disturb him which, of
course, meant war. That was the point. The innocent rabbit who then turns into Groucho Marx, and you can't get
rid of him with a pair of tire irons, as we used to say. There
was a young animator there—Herman Cohen, he was from
Texas, I think—and he had this expression he used, no matter
what the situation, he'd come over and say, 'What's up,
Doc?' It became a common phrase around our unit, and
Tex gave it to Bugs Bunny."

Jones mentioned, in passing, that Mel Blanc, who did all
the voices for the Warners' characters (and did them hilariously), was allergic to carrots. They tried turnips and celery
and everything else but, it turns out, nothing sounds like
carrots except carrots. So all those years Blanc was chomp-
ing for Bugs, they had to have a basket next to him so he
could spit out the stuff as soon as he'd done his funny
chewing noises.

Just as Bugs grew from Avery's personal characteristics,
many of Jones' and Freleng's inventions were at least partially autobiographical. Jones' Wile E. Coyote, for example, who dreams up the most elaborate traps for the
Road Runner only to have them backfire spectacularly on

him: "I didn't have to leave home to find out about the mistakes the coyote would make. I mean, give me any tool and I'm in trouble. I have yet to learn the mysteries of a screwdriver. My wife and daughter would go hide when I'd start to hang a painting. Now, the other side of the picture for me was Pepe Le Pew, the amorous French skunk. There's the man I always wanted to be. Everybody wants to be a person who's so sure of himself with women that he could never even dream he'd offended. So I was very personally involved with Pepe—I was trying to get his personality inside me so I could get what I want in terms of women!"

Many of the ideas came from personal experiences as well, or chance observations. One of their writers, Warren Foster, heard a child in a park say, "Mommy, Mommy, I taut I taw a twirl!" He brought this back to the studio and the "twirl" became a "puddy tat" so they could get a cat-vs.-canary thing going. Freleng developed it into the Sylvester-Tweetie Pie series. There was also a generous interplay among the men, which came out of regular conferences or, as Bugs did, from refining and redeveloping early drawings. Occasionally, too, inspiration came simply from rebellion against authority.

"Eddie Selzer, who was a thorn in my ass for twelve years, was put in charge of the animation division by Jack Warner, mainly because Warner wanted to get rid of him as head of publicity, which he'd been. Well, Eddie was a real beast. One of the men at U.P.A. made a caricature of him which became Mister Magoo—Selzer was the prototype for that character. I remember we were having a little jam session, laughing it up, when we looked over and there he was frowning at us from the door. He said, 'And just what the hell has all this laughter got to do with the making of animated cartoons!?' That was Eddie. One time, I was drawing a bull—just for the fun of it—when Eddie came in, looked over my shoulder and said, 'I don't want any bullfights. Bullfights aren't funny.' Now, I'd had no intention of making a bullfight picture, but after he said that I went ahead and did one–*Bully for Bugs*–and it turned out great, one of the best Bugs Bunnys we did. Eddie was always doing that. Friz made one of *his* best pictures because Eddie Selzer told him he didn't want any camels. Of course, he was adamant about Pepe Le Pew–he said nobody would think that was funny. I had a real war with him. And the first one I did–*For Scent-imental Reasons*–won the Academy Award. And *he* went up to receive it!"

Discussing the evolution of animated cartoons, Jones gives a lot of credit to Walt Disney, whom it has become fashionable in recent years to disparage. "The biggest thing Disney contributed was that he established the idea of individual personality. You may not like the personalities he developed, but they were brilliantly done. Walt didn't draw very well, but he and a fellow named Ub Iwerks were really, in a sense, one man–they came from Kansas City together (for some reason most cartoonists came from Kansas City, I can't figure out why)–and Ub was one of the greatest technicians who ever lived. It was they who created the idea that you could make an animated cartoon character who had a personality and wasn't just running and leaping up in the air like Terrytoons. The breakthrough really was *The Three Little Pigs*–that's where personality was developed. All of us who followed were obviously keyed off by that–and it's just bad history to ignore it. If you have a cartoon festival and ignore Disney, it's like having a film festival and ignoring Griffith. Because all the tools were invented over there."

In 1962, Warners disbanded its cartoon division and everyone went his separate way. Freleng invented the Pink Panther and began doing main titles for features. Jones went to M-G-M for a while, did some exceptional Tom and Jerrys, and has since done some fine adaptations of books like *The Dot and the Line* and Dr. Seuss' *How the Grinch*

Stole Christmas. But he misses the old characters, all of which are owned by the studio, and none of which can therefore be given new life.

"There was a time when animation was really nutty. It isn't now—it's business. And I'm one of the few people who has refused to have anything to do with the Saturday-morning TV stuff. At Warner Brothers I did ten or twelve pictures a year, which would amount to little over an hour's running time. Now you're supposed to come in and do seventeen hours for a series, which would be like seventeen *years* at Warners. I'd spend five weeks on a cartoon—each composed of, say, six thousand drawings. Today, they use less than a thousand. So for a half-hour program, they'll make three thousand drawings while we'd put six thousand into one six-minute cartoon. That's how you'd get the subtlety of the movement. I have great respect for a single frame of action—I feel sometimes that the difference between three or four frames makes the difference as to whether people laugh or not. But you'll notice on the Saturday-morning shows they always move parallel to the screen, because to go into the background takes a lot more drawings. Also everybody runs the same, moves the same, walks the same. The reason is that they've developed a kind of shorthand.

"If you want to hire an animator today to do something for you in a classic style—if ours was classic—you'd have to hire the same man you hired in 1940. The new fellows can't do it—they have only learned to answer the needs of Saturday morning. Well, you can learn *that* in six months or less if you can draw. But if you want to animate, it takes almost as long as it does to become a doctor—six years of hard work to become a full animator. All the directors you could depend upon started that way. The thing they're doing on Saturday mornings is what I call illustrated radio. They make a full radio track and then put together as few drawings to go along as they can get away with. Here's the difference: if you can turn the picture off and know what's going on, you're listening to radio. And if you can turn the sound off and know what's going on, then you're seeing animation. Even with Bugs Bunny, where the dialogue's important, you can still follow the story easily without it. But you turn any of those things off on Saturday morning and bad as it is *with* dialogue, it's *impossible* to follow at all the other way. But it's a craft that is dying. Unless something is done about it, our army is going to march over the cliff and disappear. You know, Walt went over and the legions follow. There's nobody learning the trade. It's pitiful."

Since Jones and Freleng never made topical jokes, their stuff remains, like all good fables and only the best art, both timeless and universal—and salable. "They had The Bugs Bunny Show and The Road Runner Show playing on network time and probably got $45,000 a week out of them—that's $15,000 per cartoon. And the cartoons only cost $30,000 to start with. The Bugs Bunny Show ran for two years in prime time on ABC, and both shows are still on the networks on Saturday mornings. And yet the studio feels that unless they get their money back right now it isn't a good investment. That's why they stopped them originally—they couldn't get all the money back on theatricals because of the cutbacks in theatres and so forth, and of course prices did go up. Today it would probably cost close to $50,000 to make the kind of cartoon we made before at $30,000. But it would still be a hell of an investment because we got classic cartoons—they're as valuable today as they were when we did them."

Jones was reasonable as he said all that, but now he just seemed bewildered, even a little lost. "God, I'd love to do even two a year. I had so many ideas, particularly ideas that went far beyond the things that I'd done. I was just beginning to spread out, as you'd see in things like *High Note* and *What's Opera, Doc?* and a couple of others. After all these years, animation is still thrilling to me. Because, as far as I'm concerned, it's a brand-new game every day."

Dear Warner Brothers,

If you knew that for a few thousand bucks you could bring back Bogart, Tracy, Lombard, Gable, Cooper, Monroe —wouldn't you do it? Well, Bugs and the other boys are stars too. Why let them die if they can be brought to life? Don't keep our modern Aesops silent. Let there be one episode in the history of the movies that has a happy ending.

March 1972

My little letter to Warners did no good at all. And if you have seen the movie of Charlotte's Web, *you also know that the low state of animation Jones talks about is not confined to the Saturday-morning TV tube.*

A short while after the column appeared, Tex Avery wrote me to amend a couple of Jones' remarks:

"If I were younger—I would fight anyone who lays claim to Bugs' signature line—'What's up, Doc?' . . . I brought this line out from Texas in 1929. In Dallas High Schools and with S.M.U. freshmen, it was always the opening line when two friends met—never, 'Hi, Tom, whatta know?' If you care to dig thru the Dallas News morgue from the middle twenties—you will find a collegiate cartoon strip drawn by Jack Patton—numerous times he would open the strip with "What's up, Doc?" All I did was put the line in the rabbit's mouth—it fit his personality."

Anyway, I'm actually the only one to get anything really nice out of that column—several original Chuck Jones drawings. Like this:

Screenwriters and Preston Sturges

IN THE GREENHOUSE OF FILM SCHOLARSHIP, the controversy goes on: is the writer or the director more the author of a film? The trouble with the discussion is that someone is always trying to make it a general rule, and, as in anything, there are no absolutes. It's as absurd to conclude that a director is *always* the guy, as it is to parrot Shakespeare and insist that "the play's the thing." Paddy Chayefsky and Neil Simon, to take a couple of modern examples, are both fairly dominating writers, and I'd be the first to agree that from *Marty* through *The Hospital*, Chayefsky is as much the key figure as Simon is on pictures like *The Odd Couple*, *Plaza Suite* or *Barefoot in the Park*. The directors of these movies are basically in the service of the screenwriter, and their personalities, if they have any to express, are kept firmly in check. On the other hand, I would say a picture like *The Heartbreak Kid*, which Simon also wrote, reflects much more vividly the temperament of Elaine May, its director. In other words, it bears a closer resemblance in quality and outlook, in ambience and overtone, to Miss May's *A New Leaf* (which she also wrote) than to any of the other Simon-scripted pictures I've seen. That it's also quite a bit better than any of those others is another issue and one I don't want to get into now, though I will say that it confirms my opinion that a director who dominates is more vital to a good movie than a writer who does.

But we are moving into deep and somewhat murky waters. The recognition of a director's signature is sometimes a difficult thing to define, unless we all have the same familiarity with the films under discussion. However, it should be clear to everyone the moment they step into a movie house that

The Searchers, Fort Apache, The Man Who Shot Liberty Valance, Wagon Master, The Wings of Eagles, My Darling Clementine and *Young Mr. Lincoln* all have the same visual style, the same unmistakable personality behind them. And, while they were all written by different people and shot by various cameramen, they were also all *directed* by John Ford. Miss Pauline Kael tried valiantly to argue that Herman J. Mankiewicz was mainly responsible for the thrust of *Citizen Kane.* However, about six hours in a projection room would have been a convincing defense. A look at *Kane* beside *The Magnificent Ambersons* and *Othello,* for example, or beside *Touch of Evil* and *Chimes at Midnight,* would be enough to convince anyone but the most myopic that Orson Welles was the unquestioned author of *Kane,* as well as the others, though they are variously *based* on material by Tarkington, Shakespeare and Whit Masterson. Verdi composed an opera called *Otello,* but surely we are not meant to split the credit for his musical achievement with Shakespeare (who didn't invent the story anyway), any more than Beethoven should have to take a backseat to Schiller because he was moved by that man's poetry to write the choral part of the *Ninth Symphony.* Only in movies is the inspiration one artist takes from another considered as some odious form of plagiarism or, worse, say the critics, lack of originality. Shakespeare and Beethoven and just about anyone worth talking about stole (if that's the word for it) like thieves, but their work transcends, by now, that sort of academic nit-picking.

I'm afraid it's largely a twentieth-century critical fashion to value originality as the main criterion of a work of art. And yet, Ecclesiastes tells us, "There is no new thing under the sun," and around 1785 a certain Mme. Bertin, milliner to Marie Antoinette, is supposed to have said, "There is nothing new except what is forgotten." She *must* have been thinking of movie history—in a kind of advanced state of foresight—because most of what is acclaimed as new in pictures has been done years ago and indeed has been forgotten or perhaps never known, by the ones giving out kudos. Griffith did scenes in the CinemaScope shape forty years before *The Robe* and, if you thought the quick cutting that a lot of directors fell in love with in the Sixties was something novel, take a look at *Intolerance* sometime. That goes for split screen, sound, color and most of the other "technical" advances we're supposed to have made. Most of these are, at best, adornments, at worst, self-indulgent decadence. Allan Dwan, who started making movies a couple of years after Griffith, told me once, when we were discussing some of the so-called modern techniques: "Oh, yeah, we fooled with that stuff—but we stopped all that when we grew up."

Pardon the tangent—back to Directors vs. Writers. Those directors who dominate their writers in the final product often direct the writer as they would an actor or a cameraman—they tell him what they want and how they want it. The writing is done to order. No wonder it's always been such an unsatisfying job for most of the major writers who've been out here. Mailer hated it (*The Deer Park*), Nathanael West loathed it (*The Day of the Locust*), Fitzgerald tried to understand it but couldn't quite (*The Last Tycoon*); only Faulkner seemed to have the right attitude—he'd come out and help a friend (Howard Hawks), take the money, and run back to Yoknapatawpha.

But they weren't screenwriters, who are a special breed. All the really valuable and inventive ones only had one desire: to become writer-directors, either because (a) they thought they could direct the pictures as well or better than the bums doing it, or (b), and more significant, they knew it was the only way to control the work and make it completely their own statement. Dudley Nichols (Ford's collaborator for several years), Robert Riskin (Capra's for even longer), Nunnally Johnson, Charles Lederer, Ben Hecht and Charles MacArthur—all exceptional screenwriters—made the transition with unexceptional results. Billy Wilder, Sam Fuller, Frank Tashlin, Richard Brooks, Joseph L. Mankiewicz, John Huston, Blake Edwards—all of whom began as writers—found their best expression when they became "hyphenates," as they are disgustingly called in Hollywood. Each of them—to varying degrees—also found a visual style that was expressive of his particular verbal talents—several of them, as a matter of fact, far more interesting in that light than as writers.

Probably the most explosive—and, sadly, the most short-lived—of these was a marvelous man named Preston Sturges, who led the way in the early Forties and made it possible with his success for all those other writers to follow his example. Having written several fresh, unusually vigorous scripts which quite overpowered their directors—*The Power and the Glory, The Good Fairy, Diamond Jim, Easy Living, Remember the Night*—Sturges in five short years (1940-1944) wrote and directed eight of the funniest, most joyfully inventive and at the same time profoundly human comedies (in at least two instances they are more properly called comedy-dramas) ever produced in America, or anywhere else for that matter: in order of release, *The Great McGinty, Christmas in July, The Lady Eve, Sullivan's Travels, The Palm Beach Story, The Great Moment, The Miracle of Morgan's Creek, Hail the Conquering Hero.* I think the speed and sparkle of their wit, the wisecracking, typically American exuberance of their dialogue, have never been equaled. Sturges was at heart a *writer*, and the distinguishing quality of all his films lies in the stories and the speech of his characters rather than in any particularly expressive visual style. He has, in fact, been criticized through the years for this lack, but I believe it's a misplaced judgment. The pictures are directed and shot the way those scripts should have been. As director, he remained in the service of the writer—himself—but he was infinitely more capable than the directors who had handled his scripts before he moved up.

He was obviously most adept at eliciting the proper spirit from his actors, and his films abound with mad, wildly extravagant performances—none of them out of key or excessive—from a group of character actors, in the main, who never before or since were so challenged or rewarded by their material. Talk about John Ford's stock company—Sturges used almost the same actors in every picture—and what a precious cast of irreplaceable eccentrics they were: William Demarest, Raymond Walburn, Franklin Pangborn, Jimmy Conlin, Porter Hall, Alan Bridge, among many others. Eddie Bracken was the perfect Sturges "hero" twice, Joel McCrea (in another mood) three times (McCrea told me he never enjoyed any other director as much as Sturges). And then there was Rudy Vallee, whose own favorite film is *The Palm Beach Story* despite the fact that in the movie Sturges mercilessly exploited and lampooned the Vallee image: while Vallee is sweetly serenading Claudette Colbert from outside her window ("Goodnight, Sweetheart, though I'm not beside you . . ."), she goes happily off to bed with McCrea.

He gave these people dialogue of the finest quality imaginable—it was as rich in slang and jargon as it was filled with unorthodox, poetic (but never pretentious) turns of phrase that managed to bring considerable complexity to his characters. His skill was such that in the repressed Forties, he was able to sneak the most audacious material past the censors without raising so much as an eyebrow. *The Miracle of Morgan's Creek*, after all, is about a girl tricked into marriage by an on-leave soldier for a night's drunken lay, and about what happens when she finds herself pregnant and can't even remember the experience, much less the father's name. *The Palm Beach Story* is a sexual quadrille of much more suggestive and amusing dimension than *Bob and Carol and Ted and Alice*, for all its liberation. He was able to switch moods and plots in the middle of his films—as he did in *The Lady Eve* or *Sullivan's Travels* or *The Great Moment*—with the most amazing dexterity and sense of balance. His scripts must seem more modern today than when they were produced.

After 1944, when he left Paramount for "independence" with Howard Hughes, Harold Lloyd, then Fox and finally Europe, his work quickly, inexplicably and shockingly deteriorated. There is no doubt an explanation—some say he was simply burned out—and I would love to have heard Sturges' own reasoning. Unfortunately, he died shortly after making his last and worst film, *The French They Are A Funny Race* (1957), keeping himself afloat for a year or two as a bit player in the films of a couple of directors who took pity on what was once a great and flourishing talent.

I guess my favorite Sturges is *Sullivan's Travels,* probably because it is at once his most personal and, together with *The Great Moment,* the one which most daringly flashes from comedy to drama and back again—a feat I admire in movies more probably than any other. A film director (Joel McCrea), noted for making light comedies, decides that he wants to make a meaningful social document about "life," about poverty and suffering. So he goes out into the world with a dime in his pocket to discover what it's all about— being poor and homeless and on the run. After a series of incredible comic adventures, he finds himself in serious trouble on a Southern chain gang where the only recreation for the miserable prisoners is the Sunday movies they are allowed to see at the nearby Negro church. There he sees a silly Disney cartoon that gives him and his fellow convicts the only laugh, the only pleasure they've had the whole week. After he is saved, through a bit of Sturgesean contrivance that always manages to reprieve his hapless heroes at the last moment (something that when done by a German like Murnau in *The Last Laugh* or Brecht in *The Threepenny Opera,* is called irony by our critics, but that when done by an American is called compromise) he is surrounded again by his happy producers and his overjoyed girl friend (they all thought he was dead) flying back to Hollywood. The moguls tell him they are now really ready to back him in his serious film (they were reluctant before but now *think* of all the great publcity!), and he tells them, a little embarrassed, that all he wants to do is make comedies. Consternation. McCrea explains, with not a little humility, what was, finally, Sturges' own testament: a good laugh may not be much, he says, "but it's all some people have in this crazy caravan. Boy!"

March 1973

Ernst Lubitsch

I WAS SPEAKING WITH JACK BENNY the other day and he told me about working with Ernst Lubitsch. The director had called Benny in 1939 and asked if he'd be available to do a film. "I said, 'I'll do it!' And he said, 'But you haven't read the script?' And I said, 'I don't *have* to read the script. If you want me for a picture, I want to be in it!' I'd have been an *idiot* to say anything else. It was always impossible for comedians like me or Hope to get a good director for a movie—that's why we made lousy movies—and here was *Ernst Lubitsch*, for God's sake, calling to ask if *I'd* do a picture with him. Who *cares* what the script is!"

The film became *To Be or Not To Be* (Carole Lombard's last—she died in a plane crash before release) and it caused not a little controversy at the time for being a purportedly frivolous look at Nazism, dealing as it did with a troupe of Polish actors in occupied Warsaw and their comical confrontation with Hitler's gauleiters. But those who objected missed the point, having forgotten Thomas De Quincey's famous maxim: "If once a man indulges himself in murder, very soon he comes to think little of robbing; and from robbing he comes next to drinking and Sabbath-breaking, and from that to incivility and procrastination." For Lubitsch, the Nazis' most damning sin was their bad manners, and *To Be or Not To Be* survives not only as satire but as a glorification of man's indomitable good spirits in the face of disaster—survives in a way that many more serious and high-toned works about the war do not. Lubitsch had a habit of establishing his European locales by showing a series of stores, each featuring a more unpronounceable name on its façade. He does this in *To Be or Not To Be*, then follows it with an identical sequence of the same shops as they looked after the bombing. The simplicity of this is deeply affecting, especially realizing the significance it must have held for Lubitsch, who was, after all, a European and to whom those "funny" names—like his own—meant more than the easy laugh he enjoyed giving his American audiences.

"The Lubitsch Touch"—it was as famous a monicker as Hitchcock's "Master of Suspense"—but perhaps not as superficial. The phrase does connote something light, strangely indefinable, yet nonetheless tangible, and seeing Lubitsch films—more than in almost any other director's work—one can feel this spirit; not only in the tactful and impeccably appropriate placement of camera, the subtle economy of his plotting, the oblique dialogue which had a way of saying everything through indirection, but also—and particularly—in the performance of every single player, no matter how small the role. Jack Benny told me that Lubitsch would act out in detail exactly how he wanted something done—often broadly but always succinctly—knowing, the comedian said, that he would translate the direction into his own manner and make it work. Clearly, this must have been Lubitsch's method with all his actors because everyone in a Lubitsch movie—whether it's Benny or Gary Cooper, Lombard or Kay Francis, Maurice Chevalier or Don Ameche, Jeanette MacDonald or Claudette Colbert—performs in the same unmistakable *style*. Despite their individual personalities—and Lubitsch never stifled these—they are imbued with the director's private view of the world, which made them behave very differently than they did in other films.

This was, in its own way, inimitable—though Lubitsch has had many imitators through the years—yet none has succeeded in capturing the soul of that attitude, which is as difficult to describe as only the best styles are, because they come from some fine inner workings of the heart and mind and not from something as apparent as, for instance, a tendency to dwell on inanimate objects as counterpoint to his characters' machinations. Certainly Lubitsch was famous for holding on a closed door while some silent or barely overheard crisis played out within, or for observing his people in dumb show through closed windows. This was surely as much a part of his style as it was an indication of his sense of delicacy and good taste, the boundless affection and respect he had for the often flighty and frivolous men and women who played out their charades for us in his glorious comedies and musicals.

No, closer to the heart of it (but not the real secret, because that, I believe, died with him—as every great artist's secret does) was his miraculous ability to mock and celebrate both at once and to such perfection that it was never quite possible to tell where the satirizing ended and the glorification began—so inseparably were they combined in Lubitsch's attitude and manner. In *Monte Carlo*, alone in her train compartment, Jeanette MacDonald sings "Beyond the Blue Horizon" in that pseudo-operatic, sometimes not far from ludicrous way of hers, and you can feel right from the start that Lubitsch loves her not despite the fragility of her talent but *because* of it: her way of singing was something irrevocably linked to an era that would soon be dead and whose gentle beauties Lubitsch longed to preserve and to praise, though he could also transcend them. For while her singing may be dated (but see her in the Nelson Eddy pictures she did and note the difference), Lubitsch's handling of the number is among the greatest of movie sequences. As she leans out the train window, her scarf wafting in the wind, she waves to the farmers along the countryside and they—in a magical display of art over reality—wave back and join in the chorus to her song. Of course, Lubitsch is making fun of it as much as he is *having* fun with it—indeed, it's this tension between his affection for those old-fashioned operetta forms and his awareness of their absurdity that gives his musicals such unpretentious charm, as well as a wise and pervasive wit. And he is never patronizing, either to his audience or to his characters, and when Miss MacDonald and the brittle and ingratiating Jack Buchanan sing a reprise of that song at the close of *Monte Carlo*—leaning together now from their train window—their fond wave

222 PIECES OF TIME

to the people they pass can be enjoyed both for its innocence and gaiety as for the deeper sense of farewell to old
times that Lubitsch's ineffable touch imparts.

Of course, it follows that Lubitsch made the very best of
musical movies—not just the first great one in the first full
year of sound—*The Love Parade* (1929)—but also just the
best period—*Monte Carlo, The Smiling Lieutenant, One
Hour with You, The Merry Widow:* no one has quite
equaled or surpassed their special glow. (I guess *Singin' in
the Rain*, directed by Stanley Donen and Gene Kelly and
written by Comden and Green, is the best of the "modern"
ones, and I love it, but really it's of another breed.) Truth
to tell, no one even came close: the Astaire-Rogers shows
of the Thirties—and I'm quite fond of Mark Sandrich's *Top
Hat* and George Stevens' *Swing Time*—seem tawdry by
comparison, and Rouben Mamoulian's *Love Me Tonight*—
a forthright imitation of Lubitsch with his usual stars, Chevalier and MacDonald—though remembered fondly by many,
looks pretty labored today next to the genuine article.

Lubitsch had a terrific impact on American movies. Jean
Renoir was exaggerating only slightly when he told me
recently, "Lubitsch invented the modern Hollywood," for
his influence was felt, and continues to be, in the work of
many of even the most individualistic directors. Hitchcock
has admitted as much to me and a look at Lubitsch's *Trouble
in Paradise* and Hitchcock's *To Catch A Thief* (both plots
deal with jewel thieves so the comparisons are easy) will reveal how well he learned, though each is distinctly the
work of the man who signed it. Billy Wilder, who was a
writer on a couple of Lubitsch films—including the marvelous *Ninotchka*—has made several respectful forays into the
world of Lubitsch, as have many others with less noteworthy
results. Even two such distinctive film makers as Frank
Borzage and Otto Preminger, directing pictures which Lubitsch only produced—*Desire* (Borzage), *A Royal Scandal*
and *That Lady in Ermine* (Preminger)—found themselves

almost entirely in the service of his unque attitudes, and these
movies are certainly far more memorable for those qualities
than for ones usually associated with their credited directors. (Actually, Lubitsch *is* credited for *That Lady in
Ermine,* but this was a sentimental gesture since he suffered
a fatal heart attack and only shot eight days of it before
Preminger took over.)

Lubitsch brought a maturity to the handling of sex in
pictures that was not dimmed by the dimness of the censors
that took over in the early Thirties because his method was
so circuitous and light that he could get away with almost
anything. And that was true in everything he did. No
other director, for example, has managed to let a character talk directly to the audience (as Chevalier did in *The
Love Parade* and *One Hour with You*) and pull it off.
There is always something coy and studied in it, but Lubitsch
managed just the right balance between reality and theatricality—making the most outrageous device seem natural and
easy; his movies flowed effortlessly and though his hand
was felt, even seen, it was never intrusive.

But finally, of course, it was another world; it's no coincidence that several of Lubitsch's films were set in mythical
Ruritanian countries, and that those set in "real" places have
the same fanciful quality. Lubitsch achieved what only the
best artists can—a singular universe where he sets all the
rules and behavior. As Jean Renoir said in a recent interview: "Reality may be very interesting, but a work of art
must be a creation. If you copy nature without adding the
influence of your own personality, it is not a work of art.
. . . Reality is merely a springboard for the artist. . . . But
the final result must not be reality. It must only be what
the actors and the director or author of the film selected
of reality to reveal." Lubitsch had his own way of putting
it; he once told Garson Kanin, "I've been to Paris, France,
and I've been to Paris, Paramount. I think I prefer Paris,
Paramount. . . ."

Lubitsch had also the unique ability to take the lightest of material and give it substance and resonance far beyond the subject. *The Shop Around the Corner*, a charming story of love and mistaken identities in a Budapest department store, becomes under Lubitsch's hand both a classic high comedy and a remarkably touching essay on human foibles and folly. Another movie, *In the Good Old Summertime*, and a stage musical, *She Loves Me,* both used the same story but they are to Lubitsch as George S. Kaufman is to Molière. The most profound expression of this particular aspect of his work is in *Heaven Can Wait*, which tells a ridiculously simple and unassuming story of one fairly insignificant man's life—from birth to death—which Lubitsch turns into a moving testament to the inherent beauty behind our daily frivolousness and vanity, our petty crises, our indiscretions, our deepest vulnerability. It is Lubitsch's "divine comedy," and no one has ever been more gentle or bemused by the weaknesses of humanity. When the hero of the picture dies behind (of course) a closed door, Lubitsch's camera slowly retreats to take in a ballroom, and an old waltz the man loved begins to play, and death has no dominion. No other image I can think of more aptly or more movingly conveys Lubitsch's generosity or tolerance: the man has died—long live man.

After Lubitsch's funeral in 1947, his friends Billy Wilder and William Wyler were walking sadly to their car. Finally, to break the silence, Wilder said, "No more Lubitsch," and Wyler answered, "Worse than that—no more Lubitsch films." The following year, the French director-critic, Jean-Georges Auriol, wrote a loving tribute that made the same point; titled "Chez Ernst," it can be found in Herman Weinberg's affectionate collection, *The Lubitsch Touch* (Dutton). After comparing the director's world to an especially fine restaurant where the food was perfect and the service meticulous, the piece ends this way: "How can a child who cries at the end of the summer holidays be comforted? He can be told that another summer will come, which will be equally wonderful. But he cries even more at this, not knowing how to explain that he won't be the same child again. Certainly Lubitsch's public is as sentimental as this child; and it knows quite well that 'Ernst's' is closed on account of death. This particular restaurant will never be open again."

November 1972

5
RECENT IMPRESSIONS

To the Western White House

MRS. NORMAN TAUROG WAS ON THE PHONE (her husband won an Oscar in 1931 for directing *Skippy*); being on a committee to Re-Elect the President, she was calling to find out how I was voting this year and whether I'd endorse Mr. Nixon. I told her I wasn't endorsing anyone.

"Don't you *like* our President?" she said.

"I don't know him."

"Would you like to meet him?"

"Sure."

That's how I happened to be invited last August 27th to a reception for some four hundred Hollywood folk at the Western White House. It was a grey afternoon—looked like rain; the drive from Los Angeles to San Clemente is not exactly scenic even on a good day, but now there was nothing to counterpoint the dreary freeway route of factories and gas stations and fast-food joints. The engraved invitation said five P.M., but at twenty-five after I was just getting off the freeway, and then wasn't sure I was headed in the right direction; I stopped at a Shell station. The young attendant was cleaning a windshield. Cybill Shepherd, who was with me, called out her window: "Where's Nixon's house?"

The boy grinned and pointed, "Straight ahead."

"Lotta people been asking today?"

His grin broadened. "Everybody."

He was right, La Casa Pacifica *was* straight ahead. There were about twenty-five spectators waiting at the gates, straining to see who was driving in. At first, it looked like an Army camp—chain link fence, some small buildings with soldiers hanging around, two huge green helicopters with

"The United States of America" painted on the sides. But there were also Secret Service men and uniformed guards with walkie-talkies and young Presidential aides, each wearing red, white and blue star-spangled cloth ties.

The check-in point was attended by several of these, presided over by a Los Angeles TV personality named Johnny Grant, who looked a little overwhelmed by his job today; he leaned in, smilingly pretended to recognize us both but couldn't quite come up with names. Still, he seemed content to let us go, but the grim-faced official beside him, clipboard in hand, was less enthusiastic. He wanted the names, please. It took me a while to figure out why Johnny Grant was there at all, but I now suppose the idea was that he would more readily recognize the celebrities as they drove up than any of the officials who might have been given the job, thus saving famous people from identifying themselves; it was also a precaution, perhaps, against some people giving away their invitations to others (they were clearly designated: Nontransferable).

We were cleared, the car was taken to be parked and we walked up the blacktop road, several other latecomers behind us. Mexican music could be heard now, and pretty soon we passed the five-man band of smiling sombreroed musicians playing away exuberantly. Then we were on a receiving line that led from the road through a little alcove and into a courtyard of the sprawling and impressive Spanish villa. Debbie Reynolds was right ahead of us, Glen Campbell was ahead of her, and Charlton Heston came up behind us, followed by Jim Brown in a zippered blue windbreaker. He *was* a little more casually dressed than anyone else, but nobody was really done up grand. (The instructions had been "less than cocktail dress.") One of the aides in patriotic ties told us the men should please precede the women.

"I thought you were a Democrat," I said to Heston.

"I was . . . well, I've always been an *Independent*." He said that significantly, and then mumbled something about preferring Nixon this year. He was wearing sunglasses but took them off as we came into the courtyard.

At the end of the line, in the beam of a floodlight that stood on a stand in the grass, the President and Mrs. Nixon were greeting their guests. Photographers were snapping away, aides stood around, Secret Service men scanned the line. (Heston pointed out that they never look at the President but only at what is going on around him, which was true.)

While Miss Reynolds and her escort were greeting the Nixons, a young man in another star-spangled tie shook hands with me. I gave him my name.

"Mr. McDonavich," he said.

"*Bog*danovich," I said.

"Of course, *Bog*danovich," he said, jocularly. "That's why I repeated it—wanted to make sure I had it right."

I introduced Cybill, and then the young man introduced us both to the perspiring middle-aged man standing beside him. I didn't get the name. The man smiled and we shook hands; his was wet. "Turn a little to your left as you greet the President," he said. "It'll make a better picture."

I turned to watch the President, and the perspiring man lightly held my arm, I suppose to prevent me from jumping my cue. From a distance, under the light, Mr. Nixon had looked as though he were wearing makeup. I could see now that he was only quite tanned from the sun. He turned to me and the perspiring gentleman gave me a light push forward, at the same time supplying my name. I shook hands with the President and introduced Cybill to him and Mrs. Nixon, who continued to smile as she had been before we came up.

"I've seen your name," the President said to me, waving one arm to indicate a movie screen, "on many *productions*." He made the word sound important.

I mumbled something or other. There was a pause. Some years before—after losing in 1960, while he was practicing law, and before he ran for Governor in California—a mutual

friend of the Nixons and of my parents had given them a
present of one of my late father's still lifes. Mrs. Nixon,
however, had not liked it. This happened in New York.
"My mother met you some years back," I said. "She'd come
to your apartment to pick up a painting of my father's."

I'm not at all sure that either the President or Mrs. Nixon
remembered this incident, but Mr. Nixon shifted his look
momentarily. Mrs. Nixon's smile remained fixed—she didn't
say anything—but the President nodded pleasantly.

"My father was a painter," I said.

"Of course I know your father is a painter," said Mr.
Nixon, a little too genially.

There was another pause—a little longer than the first one.
The perspiring gentleman was not looking any better. We
backed off. Mrs. Nixon kept right on smiling at us as the
President turned to Chuck Heston.

More star-spangled ties indicated the way to the party:
a winding path that led suddenly to a striking view of the
ocean—grey and dangerous this afternoon—a left and we
were at the pool, by the side of which Freddy Martin's
band was playing and the four hundred Hollywood people
were talking, drinking, eating. There was Vince Edwards
and Red Skelton and Zsa Zsa Gabor and Lawrence Welk,
Desi Arnaz Sr. and Chuck Connors. Frank Sinatra flashed
by, followed by several others, on the way to something
important, from the look of the exit.

John Wayne waved and came over, puffing a small cigar.
I told him my presence didn't mean I was a Republican.
"*That's* O.K.," said Duke. Mrs. Taurog bustled up with a
lady from the White House staff who said I shouldn't *move*
because Robert Semple of *The New York Times* had asked
to speak with me and she was going to find him. Just then
the music stopped and there was some applause; President
Nixon had stepped onto the bandstand in front of a microphone. He looked smaller and thinner than he had before.
"I am not going to impose on you another speech," he said,
"after what many of you had to endure last week [at the con-

vention] in terms of so many speeches." He then made a speech that lasted fourteen minutes. The emphasis was on movies:

"I would like to express appreciation as an individual, and also speaking as the President of the United States, for what you, the people of Hollywood, have done for America and have done for the world. I can speak with some feeling on this point. Let me begin by saying that my wife and I like movies. We like them on television. We fortunately now have our own projection set in the White House. [Laughter. Personally, I liked the lack of hip to 'projection set.'] That is one of the reasons I ran again. [Another laugh.] I just can't stand those commercials on the Late Show. [Laughter.] But we have seen many movies. We haven't yet shown an X-rated movie in the White House. We had an 'R' one night, and I said, 'That is as far as you can go.' " [Laughter.]

I remembered then meeting Dr. Henry Kissinger at a Hollywood party a few weeks before; he had been most complimentary about a couple of films I'd directed. When I asked if he'd seen them at the White House, he said no. Since one of them, *The Last Picture Show*, was rated "R," I said I doubted it would be a movie for the President, and Dr. Kissinger agreed.

Mr. Nixon was still talking: "But I like my movies made in Hollywood, made in America, and I don't mean that I can't appreciate a good foreign movie, or a foreign movie star or [slight pause, looking for a word] . . . or starlet, or whatever the case may be. . . . In all the countries that my wife and I have visited, about eighty, I can assure you that Hollywood, in most of them, has been there before. We go along streets in the cities of Africa and Asia and Latin America, and everyplace, and on that marquee you will see the Hollywood names that we are so familiar with. It makes us feel at home as we see those names. . . . The other day at Camp David we were looking over the movie list, and there wasn't anything that had been made recently that particularly appealed, so we wanted to get something that could be shown to younger people safely, and consequently, we ended up selecting a John Wayne movie. I asked Manolo [Sanchez], my very wonderful aide, I said, 'Manolo, do you think this would be a good movie?' He said, 'Oh, yes, sir. I saw it thirty years ago in Spain.'"

Big laugh here. Wayne was standing a few feet away from us. He nodded, lifted his drink in a toast and said quietly, "Keep those *com*in'."

The next part of the President's speech was drowned out by the noise of a train going by. At first I thought maybe it was a missile being launched or a helicopter landing or taking off—it was very loud. But pretty soon you could tell it was a train. Still we never saw it, since the tracks must be down below, between the greenery at the edge of the property and the ocean beyond. It seemed inconceivable that the President's house was next to a train route, since the sound would wake a bear in hibernation, but there it was anyway, rattling and screeching its way through Mr. Nixon's speech. If anyone else was surprised or disconcerted, you couldn't tell—they just listened intently to the President's words which they couldn't possibly hear. Mr. Nixon, himself, made no reference to it.

He was closing with an anecdote concerning a Harlem Congressman named Rangel, a Democrat, who had spoken to him about stopping the export of heroin poppy from Turkey and, after working out an agreement with that country, the President had called Rangel on the phone to tell him: "The Congressman was somewhat overwhelmed by the call, and we talked a bit, and he said he appreciated the follow-up. Then he said, 'You know, Mr. President, when I was growing up in Harlem, if I had told my old man that someday I would be talking to the President of the United States, he would have told me I was crazy.' And I said, 'Well, Mr. Congressman, if when I was growing up, in Yorba Linda, had I told my old man that someday I would be talking to a Congressman on the phone, he would have thought I was crazy.' [Laughter.] I will simply close my remarks tonight by saying . . . if I had told my old man when I was growing up in Yorba Linda that someday I would be talking to Jack Benny, he would have said I was crazy!"

He stepped down to laughter and applause, the band struck up again, and a couple of minutes later, Bob Semple of *The New York Times* was brought over and we were introduced. He asked me a few questions, mainly why I was there and who I thought people my age in the movie business were supporting this year. I told him I had no idea but that I had come mainly out of curiosity and for the experience of meeting the President of the United States. Bob seemed very distracted, mainly by Cybill, off whom he didn't take his eyes the entire time. She pointed at the drink he had in his hand. "There's a bug on your glass," she said.

He grinned happily and shrugged. "These Margaritas'll kill anything." Ron Zeigler came over and told Bob the Press was leaving, so he excused himself to leave and, as he did, bumped right into Dorothy Lamour going the other way. Apologies, a wave to Cybill and he was gone.

We wandered around, taking in the sights: Clint Eastwood, Rhonda Fleming, Glenn Ford, Art Linkletter, Hugh O'Brian, Jack Warner, Dick Zanuck, Joanne Carson. Billy Graham was there too, standing on a rise—overlooking the golf course, and surrounded by a bower of branches, with a kind of glow around him as he talked to several people. Then I noticed he was standing in a floodlight too. Dr. Kissinger was as charming as ever, Jill St. John by his side. Jack Benny was trading jokes with George Burns, George Jessel, and Vice-President Agnew, and when the opportunity came I said hello to Jack, who said that after the President's "plug," he'd calculated he had to be a Republican for "at *least* another eight years."

Mr. Nixon made one more short statement, telling us that a little memento was waiting for us as we left—cuff links with the Presidential seal on them for the men, a similar pin for the ladies. He said his initials weren't on them so that Democrats could wear them too. Then "Scat Man" Carothers sang with gusto a song about Mr. Nixon which he'd written for the occasion.

It was getting late. We worked our way through the crowd and came over to the President, still standing near the band, shaking hands with everyone as they were leaving. We stepped up.

"Well, thank you, Mr. President," I said as we shook hands. "I haven't been won over, but it's been a nice party."

He rode right over that—didn't hear it—but also didn't let go of my hand. "I had no idea you were so young," he said.

"It's my name—makes you think of an old fellow with a beard."

"Yes—*Bogdanovich*," he said as though to confirm the age in the sound of it. He still held my hand, but without awkwardness—not as though he couldn't find the right moment to let go—but just because he wanted to hold it, I guess. I certainly wasn't going to pull it away. It reminded me of times my headmaster in high school had held my arm as he walked me down a hallway—it was friendly and rather warm in fact.

"But, you know," he said, "when you think of some of the great directors of the past—John Ford, for example—he started very young, didn't he?"

"He was twenty-two," I said. "I did a documentary about him."

He didn't seem to hear that either—went right on with his thought—but he finally took his hand away to make a gesture. "You know, I ran a couple of his films the other day —*Apache*—ahm, *Fort Apache* and *She Wore a Yellow Ribbon* —was he twenty-two when he made those?"

"No—oh, no—that was later in his career—I guess he was around fifty when he did those." I was still trying to get over the odd sensation of discussing with the President of the United States not only one of my favorite directors but also two of what I considered his best films.

"Well," Mr. Nixon said, "then you have a long time ahead of you, too."

I grinned. "You know, Mr. President," I said, "you were mentioned in a review of one of my pictures."

"Really?" he said, leaning his ear closer, looking down. "What was that?"

"Well, this critic [it had been Pauline Kael in *The New Yorker*] said that the movie I'd made was one that 'even President Nixon would like.' "

He threw his head back and laughed. I think he even slapped his thigh. "Well!" he said, "you don't know if that's a compliment or not!"

"Yeah," I said and laughed too. "But, you know, Dr. Kissinger told me he thought you hadn't seen it."

"Well, I will," he said. "I will."

Cybill was wearing a red, white and blue striped dress. "I wore this dress for you, Mr. President," she said. "I thought it'd be appropriate."

Mr. Nixon looked at her and paused a moment. "Well—it *becomes* you. You know, with your blonde hair and your height . . ." and he continued for several moments, either really missing the point or purposely avoiding it. In any event, any joke about the red, white and blue was neatly squelched. He shook hands with Cybill and we started away.

"You ought to put her in a picture!" he called after us.

"I did. That's the one you haven't seen."

"Oh?" He came after us and leaned in toward me confidentially. "What was the *name* of that production?"

"*The Last Picture Show.*"

He looked up at me and there were several seconds of silence. He knitted his brow intently. "Ahm—the one in Texas?" he said tentatively.

"That's right."

"In—ahm—in black and white?"

"Yes."

"But I saw that! Why, that's a *remarkable* picture! We

ran that at Camp David!" And to my amazement, he launched into a very flattering paragraph about the movie and the actors in it—Ben Johnson in particular—generally confirming Miss Kael's prediction. Then he turned to Cybill, putting a hand on her arm. "And what part did *you* play?"

"Jacy," she said.

I said, "She was the one who stripped on the diving board."

The President paused. He looked at me, but kept his hand on Cybill's arm. "Well, *everyone* gave a remarkable performance in that film," he said, and then, still not looking at Cybill, but patting her arm as he spoke and with the barest flicker of a smile: "And, of course, I remember *you* very well now, my dear."

We said good-bye again, shook hands and left. On the way out, I picked up the handsome set of Presidential cuff links—the little white box had Mr. Nixon's signature on top. Cybill took a pair too, because she preferred them to the pin.

December 1972

Q and A

FLYING AROUND the world flogging your movies has become, for some directors, an almost mandatory part of the job. A kind of extended journey for the ego, it's also supposed to help increase the box-office receipts on your pictures; truth to tell, after a week or so, the ego-building aspects of the trip dissolve in tedium or exhaustion and it becomes solely a publicity tour to sell seats. Having discovered that no matter where you are—whether it's Sydney, Australia or St. Louis, Missouri, Paris or Copenhagen, Belgrade or Stockholm—the questions asked are identical, a good part of the fun goes away. No matter how plush the surroundings—The Plaza, Claridge's, the George V (and when you're on one of these tours all you ever see is the inside of your hotel suite)—at some point you become positive you'll go insane if one more person asks you why you shot your movie in black and white. (That happened to be the *one* surefire opener from nearly every interviewer while I was beating the drum for *The Last Picture Show*, though I know any director or actor on that hoopla trail has some identical sort of constant repeater.) At first you tell the truth—amusingly, you hope, and without too much pretension—but after the twelfth or twentieth time (depending on your stability) the nature of the truth slowly changes, if not because of perversity, then for the sake of your own diversion. By the end of my trip, for example, I'd reduced the answer to a terse, "Because Orson Welles told me to," which at least had the effect of closing the subject. The fact that it was also partially true didn't change the expression of uncomfortable disappointment on the faces of my inquisitors, who'd hoped for something much grander about the art of the cinema. I think it was in Melbourne that one interview just about ended before it had begun when a hapless reporter—laden with tape recorder and cameras—arrived at the end of a day-long stream of questioners to ask the old black and whiter. I stared at her one miserable moment, said, "Cheaper that way," and left the room to compose myself.

It's not always so bad and let's face it, sure is nicer to be asked something than ignored; also, the people are generally polite and earnest and interested, the trip is free and the p.r. personnel usually try to make it as bearable as possible; it's the game itself that's debilitating. I think my favorite moment was in Atlanta, Georgia, with Ben Johnson. We were having drinks late in the day with the two major local newspaper critics, and as I'd just got back from Europe and the same old routine, Ben, who'd only just started this trip, was trying to distract them from my ill humor and monosyllable answers. The Academy Awards were coming around, Ben had been nominated and after several weighty questions and about three drinks, he leaned back expansively and said to the two journalists, "Why don't y'all come on out fer the Oscars an' get some a that Hollywood puss?" One of the writers was in mid-swallow, I think, and nearly had a bad moment all over the table but, to their credit, they rapidly collapsed, with me *and* Ben, into total hilarity and there wasn't another serious question the rest of the night. If only Ben could always be around.

I don't know what previous sins the other directors or actors are paying for, but in my particular case I deserve all the discomfort I get since I myself used to be on the other side of that tape recorder-note pad. As a journalist-critic-film-historian type, my questions were I'm sure just as tough to take as I now find many of those directed at me. A particularly awful habit I had—and one common to most interviewers, I'm afraid—was to dig out in the course of one's homework several select statements the victim had been quoted as making. These I would then read to the poor man and ask him to elaborate or qualify. However, as Mr. Welles pointed out to me rather less than politely when I'd done this to him once too often, if a pithy remark is good enough to be quoted, it really requires no amplification, and if it does, wasn't worth quoting in the first place. Of course, that's if one can even remember the damn thing you said. It reminded Orson of the old Robert Browning story: asked to explain a line of poetry he'd written, Browning answered, after a little thought, "When that was written, only God and Robert Browning knew what it meant. Now, only God knows."

Older directors find various ways of coping with all this —the younger ones are stuck with being either boyishly enthusiastic, pompous, pretentious or rude. Now John Ford, for instance, simply pretends not to recall any single shot, scene, actor or incident in any one of his films. He remembers them all, of course, vividly, but it sure cuts an interview short when a question that begins, "In *Young Mr. Lincoln*, did you . . ." is interrupted with, "Did I make that?" If the question is really complicated and profoundly intellectual, Ford enjoys himself by pretending to be deaf so that you must repeat it. And repeat it—each time louder. Now believe me, there is no question on earth that can sound anything but inane after it has been asked five times at an ever-increasing volume. When he has made you say it as loud as possible and is sure you now realize yourself how stupid the whole train of thought was, he looks at you with a fleeting expression of pity and lets you off the hook with, "I don't know."

Josef von Sternberg's answers were generally designed to make you sure you were nuts. "Why did you always have Dietrich wearing feathers?" you'd say, and he'd answer, "She *never* wore feathers." "But Mr. von Sternberg, in *The Scarlet Empress*, the egrets she. . . ." "I don't remember." And that was the end of that. Hitchcock goes around any question he doesn't like by telling an amusing story that usually has little to do with what was asked, but is so diverting or elaborate that by the time he's finished, the interviewer has himself forgotten what he wanted to know. Charlie Chaplin, at an advanced age but otherwise quite healthy, turned to an over-enthusiastic interrogator recently and told her he was terribly sorry but he had trouble remembering anything because he'd recently had a stroke.

Then, abroad, of course, there's the language barrier. It's a problem sometimes even in England. I spent the better part of a half hour telling one London journalist a bunch of my favorite Jimmy Stewart stories and when I was finished he asked who Jimmy Stewart was. "Jimmy Stewart!?" I said. "You don't know who Jimmy Stewart is?" He wasn't *that* young—nobody's that young, I said. He got a little irritated. I tried again. "*Mr. Smith Goes to Washington*," I said, "James Stewart!" "Oh," he said, "*James* Stewart"— and then, with a definite edge in his tone, "I don't know him well enough to call him 'Jimmy.'" Well, now I had to explain that I wasn't trying to indicate familiarity by calling him Jimmy, since everyone in America knew him by that name, that even his late, unlamented U.S. television program was called *The Jimmy Stewart Show*. I don't think the reporter was convinced. I'm sure he continued to think of me as a hopeless name-dropper who would probably even call James Mason "Jimmy."

Speaking of Mr. Stewart, he was also the cause of considerable dismay for me in Italy. I'm afraid one of my most often repeated parlor turns is to mimic Stewart's distinctive voice—not to mention Cagney's, Cary Grant's and a few others. I'm no Rich Little (who, by the way, must be the best mimic-actor ever born), but these little numbers of mine usually meet with some small amount of success. Well, there I was in Rome doing Stewart for the press and receiving only the most icy and incomprehensible looks until a merciful friend clued me in to the fact that *all* American movies are dubbed in Italy and that no Italian *had ever heard* Jimmy Stewart's voice—or Grant's or Cagney's or, in fact, any American movie star's voice in history. It was always some fine Italian actor speaking for them. So, Rich, don't *ever* go to Italy—or Japan, either, for that matter. If you see a John Wayne movie in Tokyo, I'm told, he sounds just like Toshiro Mifune. A shattering thought which speaks well for a return to silent movies as the only true universal language and reminds me again of that great quote of Jean Renoir's. "In a truly civilized time," he said, "like the 13th century, a person who dubbed another's voice would have been burned at the stake as a heretic—for presuming to imply that a man could possibly have two souls."

(I reminded M. Renoir of this quote recently and later, when the topic of our conversation turned to President Nixon and his strangely disjointed manner of delivery on television, he said, "I have the answer! Nixon is dubbed!")

Anyway, perhaps the whole question-answer business should be put to rest. After all, a good movie, like any good work of art, shouldn't really need elaboration from the author. As comics used to say about their jokes, "When you gotta explain 'em, they must be pretty bad." Of course that would put critics out of business too, and as one who used to enjoy the press-screening circuit, I stop short of suggesting such harsh measures. I wouldn't like to stop anyone from seeing and talking about the movies, though I do sometimes get the eerie feeling that we're speaking in a void. Does anyone care? In America, fewer people go to pictures than ever before, just as there are fewer newspapers and magazines to write about them. The movies and the reporters are slowly but irrevocably being fried into extinction by that all-seeing laser eye of the television. Maybe not by Mr. Orwell's deadline, but perhaps by Mr. Kubrick's, there'll be no movie theatres at all, and no written press. Just TV. In that gloomy crystal ball, I can see that the only critics then will also be on TV, and surely they won't *precede* the TV movies to tell you whether to watch or not—no sponsor would allow that even in 2001—but no doubt they'll follow it to fill you in on what you missed or to tell you what a boob you were for liking it. And will the old Q and A form be dead? Will the directors and actors of those new milestones be asked to explain what on earth they've done and why? Probably so. What is there that could possibly stop this mania we have that has led us to an age Welles has described as, "A time when most books are books about books." And then, of course, you can't kill the talk shows. By the turn of the new century, they are sure to be the only form of conversation known to mortal man. And, after all, Dick Cavett's first question to me was, "Why did you shoot your film in black and white?" And, in front of more people than might ever have seen my picture, I told him as though I'd never been asked before.

May 1973

On Location

HAYS, KANSAS, where we've been shooting *Paper Moon*, is geographically almost directly in the middle of the country. It's an old town—Custer rode out from Fort Hays on the way to his fatal encounter at Little Big Horn—and a couple of remnants of the fort have been preserved as an almost touchingly tacky tourist attraction. There are even five or six lonely head of buffalo in a field across the way as a pitiful reminder of the days when thousands of them roamed the plains of the territory. Whatever other historical relics might have been around have been cleared away to make room for Colonel Sanders' fried chicken, Foster's Freeze ice milk and Sandy's hamburgers, an assortment of garish gas stations, a Ramada Inn, a Holiday Inn (side by side in all their glory) and a huge plastic shopping center called The Mall and featuring a Safeway, a J.C. Penney's, a duplex movie house (Cinema I and II, of course), and a drugstore with the paralyzing name, Skagg's. In other words, a town not unlike hundreds of others found at regular intervals along the road east, west, north and south. It's a dreary and sterile landscape best described, I think, by Nabokov in *Lolita* (and, incredibly, completely ignored by Kubrick in his movie version of the book). Mailer, too, has written vividly and accurately about the terrible sprawl of our modern way of life in *Cannibals and Christians;* his material is virtually a polemic on the issue, but it has unfortunately in no way impeded the rapid, dizzying growth of ugliness across our proud land.

Of course, that old wise guy, H. L. Mencken, saw it coming as long ago as 1927, but his harsh, prophetic essay, "The Libido for the Ugly," didn't change anything either. "On certain levels of the human race," he wrote in *Prejudices: Sixth Series*, ". . . there seems to be a positive libido for the ugly, as on other and less Christian levels there is a libido for the beautiful. It is impossible to put down the wallpaper that defaces the average American home of the lower middle class to mere inadvertence, or to the obscene humor of the manufacturers. Such ghastly designs, it must be obvious, give a genuine delight to a certain type of mind. They meet, in some unfathomable way, its obscure and unintelligible demands. . . . Here is something that the psychologists have so far neglected: the love of ugliness for its own sake, the lust to make the world intolerable. Its habitat is the United States."

But that's not what our movie is about; it's set in 1936, when things weren't so bad—there was only a Depression then. And on the outskirts of towns like Hays are a score of little communities like Wilson and Dorrance, Liebenthal and Gorham, Russell, Natoma, Lucas and Hoisington and Luray, where you can still find locations that haven't been affected too obviously by progress, and so a period can be pieced together for the camera by taking a house here, a field there, an old hotel in one town, a granary in another, a dirt road, a barbershop, a hardware store, a train depot, all within a fifty-mile radius of our home base. A not uncommon practice in making movies—we'd done the same thing in creating Anarene, Texas, out of several small towns near Wichita Falls for *The Last Picture Show*—chief among them Larry McMurtry's hometown, Archer City, to the people of which he had dedicated his novel with pity and malice in almost equal measure. And what do these nice people think when a movie company commandeers their community for a week or two or eight or ten?

Well, somehow, movies still manage to retain some glamour out here and Hollywood-on-location is a kind of haven for the girls who come out of the cold in droves to touch some small part of that fabled fairyland. Ryan O'Neal is otherwise occupied, but the associate producer will do or an assistant director, a grip or a gaffer, for each of them is some connection with a world that lies beyond the endless horizon, a distant mecca most of them will never see. The

local boys aren't terribly happy about it—a couple of skir-
mishes between the crew and the townies in the Rose Room
of the Holiday Inn—but nothing much more serious. I've
heard from other companies on similar out-of-the-way locations that overprotective parents have sometimes taken measures like having their teen-age daughters committed to
psychiatric hospitals to prevent them from getting overly
involved with the movie people (or, indeed, with any boy
of whom they didn't approve). The worst we had was
one young girl threatening to beat up two others her age
if they went "home" with the fellow from the crew she
had her eye on. But still, as we leave, the Holiday Inn
marquee puts it quite succinctly: THANKS FOR HAVING SLEPT
WITH US. GOODBYE, PAPER MOON.

We cast many of the smaller roles here—the bits, the stand-
ins, the extras—and they come by the hundreds from miles
around to try out: mothers, grandmothers, spinsters, teachers, children, farmers—many of them with some faint connection to the theatre, having played a small role or the lead
in a school production two decades ago. I remember a man
of thirty-five (in Archer City) who looked at least ten
years older, passionately auditioning for several roles. He'd
been in the Army, he'd been a salesman, but what he remembered most was that one big part he'd played in high
school before he didn't go to college, before he realized he'd
never be what he wanted to be. He did a silent bit for us
excellently, and hung around most of the time we were
there hoping for more. It was not a little depressing to see the
kids come in and tell of their ambitions and know that most
of them would end up like my middle-aged friend.

A twenty-seven-year-old mother auditions in Hays—six
children at home, married when she was fifteen—desperately
nervous, she reads poorly for the part of a waitress with two
lines. She doesn't get the part; I see her on various location
sites just watching. She is an extra in one sequence. A thin,
never-married lady who writes love fantasies for magazines
like *Modern Romances* reads for the part of a just-widowed

mother of six and she is very good. Standing before the camera, clearly terrified out of two years of life at least, she is a complete professional and more moving than any actress could have been. A little girl has been the stand-in for the leading actress in the film (who is Ryan O'Neal's nine-year-old daughter, Tatum) and she has sat endlessly in front of the camera while lights are adjusted on her and lenses focused, brusquely asked to sit still and be quiet, moved quickly aside when the star arrives—and now her father comes up to me after two weeks of this work, shakes my hand shyly and thanks me for making his daughter so happy.

Most of the citizenry cooperates beyond the wildest dreams of a "totalitarian director," in Mr. Mailer's apt phrase. We close down their streets, we clog up their traffic, we forbid them to go into their own homes, to cross their streets, to buy at their stores, and still they turn out to watch us, starry-eyed and fascinated. With what? After all, movie-making is not the most interesting activity to watch from a distance—the only action is near the camera and that is usually hushed, muted; much of the rest is noisy, incomprehensible preparation for a bit of film that will last twenty seconds, a minute. But the schools let out and grade by grade the buses bring the children to watch the movie company—surely a meaningless field trip—what can they learn from seeing thirty or forty men moving lights, adjusting reflectors, scurrying about under pressure? And, of course, the movie people themselves are generally quite rude, preoccupied with their own business, intolerant of any interference or delay. We have changed a Gorham Hotel sign to read White Cloud Hotel and an indignant native comes up to complain while we are rolling a shot, thus ruining the sound. He is asked to be quiet. "But this is the Gorham Hotel—this ain't White Cloud!" The assistant director explains patiently that we know that, but we've already had Gorham in the movie and our characters have supposedly moved. The man is not mollified—he continues to complain. Now several members of the crew turn toward him menacingly. He backs away—his passion for accuracy suddenly dispelled.

I remember on *The Last Picture Show* we were shooting an exterior, and across the street the camera could see the backyard of a house in which two children were playing. Their presence there was wrong for the spirit of the scene in the foreground, so I impatiently asked the assistant director to please remove them and he yelled out loudly what is I think the archetypal line of a movie company on location: "Hey, you two kids, get *out* of your *yard!*"

In our cutting room at Hays' Ramada Inn, a phone call— a man tells my cutter he'd like to drop off a bottle of whiskey as a present for me. I didn't recognize the name so she put him off, mentioning that I didn't drink and that I'd be satisfied with a note. I had no idea what I was being thanked for. The next day a bellboy brings to my room a small gift-wrapped box, a note attached. It reads:

"Dear Sir,

"I want to thank you for making my Grandmother feel like a person with a purpose. Words can't really express my feelings about what it means to see her smile all over and because of you she seems to glow a little. She knew nothing about the filming you did at her house and it took her by surprise. However, she has one more item to put on her list of memories and I'm sure she'll never forget you. Even if you already forgot her, I'm sure she'll never forget you.

"Yours . . ."

And within the gift-wrapping the whiskey had been replaced by a Bible. I asked an assistant which house the man was talking about and when he told me I remembered the grandmother. She'd come in the back door with a neighbor lady while we were shooting on the front porch. I suppose she hadn't noticed that we were in the middle of a take, if in fact she knew what such an obscure thing was. But anyway,.

the camera was turning, and in she came chatting happily with her friend; I turned and in a loud, notably unpleasant tone said, "Quiet back there—we're shooting!" Of course, it was her own home but that didn't seem to bother her—she smiled and apologized and sat, meek as a mouse, eyes filled with wonder in a corner chair while the scene continued. I didn't notice or speak to her again. We were there maybe an hour. And now I had a note from her grandson and a Bible of thanks for a glowing memory I had given his grandmother.

And there was the elderly German from Russia, whose wife had died a year ago, living in a small house, his four daughters married, all with grander homes. We came to "take a picture" (his words) in and around his house, and in front was our Model T Ford which was something he had to see. So he put on his coat and his hat and walked out slowly with his cane. It was the first time he'd left the house in a year.

Of course not everybody's so happy to have us. A Baptist minister in Archer City preached against us from the pulpit, condemning us as pornographers and wicked, and the vote was very close on the high-school board in Archer City as to whether or not to cooperate with us and let us film within their institution. And then there was the man in Hays whose house was rented for Ryan O'Neal; Ryan stayed there one night and moved out because he didn't like it, and the man sued—on a multitude of charges—for $900,000. The local judge awarded him the eight-weeks rent he'd supposedly been promised: $3,600. The man was disgruntled and convinced he'd been cheated by the Hollywood names.

Strangely for a director there is no nostalgia connected with any place in which he shoots a film. If the location is bleak and lonely like Archer City or Wichita Falls or Hays, there is never any desire to return to the scene. And even if it's a city like San Francisco, where there are things to do—having shot there for eight weeks, the impulse is never to go back again—and certainly not to those particular areas at which he's shot. Orson Welles put it very well: "When I shoot on location, I sense and see the place in such a violent way that now—when I look at those places again—they're like tombs, completely dead. There are spots in the world that to my eyes are cadavers; because I have already shot there—for me, they are completely finished." In another vein, for a movie he's making called *The Other Side of the Wind*, he wrote these lines, spoken by an aging and disillusioned film director: "The Medusa's eye. Know what I mean? Whatever I look upon finally dies under my gaze. The Medusa's eye. Yeah. Somebody once told me about that. Maybe it's true. The eye behind the camera. Maybe it's an evil eye at that. There were some Berbers once up in the Atlas Mountains that wouldn't let me even *point* a camera at them. They think it dries up something in the soul. Who knows? Maybe it can. . . . Venice, Angkor Wat, the God-damned Pyramids—they're all so many used-up movie sets. . . ."

February 1973

Mr. Zukor's 100th Birthday Party

LAST JANUARY 7TH, Hollywood threw a birthday party. Adolph Zukor, the founder of Paramount Pictures, was one hundred years old, so the studio he used to own turned the event into a glittering gala at the Beverly Hilton hotel, a benefit ($125 a plate) for the Variety Clubs of America, a major publicity blast for itself and a tribute to the oldest founding father of the industry. Twelve hundred and fifty of Hollywood's finest turned up—a far better showing, in celebrities anyway, than the Oscars have been drawing in recent years. As Bob Hope rather unkindly put it, "If a bomb fell on this place, Troy Donohue would be back in business!" Among the hundred or so on the three-tiered dais: Anne Baxter, Jack Benny, Michael Caine, Frank Capra, Bette Davis, Allan Dwan, Gene Hackman, Charlton Heston, Alfred Hitchcock, Rock Hudson, Danny Kaye, Gene Kelly, Dorothy Lamour, Mervyn LeRoy, Jerry Lewis, Fred MacMurray, Groucho Marx, Walter Matthau, Gregory Peck, George Raft, Buddy Rogers, Diana Ross, Gale Sondergaard, Barbara Stanwyck, George Stevens, Stella Stevens, James Stewart, Liv Ullmann, Jack Warner, William Wyler, not to mention the heads and key executives of all the major studios. "A living wax museum," Hope called it.

When he was sixteen, so the story goes (and Will Irwin wrote it in a biography, *The House That Shadows Built*, published in 1928), Zukor left Hungary and came to New York with $40 sewn into the lining of his coat. He eventually became a successful furrier, began investing in penny arcades and nickelodeons, finally exhibiting two-reelers, then the first feature film, *Queen Elizabeth*, Sarah Bernhardt's only movie, her "one chance for immortality" as she called it. A pretty bad picture then, it's unwatchable now except to meticulous archivists, but its success helped to promote Zukor's movie company, Famous Players (launched in 1912), into the big time. The firm's original formula, "Famous Players in Famous Plays," was actually not a good idea since it stuck to the idea of pictures as filmed theatre—instead of moving in the direction Griffith was pointing—of a new art. Later Zukor merged with Jesse Lasky to form Famous Players-Lasky, which evolved, as movie companies did in those days, into the less cumbersomely named Paramount. ("If it's a Paramount Picture, it's the Best Show in Town" was the slogan for years.)

If you believed the speeches at the dinner, and the floor show and the little Walter Cronkite-narrated compilation of clips screened at the end (what's a Hollywood party without a movie?), Mr. Zukor was at the very least *another* D. W. Griffith. The French television crew that was there must have certainly thought so. As I was leaving, they asked me to say a few words if I could about Mr. Zukor's "visual style." I couldn't. Zukor was no doubt a shrewd and intelligent and, from the testimony of his employees, a benevolent studio executive, who made his share of the right and the wrong decisions. Paramount was, in fact—especially in the late Twenties and through the Thirties—among the best and certainly the most sophisticated of the studios. Von Sternberg made his best pictures there—from *Underworld* through *The Devil Is a Woman*; Dietrich, his star, was Paramount's answer to Metro's Garbo and I have always preferred Marlene. Here Lubitsch made his first musicals—with Maurice Chevalier and Jeanette MacDonald—and some of his most delightful comedies. In the Forties, there was Preston Sturges at his height, and Billy Wilder too. DeMille was the insurance policy. From 1914 through his last film, the 1956 *Ten Commandments*, he made almost all his blockbusters for Paramount. Without their talents, and the talents of scores of others, what would have become of Mr. Zukor? On the other hand, he was their Patron, and there has never been an art without patronage. (Without critics, yes. Check out the Renaissance.)

But, what the hell, he was one hundred years old and no one in pictures had ever made *that* before, so let's give him credit for everything! For Mary Pickford and Doug Fairbanks, for Gloria Swanson, Gary Cooper, Clara Bow, Hope and Crosby and Lamour, Dietrich too, and Veronica Lake, Alan Ladd and Chevalier and don't forget William S. Hart. If they didn't actually *say* he'd invented the movies, the implication was there, but after all it was for a good charity and no one really got hurt. The in-crowd didn't buy a second of it, and the public wasn't exposed to the harmless exaggerations—as they are to the Oscars every year—so what does it really matter?

Would I comment on Mr. Zukor's "visual style"? Well, he knew the color of money. No, I didn't say that. I was so thrown by the question—particularly as it came laden with a thick, deeply intellectual French accent (why is it we think any foreign accent in America, including British, is intellectual?)—that I stumbled through something no doubt incomprehensible to the French about Mr. Zukor's being a studio head not a director and one thing studio heads didn't really impose was a visual style. Although, when you stop to think about it, someone *did* back then because the product of each of the majors *had* a special look. You could tell it was an MGM picture or one from Warners—the first was bright and glossy and rich, the second dark and moody and cheap; indeed Paramount films also had a specific quality, a kind of veneer of polish without being too slick. Whence all this came one can't really be sure. It's gone now. Except for Universal and Disney—the two studios that still shoot much of their stuff on the back lot—you can't tell just from looking at it what studio a given film has come from. Even in the old days, however, if it was a good director, his own style predominated, and one of the ways you could tell he was good was in how different his film looked from the general product the studio turned out. Louis B. Mayer, for instance, was furious about Fritz Lang's *Fury* because it didn't *look* like a Metro film. (Even the titles used different lettering.) On the other hand, if Lubitsch's sexy elegance was the ideal to which all of Paramount's general product aspired, Hawks' shadowy and brooding mood was what Warners must have hoped all their pictures would achieve. It's not insignificant, by the way, that both these directors had virtual carte blanche at those studios even at the height of the Hollywood factory system. Lubitsch, as a matter of fact, was made for a while head of production at Paramount, a job he loathed and left as quickly as he realized the mistake he'd made accepting it. If Zukor was responsible for that sort of aspiration to quality—wanting all the company's work to look like Lubitsch—he was more than a good man. But movie history fades quicker than any other, and we'll probably never know the intricacies of the thinking that led to corporate decisions.

I certainly didn't have a chance to say all that to the French TV, even if I could have put it together, but when they pressed me for something, asking why we were honoring Mr. Zukor, I said, "Well, we should—after all, he was there at the beginning—and here we are at the end." A quick "thank you very much" after *that* and let's get on to someone more . . . ahh, here's Zsa Zsa Gabor—"Miss Gabor, could you say something about Mr. Zukor's style of working with actors?" "Oh, darlings. . . ."

It was *that* kind of night—keep it upbeat. Frank Yablans, the president of Paramount, and Charles Bludhorn, the chairman of Gulf & Western, which now owns the company, both made impassioned speeches about the health of the industry—who else should, after all, with the blasts of *Love Story* and *The Godfather* still reverberating around the community. The people would, it seems, leave their TV sets if you gave them the right picture or promoted it well enough. And these men had proved it. So the town was happy to cheer them and their words of encouragement. Even the other studio heads couldn't be too unhappy or envious. Things *were* looking up, and besides it's an old Hollywood belief—any movie that does business is good for every other movie. And, in their bigger moments, picture people do believe that. Which doesn't really mean they're being small when they gloat over another's failure—it's all part of the game, isn't it? Show biz?

It sure was show biz *that* night. Bob Hope came on with a string of nasty and brutally funny cracks—insults is the right word—but he was in his element. I haven't heard him that good for years. No political jokes, no plugs for Vietnam, just a machine-gun barrage of one-liners and jokes that took the mickey out of everyone there, even himself. If he was a little cruel, at least he wasn't sanctimonious. He got a standing ovation, by the way—the only one of the evening except for Mr. Zukor when they finally wheeled him in at the end of the affair. But Hope's was spontaneous, while Zukor's was more or less predictable, almost mandatory. It was also difficult to *see* Mr. Zukor in that wheelchair behind the dais, so everyone remained standing for quite some time —long after they brought out the fourteen-foot birthday cake which looked plastic, but turned out not to be. Backstage after it was all over, Mr. Bludhorn and Mr. Yablans encouraged me to dig a finger in and I did. Tasted O.K. too, for a fourteen-foot cake that looked plastic.

But let's go back to the beginning. The dais guests and assorted other V.I.P.s and press assembled first in the Empire Room of the Hilton, surrounded by huge movie stills and a replica of the famous Paramount gates (remember Gloria Swanson being driven by Erich Von Stroheim through the real ones on that hopeless trip to see DeMille in Billy Wilder's *Sunset Boulevard*); drinks and canapés passed about by waiters, lots of business talk and gossip, not much real conversation, it was too crowded. Then the word went out for the dais people to gather in the next room for their entrance. I was talking with Jimmy and Gloria Stewart when Howard Koch, the producer of the gala (he also did the last two Oscar shows) came over and said, pointing, "Hey, would

you guys go in there and find your names and sit on them."
He moved quickly away to the next group. Gloria turned
to Jimmy. "What'd he say?"

Jimmy looked whimsical. "He said we should . . . he
said would we find our names and *sit* on them"

"Oh," said Gloria. "Well, see you later, darling."

"Yeah," Jimmy said. "Well, I'm going to go find my name
and *sit* on it."

The names were on little cardboard signs on rows of
folding chairs. Much amusement and a little chaos in finding
them: Stella Stevens browsing absent-mindedly through the
B's—does anyone remember how terrific she was in *The Si-
lencers* and *The Courtship of Eddie's Father* (the movie,
not the TV series); Hitchcock, launching, for the benefit of
Capra and Hackman and Gene Kelly, into his story of how
he'd first worked for Mr. Zukor in England in 1920, though
of course Mr. Zukor didn't know it at the time, Hitch
being a lowly title writer then. Before anyone could really
sit down, we were being pulled to stage left for our en-
trances. Each of the hundred dais guests was announced
separately, but also very quickly. Hardly enough time for a
bow even, much less the applause to which some of them
were accustomed and, indeed, entitled. But on they came at
double time, except when the announcer got things screwed
up (he introduced George Stevens Sr. as George Stevens
Jr. and started to announce Mae West before someone
could tell him she hadn't shown up) or there was a delay
in finding someone who obviously hadn't found his name and
sat on it.

The little band on the vaudeville-designed stage started to
play the National Anthem but someone called out, "We'll
have the Invocation first please!" and they covered their
goof quite well (Nelson Riddle is unflappable!) by subsiding
as though they'd planned it that way. James Francis Cardi-
nal McIntyre made the Invocation, or at least he tried to.
He began to read the prepared text, then stopped and
apologized. The spotlight on him was so bright, he said, that

he couldn't make out what he'd written. He ad-libbed instead while everyone stood, heads sort of bowed, not quite
sure how solemn they were supposed to be. *Then* the National Anthem. Lisa Kirk sang it from the dais (the band
was 100 yards or more away at another side of the hall).
She had no doubt realized it's an impossible song to do
straight, so she sang it dramatically, with considerable emotion. I can't quite judge how this came off as I was standing
one seat away from her and that much expression always
feels a little embarrassing if you're right up next to it. (The
lady singer at the Nixon Inaugural who jazzed it up vocally
—with no musical accompaniment—was embarrassing even
from a distance.)

The Hot Bay Shrimp Savoy followed, succeeded in due
time (quite a bit of mingling between the dais guests and
the civilians here) by the Chateaubriand of Blue Ribbon
Beef with Sauce Bordelaise (that was the billing in the golden
program we all got). Then the speeches—Charlton Heston
was emcee—by Variety Clubs President Sherrill Corwin,
who told of how much money had been raised (over $100,-
000 plus another $1,000 for each of the candles on Mr.
Zukor's cake which were to be auctioned off), by Yablans,
by Bluhdorn, by Jack Valenti (all three extremely polished
after-dinner speakers). Bluhdorn got the biggest laughs of
the night by poking fun at his head of production, Bob
Evans, seated nearby, who, he told the delighted audience,
really wanted to be an actor and had begged to play Michael
in *The Godfather*.

After Hope and after Jack Benny came the "entertainment
tribute," which was staged by Tommy Tune and Michael
Stuart. It was an energetic display, I'll say that for it. Loud
and fast and boisterous, lots of balloons, jets of smoke, strings
of confetti. But I kept having the feeling—as various dancers
came on impersonating Paramount stars Swanson and Bow
and Dietrich and Grable (I thought she was a Fox star),
Veronica Lake and Mae West—that it was all really meant

as a giant put-on. That Tommy Tune—who also starred on his stilt-like legs (if you made it to Ken Russell's *The Boy Friend*, he was the lead juvenile)—had been stuck with this assignment and couldn't help but send it all up in a kind of devilishly intense, almost sadistic fashion. I can't believe he really waxed sentimental about all those old stars he was "recapturing" for us, and indeed the whole performance—in fact, the whole evening—was strikingly bereft of sentiment or, strangely, even an honest stab at sentimentality. There was something coldly calculating about that stage show, and when, at the end of it, Tommy asked the audience to join him in counting out Mr. Zukor's one hundred years as the ensemble did a hundred high kicks, no one did. I guess the idea was for the thing to climax in cheering chaos with 1250 voices counting to the beat, ending in a blasting "one hundred," but the crowd wasn't taken in. They didn't count, they just sat there watching.

If I have misread the performers' intentions, I'm sorry, but I couldn't help feeling the cold edge of derision behind it all somehow, otherwise how to explain the culminating entrance of the real Dorothy Lamour, flanked by two small chimps whom she introduced as Bob and Bing. Add to this bit of grotesquerie the fact that the animals both misbehaved, shrieking chimp shrieks loudly to the delight of the crowd and the embarrassment of Miss Lamour, who I must say handled it with the humor of a professional caught in a nightmare. I think she had really wanted to celebrate "Papa" Zukor's birthday—she's the only one who called him that all night—and felt sincerely warm toward him. Her remarks seemed most genuine, but by that time it was too late. The chimps she'd been saddled with had given a hint of the true nature of the night, and there was nothing to be done. She sang several songs she'd made famous, but the mike they'd attached to her wasn't adequate to the job and sometimes it was hard to hear her. David Butler, the veteran director who had guided her and Hope and Crosby through one of the *Road* pictures, was sitting next to me. "Why didn't they give her a mike?" he said sadly. "She never had the greatest voice, you know, she needs a mike."

Finally, it wasn't happy. The Hollywood that Miss Lamour and Mr. Zukor represent is no longer with us, and the attempt to revive it on his hundredth birthday was without real joy, without the divine madness that, rightly or wrongly, we associate with those golden years which seem now to have happened more than a hundred years ago. The one political remark of the night—Mr. Zukor said, upon receiving an achievement certificate from President Nixon (presented by Hope), "God bless the President of the United States and every move he makes"—was so glaringly out of key with recent history that even a die-hard Nixon supporter must have felt a twinge of uneasiness. These simply are not days we ask God to bless. They are gone, those easier times, gone with Griffith and Hart and Cooper and Lubitsch, gone with the Paramount Studio on Marathon Street, still standing but hardly used, haunted by the talented ghosts who used to work there so well and hard and even, I'm sure, by the spirit of Mr. Zukor, who built it, never for a moment imagining he would live to see its stages empty, its legions of dream-loving audiences gone forever. But Happy Birthday, Mr. Zukor, you helped to make it happen once, and we shall never see its like again.

April 1973

Index

The dates in parenthesis following the italicized titles indicate the years in which the films were released in America.